THE ENGLISH ROTHSCHILDS

dau.   dau.   Carl Mayer
(1788-1855)

.s Mayer
(1792-1868)

SEE ENDPAPERS AT END OF BOOK

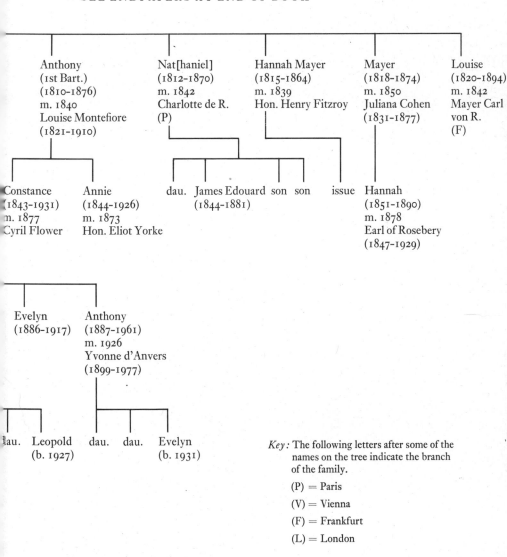

Anthony
(1st Bart.)
(1810-1876)
m. 1840
Louise Montefiore
(1821-1910)

Nat[haniel]
(1812-1870)
m. 1842
Charlotte de R.
(P)

Hannah Mayer
(1815-1864)
m. 1839
Hon. Henry Fitzroy

Mayer
(1818-1874)
m. 1850
Juliana Cohen
(1831-1877)

Louise
(1820-1894)
m. 1842
Mayer Carl
von R.
(F)

Constance
(1843-1931)
m. 1877
Cyril Flower

Annie
(1844-1926)
m. 1873
Hon. Eliot Yorke

dau.   James Edouard   son   son   issue   Hannah
(1844-1881)   (1851-1890)
                                         m. 1878
                                         Earl of Rosebery
                                         (1847-1929)

Evelyn
(1886-1917)

Anthony
(1887-1961)
m. 1926
Yvonne d'Anvers
(1899-1977)

dau.   Leopold   dau.   dau.   Evelyn
       (b. 1927)   (b. 1931)

Key: The following letters after some of the
names on the tree indicate the branch
of the family.

(P) = Paris

(V) = Vienna

(F) = Frankfurt

(L) = London

THE ENGLISH ROTHSCHILDS

By the same author

DISSENT IN POLITICS, 1780–1830:
The Political Life of William Smith, MP

POLITICAL CHANGE
AND CONTINUITY, 1760–1885:
A Buckinghamshire Study

SOMERS:
The History of a Connecticut Town

DISRAELI

THE ENGLISH ROTHSCHILDS

Richard Davis

The University of North Carolina Press
Chapel Hill

First published in the United States of America 1983
by The University of North Carolina Press

Library of Congress Cataloging in Publication Data

Davis, Richard W.
   The English Rothschilds.
   Bibliography: p.
   1. Rothschild family.   2. Bankers—England—Biography.
   I. Title.
   HG1552.R8D38   1983   332.1'092'2[B]   83-10517
   ISBN 0-8078-1575-6

Published in Great Britain by
William Collins Sons and Co. Ltd
8 Grafton Street, London

© Richard W. Davis 1983

Photoset in Bembo by
Rowland Phototypesetting Ltd
Bury St Edmunds, Suffolk
and Printed in Great Britain by
William Collins Sons and Co. Ltd, Glasgow

To the memory of
Richard B. Scandrett
who would have been interested in
the themes of this book

CONTENTS

ACKNOWLEDGEMENTS

My first and best thanks must go to Lord Rothschild. Through his kindness, I have enjoyed free and unrestricted access to the Archives of N. M. Rothschild & Sons. He has also given me every assistance in locatin₍ papers elsewhere. Last but not least, he has read every word of the book in manuscript. So has his sister, the Hon. Mrs Miriam Lane, to whom my debt is also very great. Both have taken the keenest interest in my work and given me every encouragement. One thing they have not done is to attempt to influence my interpretation in any way.

The Earl and Countess of Rosebery not only made me free of their papers at Dalmeny, they also gave me warm and generous hospitality while using them. I am very grateful.

I should also like to thank Mrs James de Rothschild for taking the time and trouble to answer my questions and give me her valuable reminiscences. Miss Mary Brassey kindly put her transcripts of 'Eddie' Hamilton's diary at my disposal. Lord Porchester has allowed me to see and quote from the letters preserved in Alfred de Rothschild's scrapbook.

I have also been allowed to consult papers in other collections. I am grateful for the gracious permission of Her Majesty Queen Elizabeth II to make use of the material in the Royal Archives, and to those who make them such a pleasant place to work. The Marquess of Salisbury has kindly given me access to the Rothschild letters in his possession, and Mr Harcourt Williams has made me feel welcome in the Archives at Hatfield. The Earl of Shelburne allowed me to see the letters in the Lansdowne Papers, and gave me a kind reception at Bowood. I am grateful for similar reasons to Mr Massell and the Board of Deputies of British Jews.

The National Trust allowed me access to the Disraeli Papers, and I should like to thank them and the staff of the Bodleian Library, where I made use of these and other papers. The Master and Fellows of Churchill College, Cambridge gave me access to the Randolph Churchill Papers, as did Lord Esher to his family papers in the same archive. I have received the kind assistance of Mr Alan Bell both at the National Library of Scotland, and more recently at Rhodes House. I am grateful as well to the trustees of those institutions. Ms Rogers at the Kress Library, Harvard, was also most kind and helpful. My thanks go as well to the Trustees of the Chatsworth Settlement and to Mr Pearman who arranged the xeroxing of papers there.

I owe special debts of gratitude to Mrs Ann Thomson, Lord Rothschild's Personal Assistant, and to Dr Gershom Knight and Mrs Yvonne Moss of the Rothschild Archives. Some of my debts to Dr Knight are acknowledged in the footnotes, but I am grateful to all of them as well for all kinds of other assistance over many months of work.

Washington University and my Department there have generously supported my work over the years. The National Endowment for the Humanities gave me a Fellowship to fund this and other work. I am grateful.

Finally, I am deeply grateful to the Master and Fellows of Christ's College, who made me one of their number for the year in which this book was written. It has meant a great deal to me.

Spelling and punctuation have been modernized
for the sake of clarity.

ILLUSTRATIONS

INTRODUCTION

JEWS HAVE HAD radically different receptions in different European societies – to state one of the more obvious facts of modern European history. These differing receptions can tell us much about the several societies, and about history generally.

The experience of the Bleichröders, for example, gives the lie to J. A. Hobson's dictum about financial power being the governor of political power. (So, in a different way, does the experience of the Rothschilds who first occasioned Hobson's pronouncement,[1] as is illustrated in this book.) There was no more powerful financial house in Germany than that of Bleichröder – yet its principal founder, Gerson Bleichröder, never ceased to be the creature of Bismarck's whim, to be cossetted or abused as it struck the Iron Chancellor's purposes. And Gerson's grandchildren would find out just how illusory was the structure he had built. They were consigned to the Nazi limbo reserved for converted Jews whose families were judged to have some claim on the Fatherland's gratitude – left to die quietly, and out of sight in one of the specially provided sanatoria. Financial power was not enough.[2]

The contrast with the English Rothschilds could hardly be more striking. Almost from the beginning, it would have been a hardy politician indeed who would have thought of toying with them. Not a decade and a half after his arrival as an obscure young cloth merchant at Manchester, Nathan Rothschild was financing Wellington's armies on the Continent. By 1828 he was being credited with bringing down Goderich's government. The Rothschilds' place in political history – or in this case myth – was already firmly established.

Their reputations, based on good and evil report, would continue to grow. Nathan's son Lionel made possible the famous purchase of the Suez Canal shares by Disraeli in 1875. He was believed by some to have Disraeli, and for good measure *The Times* in his pocket. Lionel's sons in their turn would have the

13

conquest of Egypt and the Boer War ascribed to their influence. These episodes are examined in the book.

Contemporaries were wise enough to see that Rothschild power was more than merely financial. Lord Granville, unsuccessfully arguing for a peerage for Lionel in 1869, observed that their 'influence is great by their wealth, their intelligence, their literary connexions, and their numerous seats in the House of Commons'.[3] By this time, the wealth was based not only on their banking interests, but on great landed estates which dominated the Vale of Aylesbury, where their Stag Hunt was the main feature of sporting life. Lionel's son, Natty, sat as MP for Aylesbury. Lionel himself sat for the City of London. His brother Mayer was MP for Hythe. But Mayer was better known as a connoisseur and sportsman; the former for the treasures that filled his grand house at Mentmore, the latter for the horses that raced from its stables, which two years later would produce a Derby winner. Lionel's three sons had recently come down from Cambridge, where the two elder had become firm friends of their future sovereign, Edward VII. Of that generation, Natty would become the first Lord Rothschild, a well-known figure in society and politics, as well as the banker who backed Cecil Rhodes. Mayer's daughter, Hannah, would become Countess of Rosebery, wife of the Liberal politician and future Prime Minister. The Rothschilds had sunk down complex roots, securely anchored in the subsoil of British life. Theirs were no mean achievements for the children and grandchildren of the young man who had left the Frankfurt ghetto in 1799.

True, they were the achievements of Englishmen and women, and England's was a milder and more benign climate for Jews than that in the land of their forefathers. In England there was no tradition of the ghetto to live down. The reason was a rather drastic one. There were no ghettoes in England because until a century and a half before Nathan's arrival there had been few Jews. A royal decree of 1290 had banished them. The decree was never rescinded, but in the 1650s a new tolerance emerged under the regime of Oliver Cromwell, and Jews began to return. There were still not many in 1799, no more than twenty-five thousand. They were mostly very poor, though there were a number of prominent families of merchants and bankers whom the Rothschilds would soon join, by marriage as well as achievement.[4]

No matter how great their wealth or accomplishment, Jews were excluded from the tight little world of power and influence. So, however, were most other people. Power rested with the landed aristocracy, the nobility and gentry, and with the Anglican Church to which the great majority at least nominally belonged. Other classes partook of the fruits of power, even shared in it in a peripheral way, according to their affinity with its possessors. The great landowners could not completely ignore the merchants who lent them money, and to whose daughters they married their sons. Lawyers played an important role in the lives of men of property. So did the farmers who were their neighbours and tenants. And successful individuals from these and other groups in society were always edging towards and crossing over the privileged pale. The defences were strong, in part because they were not rigid.

Barriers were similarly yielding and removable as one moved down the social scale, with like benefit in strengthening the social fabric. Yet the barriers were no less real for being flexible, and they were becoming increasingly oppressive to many.

As Anglicanism provided a definition of the social as well as the religious Establishment, so Dissent tended to be a hallmark of those outside it. Originally a brand of inferiority, it was becoming a symbol of defiance, and Protestant Dissenters were joined by Roman Catholics, and then by Jews, in demanding an end to their inferior status. The motivation was by no means entirely religious. Protestant Dissenters were prominent among all groups who had prospered from the so-called revolutions in commerce, industry and agriculture. A number of Jews, too, were leading merchants and financiers. Roman Catholicism often went hand in hand with Irish nationalism. The resulting passions were all the stronger for arising from a variety of motives, and they became ever more difficult to ignore.

A bond between religious nonconformists of all sorts was provided by the fact that in a number of cases the same statutes were responsible for excluding them from full citizenship. Proceeding on the old assumption, which seemed to them recently proved, that religious differences made unreliable subjects, the traditional elite restored to power in 1660 set about excluding non-Anglicans from positions of power and influence. The Corporation Act of 1661 was aimed particularly at Protestant Dissenters, the Test Act of 1673 at Roman Catholics; but by making the taking of the Anglican sacrament a test for municipal office and all offices under the Crown, they effectively excluded all who were not members of the Established Church. The requirement of subscription to the Thirty-nine Articles similarly limited Oxford and Cambridge degrees.

Jews suffered from other statutes not originally aimed at them. The oath abjuring the Stuart line deposed in 1688 clearly had quite another object than the exclusion of Jews; but the formula it prescribed, 'upon the true faith of a Christian', nonetheless had the effect of barring Jews from both houses of Parliament, from voting in Parliamentary elections, and from becoming a freeman of the City of London. Ironically the same formula, substituted for the sacramental test on the repeal of the Test and Corporation Acts in 1828, only made more pointed the continued exclusion of Jews. (The irony lay in the fact that the intention had been to exclude Unitarians, which it did not.)

Yet if it was not the intention in the first instance to exclude Jews, there were many who were happy with the result. Just as the Church long resisted the attempts to remove the disabilities of Dissenters and Catholics, so after 1828 and 1829 there were several decades of determined opposition to what was called after the precedent of the Catholics, Jewish 'Emancipation'. In 1816 Lord Chancellor Eldon had declared that it was the duty of every judge when told there was 'no difference between worshipping the Supreme Being in chapel, church, or synagogue, to recollect that Christianity is part of the law of England'.[5] It was not only judges who remembered it. It took Lionel de Rothschild eleven years, from 1847 to 1858, to establish the right of a Jew to sit in the House of Commons. Opposition to a Jewish peer lasted much longer, and crumbled only before his son Natty in 1885.

It was said by the defenders of discriminatory legislation at the time, and has been said by historians since, that the effects were not really onerous. Not many Jews aspired to be peers or MPs, and only a small proportion of the total number could realistically have hoped for municipal office or a university education. Furthermore the restrictive statutes were not uniformly or systematically enforced. The amount of real suffering, it is therefore contended, would have been slight.

Similar arguments and conclusions have been advanced with regard to the situation of Protestant Dissenters. Their leaders had an effective answer. If the discriminatory legislation was unimportant in its effects, they asked, why was it maintained? Even if it was not as a rule rigorously enforced, they further argued, it perpetuated prejudices which were at least as dangerous and burdensome. The only real safety lay in openly acknowledged equality before the law.

The Rothschilds and others who led the campaign for Jewish Emancipation advanced similar arguments. The latest authority believes that they too were successful in convincing a large proportion of their coreligionists.[6] Even if they were not, few today would doubt that they were right. Law does change social attitudes, and those who are objects of prejudice are ill-advised, if they can avoid it, to acquiesce in anything which sustains it.

So the Rothschilds thought and acted, and they were remarkably successful. Part of the credit for their success must no doubt go to British society, but by no means all. The exclusion itself is an inescapable fact, and it was founded on prejudice which is far from dead. The barriers did not fall of their own accord. The role of the Jews' most prominent champions was important. Not only their struggles, but the way in which they struggled, and the way in which they succeeded, helped to shape English attitudes about Jews. Throughout, the Rothschilds maintained their pride and their dignity, and they helped to give their coreligionists both. The English Jews were fortunate in having as their foremost champions an extraordinary family.

The present generation of Rothschilds retains great influence by much the same means as Granville identified over a century ago. Their name remains a synonym for wealth. Their intelligence is evident. Besides a generally acknowledged financial wizard, the family can boast several eminent scientists, an economist, and some successful authors. The artistic taste and passion for collection, though the results are often shared with the public, remain. The family is perhaps not so prominent as politicians, but the present Lord Rothschild is an outstanding example of those 'great and good' individuals whose talent, capacity for hard work, and devotion to public service make them in the eyes of many more important than the transitory holders of office.

To an extent not usually appreciated, these great and varied abilities were anticipated in the first generations of the family to gain prominence. As Mayer Amschel told his son Nathan in 1805, his original ambition had been to be a student of the

Talmud and he had learned the business of merchant and banker only out of necessity.[7] The letter was written in Judendeutsch, Hebrew characters which transliterate into German with Yiddish words interspersed. This was what he and his sons wrote most easily, and what they all used to the end of their lives in family correspondence. But Mayer Amschel also taught himself to write English,[8] and all his sons became fluent in the three main European languages. They could talk to the Duke of Wellington in English, Prince Metternich in German, and Louis XVIII or Talleyrand in French – and they did.

Even his father deferred to Nathan,[9] and all his brothers did, though not always willingly or graciously; in the end he was the dominant partner. They, however, were undeniably able lieutenants. The eldest, Amschel, born in 1773, would always retain his Frankfurt base. James, the youngest, born in 1792, was the first after Nathan to leave it. In 1811 he went to Paris, where he ably seconded his elder brother's speculations in bullion and specie, experience which was later turned to good account when Nathan undertook the financing of the Allied armies ranged against Napoleon. James had become a power in France well before Nathan died, and he would inherit the latter's dominance in the family, leading it as Nathan never had into private industrial and commercial ventures. Salomon, born in 1774 and the next eldest after Amschel, was for some time a family trouble shooter, travelling where needed. Gradually, however, he attached himself to Metternich and settled in Vienna. Finally, there was Carl Mayer, born eleven years after Nathan in 1788. He too had gone where needed, but in the 1820s, when the Continental powers began to concentrate much of their concern on Italy, he established a Rothschild house in Naples, though also continuing to spend a good deal of time in Frankfurt. These were the four brothers who, after their father's death in 1812, would play their part in the great achievements of their fifth brother in London. It is on Nathan and his descendants that I have concentrated in this book.

It will not be the last written about the English Rothschilds. It is, however, the first based on their own papers. I have enjoyed full access to the Rothschilds' archives, as well as considerable assistance in securing admission to Rothschild correspondence in other hands. My gratitude is recorded elsewhere; but because of the help I have received, I have, I hope, been able to present a fully

rounded picture of the English family in its first three generations.

It has not been an easy task. I am not an economic historian,
and I make no pretence to having written a history of the
Rothschild bank; that is a job still to be done. Nor am I a Jew,
which some may see as a lack. I have done my best, however, to
portray an extraordinary Jewish family whose wealth was based
on banking.

Some may wonder whether this kind of biography, or indeed
any biography, is called for. Those who believe that men and
women are merely the creatures of vast impersonal forces,
economic, social or psychic, will doubtless think it is not. Those
who find such deterministic systems a not entirely adequate
explanation of life may be more charitable. Few would deny the
powerful influence of impersonal forces, which often seem to
sweep the individual along willy nilly. Yet like the boatsman in
heavy and dangerous waters, we can perhaps row hard, avert the
dangerous rocks, and at least help to determine our fates. As
Jews, as bankers, as Englishmen, and as statesmen, the Rothschilds have never hesitated to take a firm grasp upon the oars,
and they may well have helped to steer through difficult waters.
Those who read this book will judge. In any case, it seems to me
that before the minute examination of the parts of the canvas
which other scholars will doubtless undertake, it is necessary to
attempt to see the picture whole. What follows is such an
attempt.

CHAPTER ONE

Nathan

AT THE START OF the nineteenth century, what most struck Mancunians, and their visitors, was the extraordinary transformation of the town in scarcely three decades. During that time it had almost literally exploded, from a provincial town of moderate size to the position of second city in the kingdom, the capital of the vast new cotton industry.

It was cotton that had done it all. Entrepreneurs like the first Sir Robert Peel had struck out, and others had followed in their wake. Thirty years before, a local guidebook marvelled, what had become Peel Street was remote from business. Then Peel 'erected a warehouse, in a retired situation where the land was cheap, but which immediately experienced an unprecedented advance. . . . Building after building arose, and dwellings after dwellings were metamorphosed into warehouses, which have spread till Cannon Street, Marsden Square, and a part of Church Street . . . have banished the accustomed *Lares* to make way for the God of Trade.'[1]

It was in Marsden Square, off Brown Street, that Nathan Rothschild set himself up as a cloth merchant. According to one authority, Nathan established his home in Downing Street, Ardwick. Little time can have been spent there. After his marriage, even his capable wife appears to have been on hand on the business premises to look after affairs in his absence.[2]

Nathan was an unashamed devotee of the God of Trade. As he was the first to admit, he was all business. Thirty-five years later, a fellow guest at Ham House remarked that he was sure Nathan did not wish his children to be too fond of money and business. 'I am sure I should wish that,' Nathan shot back. 'I wish them to give mind, and soul, and heart, and body, and everything to business; that is the way to be happy.'[3]

The young man who had arrived in Manchester in 1799[4] had

been much the same, in appearance as well as attitude. Doubtless the twenty-two year old Nathan had not yet developed the ample paunch which caricaturists would later love to exaggerate, but his was not the sort of beauty which changes much with the years. The red hair, flattish nose, slightly protruding blue eyes, massive head set squarely on the short, powerful body, all changed remarkably little with the passage of time. He was a bulldog of a man, and the resemblance was more than skin deep.

It has become almost de rigueur to start books on the Rothschilds in the dark, narrow streets of the *Judengasse* in Frankfurt, where Nathan had been born in 1777, and where the rest of the family still lived. But if Nathan had been marked by the humiliations of life in anti-semitic Frankfurt, it was only in reaction. For the truly oppressed, obsequiousness is often a condition of survival; and even in their powerful old age, his older brothers, Amschel and Salomon, never quite lost a certain cringing quality. Nathan had never had it. In 1803, when the renewal of war with Napoleon brought a tightening of regulations concerning foreigners, Nathan sent off immediately to his London agent: 'I have spoken today with a particular friend of mine, one of the principal Justices of the Peace of this town, who told me that I need not be anyway uneasy for that he would protect me and procure my leave of residence in Manchester, but I should rather if you can procure me a renewal of my passport, that I may not put myself under any obligation.'[5] Nathan was determined to stand independently, on his own two feet – and so he always would.

A good deal of what has been written about Nathan's early life is based on the 1834 interview with Sir Thomas Fowell Buxton at Ham House, quoted above. The evidence, however, should be treated with some caution. Middle-aged men's memories of the springtime of their powers are notoriously unreliable. Furthermore, it is fairly evident from Buxton's account that Nathan was making the most of a good story and a fascinated audience. Finally, we have only Buxton's version; and it is clear that the great and pious philanthropist was more than a little bemused by this unrepentant, ebullient son of Mammon.

The story was a good one. According to Nathan, on a Tuesday he had a falling out with the largest trader in English goods in Frankfurt, who thereupon refused to show the Rothschilds any more of his wares. The same day, Nathan announced to his father that he would go to England himself, and duly departed on Thursday. He could speak nothing but German, but this held him back not at all:

> As soon as I got to Manchester, I laid out all my money, things were so cheap; and I made a good profit. I soon found out that there were three profits – the raw material, the dyeing, and the manufacturing. I said to the manufacturer, 'I will supply you with material and dye, and you supply me with the manufactured goods.' So I got three profits instead of one, and I could sell goods cheaper than anybody. In a short time I made my £20,000 into £60,000. My success all turned on one maxim. I said, I can do what another man can, and so I am a match for the man with the patterns, and for all the rest of them![6]

Thus Nathan, *pace* Buxton.

The truth was a little less startling. It seems unlikely that he began with a capital of £20,000, and it is quite certain that it did not grow at such a dramatic rate. In 1815, after he had been primarily a financier for several years, and a spectacularly successful one, his total capital amounted only to £90,000.[7] In 1805, before Nathan's marriage and probably as part of the preliminary arrangements, his father sent him £16,000 through his future father-in-law, the London merchant Levi Barent Cohen.[8] Before that, at least up to the Peace of Amiens when he began to export to the Continent on his own, Nathan had acted as the agent of the family firm in Frankfurt, drawing on his father's credit in London for working capital.[9]

Yet, though the sums involved may have been exaggerated, it is clear from contemporary evidence that from the beginning Nathan carried on his business with determination, tireless energy, and considerable imagination and flair. He was far from the only one to combine the functions of merchant and master manufacturer. The middleman he cut out was the one operating between the Manchester and Frankfurt markets, which allowed him to promise his Continental customers that they would have 'every kind of goods that are manufactured here and you may depend upon having them 10 per cent cheaper than you will find them in any house at Frankfurt'.[10] The main advantage of being engaged directly in manufacturing was that he could tell his customers that, 'If you have any other patterns which you prefer

23

in printed or dyed goods, you can send them to me and I can finish them exactly to pattern.'[11] The primary secret of Nathan's success, however, which allowed him to offer goods cheaper than other merchants and still make a profit himself, appears to have been something else:

> On Tuesdays and Thursdays the weavers who live in the country twenty miles round Manchester bring here their goods, some twenty or thirty pieces, others more, others less, which they sell to the merchants here at two, three and six months credit. But as there are generally some of them in want of money and willing to sacrifice some profit to procure it, a person who goes with ready money may sometimes buy 15 or 20 per cent cheaper . . .[12]

Now, as later, the basic explanation of Nathan's success was that he bothered to find out what people wanted, and gave it to them. Weavers wanted cash on the nail, and his Continental customers wanted cheap goods. Nathan saw to it that both sides got what they wanted.

In his twenties, Nathan was already full of salty aphorisms. Many were based on his own stint as a commercial traveller. As he told his own, whom he had sent to exploit the French market after the peace in 1802: 'I have been a traveller the same as you and know it is very easy to get commissions but not quite so easy to get paid for them.' His experience had also given him a variety of contacts. 'As I have had the pleasure of knowing Madame Steiner about six years since when I was traveller for another house, I have enclosed a trifling present.'[13] Nor was he without other sorts of guile. He cleverly exploited one of the oldest tricks of all. He would be delighted, he told one Frankfurt firm, to send them goods on his advantageous terms – but they would please keep it a secret, as two large and important firms were under the impression *they* had the exclusive benefit of his services.[14] Special treatment is flattering, especially, it seems, if it is under the counter.

All Nathan's attractions and blandishments would have been in vain had he been unable to deliver the goods, which in the time of Napoleonic wars was not always easy to achieve. But he also proved himself adept at this. The normal route for British textiles to take to German markets was from Hull to Hamburg. Nathan, however, was a keen reader of the newspapers and kept abreast of

24

the latest reports from other sources. Armed with these, he aimed a constant stream of queries and instructions at his agents. Communications with Hamburg seemed to be suspended. Would it be advisable to try the London to Emden route? The London papers reported that the port of Lubeck had fallen under French control. Nathan's goods should therefore be shipped to Tonningen. And so on.[15] The trade required constant vigilance, and Nathan exercised that vigilance – wherever he was, for a good deal of his time was spent seeking the cheapest and best sources of supply from Glasgow to London, Hull to Nottingham.

Even for a man of Nathan's boundless energy, it must have been a gruelling regimen; and, as Napoleon tightened his Continental system of exclusion, getting British goods through the contracting meshes became ever more difficult. This was partly responsible for a shift in emphasis in Nathan's business dealings, from goods to the various mediums of exchange, bills, bullion and specie, as well as government securities. But there were other reasons for the transition from merchant to banker to financier.

One may have had to do with his marriage in 1806 to Hannah, the daughter of Levi Barent Cohen, a large London merchant who had been one of Nathan's customers and by this time had become his banker.[16] L. B. Cohen came from a family of rich Amsterdam linen merchants, but he himself had moved to London as a young man. There he prospered, becoming a leading member of the Jewish community, noted for his philanthropy. Though Hannah's portion was only £3,250, a respectable but hardly princely sum, which in any case was all settled on her,[17] it was a good marriage for Nathan. The Cohens had a position which he did not have, and through L. B. Cohen's numerous progeny Nathan became connected with the Montefiores, the Goldsmids, the Salomons, indeed with almost everyone who counted in Anglo-Jewish society.[18] There are a number of stories that Cohen was concerned that Nathan was not a man of sufficient substance to marry his daughter.[19] It may have been this that prompted Mayer Amschel to make his son a man of independent means, which, as has been seen, seems to have happened not long before the latter's marriage and through the medium of his future father-in-law.[20]

Hannah, however, brought Nathan much more than her

portion and a more secure social position. She was a woman of beauty, poise and charm. At the time of his marriage, his friends complimented him on his discernment. 'I had the pleasure of seeing your fiancée yesterday,' wrote Moses Alexander. 'You showed good taste in choosing her. I find her most charming.'[21] And in 1817 Nathan's brothers were lost in admiration at the ease with which she moved through Paris society. She was, Salomon and James wrote to Carl, a lady of great distinction, who could take her place on any social occasion.[22]

Nathan, for his part, doted on her. On the occasion of the same Paris trip, Amschel wrote to his brothers in Paris urging them to let Nathan have his wife back:

> That good man is of decent morals. This is rare. He should not be put on too hard trial . . . I beg Madame Hannah to return. Nathan is pitiable.[23]

He always would be. 'I suppose,' wrote his eleven-year-old daughter Louise from Brighton in 1831, 'you are rather impatient to see Mama, as you can scarcely be a day without her.'[24]

Hannah's hold on her husband was more than physical. Nor did it depend on the fact that she cossetted and spoiled him, though she did. It was more than that, as Nathan made clear in the will he dictated on his deathbed in Frankfurt five years later:

> My dear wife Hannah . . . is to co-operate with my sons on all important occasions and to have a vote upon all consultations. It is my express desire that they shall not embark in any transaction of importance without having previously demanded her motherly advice, and that all my children sons and daughters are to treat her with true love, kind affection and every possible respect, which she deserves in the highest degree, having shared with me joy and sorrow during so great a number of years, as a fond, true and affectionate wife.[25]

Fond, true and affectionate she undoubtedly was, but all these qualities were mixed with firmness and directness. When she wrote it was to 'Dear Rothschild', in letters full of advice on business and politics.[26] As a young bride, she had stepped in to manage her husband's business when he was away from Manchester. Age and family responsibilities would not make her any less a woman of affairs. In February 1829 Moses Montefiore

26

noted in his diary a call on his Rothschild sister-in-law and her husband:

> We had a long conversation on the subject of liberty for the Jews. He said he would shortly go to the Lord Chancellor and consult him on the matter. Hannah said if he did not, she would.[27]

'Brief but impressive language', was what Montefiore called it. And the Duke of Wellington, though himself given to such language, had no desire to expose himself to Hannah's. In the 1840s when Sir Robert Peel asked the Duke to attempt to use his influence with the Rothschilds to secure a more favourable attitude on their part towards Conservative aspirations in the City of London, the victor of Waterloo declined:

> The Rothschilds are not without their political objects, particularly the old lady and Mr Lionel. They have long been anxious for support to the petitions of the Jews for concessions of political privileges. I should doubtless hear of these objects.

Though the Duke thought 'the old lady' well inclined towards him personally, he was under no illusion that this would sway her on political matters.[28] Hannah was a strong and forceful personality. Such was the woman with whom the young Nathan Rothschild chose to share his life.

It would not long be shared in Manchester. Their first child, Charlotte, who would later marry her cousin Anselm, was born there, but their next child, Lionel, was born after their removal to London. That happened around June 1808, when they took up residence at 12 Great St Helens.[29] The timing of the move probably had something to do with the death of Hannah's father, which took place early in March 1808.[30] Certainly Cohen's second son Solomon would soon become closely associated with Nathan in business; by 1814, Nathan's brothers were referring to him as the 'Commanding General', and to Cohen as the 'General'.[31] And the youngest son Benjamin would later become another close associate, to whom Nathan would leave £10,000 in his will.

Possibly his father-in-law's death brought Nathan a new infusion of capital, but this was not the most important factor in his swift transition from cloth merchant to a powerful position in the banking world. His brother Carl, writing in September 1814, quotes Nathan to the following effect:

> Nathan writes again about the Kurfürst. The Kurfürst made our fortune. If Nathan had not had [his] £300,000 in hand, he would never have become anybody.[32]

The Kurfürst was Wilhelm IX, the Elector of Hesse-Cassel. Whether Nathan would have been a nobody without him is perhaps doubtful. Carl, who had handled the negotiations with the Elector and who was at this time somewhat raw from the rough edge of his elder brother's tongue, was doubtless adding his own comment in the last clause. It is, however, true that without the use of the Elector's capital, Nathan would not have risen so fast, and in all likelihood never to such dazzling heights.

The story, one of a minority about the Rothschilds for which there is outside documentation, as well as their own testimony at the time, has often been told. The Elector, who before he succeeded his father had lived and ruled in the small principality of Hesse-Hanau, was an eighteenth-century Croesus. He had grown rich, among other things, from the profits of the famous Hessian mercenaries, and latterly from lending to royal relatives – George III and the future George IV had been his customers in their respective ways. Mayer Amschel, aided by the Elector's close adviser and confidant Carl Buderus, with whom he established an intimate and mutually profitable relationship, succeeded in gradually establishing himself and his firm in Frankfurt as the Elector's main financial agent. Especially after the threat of Napoleon caused the Elector to flee his Electorate, this business became an extremely important one for the Rothschild family.

The Electoral Prince had large, and ever growing, amounts of money for which he wanted an investment that was both profitable and safe. Much of his money was already in England, and for obvious reasons such a haven for the Electoral hoard looked increasingly attractive as time, and Napoleon's victories went on. On 30 June 1803, just after war had broken out following the uneasy peace established at Amiens, Nathan wrote to Harman and Co., his London agent: 'Agreeable to the direction I have just received from my father Mr M. A. Rothschild, I take the liberty to request you to favour me with your opinion whether it is probable *3 per cents* will be much lower in a short time, as he has given me orders to purchase for his account £5000 if at 50/-.'[33]

28

Whether this purchase was on behalf of the Elector, it is impossible to say, but there is no doubt that beginning in 1809 very large sums of the Elector's money were put into this British government stock, with Nathan acting on the Elector's behalf. Especially in wartime, the transfer of title was a long and complicated business. In any event, for long periods Nathan had a great deal of money and valuable assets in his own hands.[34]

Here we might take up Nathan's own account of his progress once again, or at any rate, Buxton's recollection of Nathan's account:

> Another advantage I had. I was an off-hand man. I made a bargain at once. When I was settled in London, the East India Company had £800,000 worth of gold to sell. I went to the sale and bought it all. I knew the Duke of Wellington must have it. I had bought a great many of his bills at a discount. The Government sent for me, and said they must have it. When they had got it, they did not know how to get it to Portugal. I undertook all that, and I sent it through France; and that was the best business I ever did.

When Buxton had finished his letter recounting the previous day's dinner conversation to his daughter, he remembered something else: 'The Prince of Hesse-Cassel,' said Rothschild, 'gave my father his money; there was no time to be lost; he sent it to me. I had £600,000 arrive unexpectedly by the post; and I put it to such good use, that the prince made me a present of all his wine and his linen.'

'Very amusing', was Buxton's description of his dinner-table talk.[35] Indeed it was. Clearly, Nathan told a good story, and told it well. It also seems clear that he was what some of those who deal professionally with the human personality would call a controlled manic. His garrulousness and ebullience in conversation suggest it. So does the matter of the conversation. One gets a strong impression of a man of immense self-confidence and boundless energy, of a man willing to take great risks.[36] Nathan was all these things, and he was also brilliantly successful in his new enterprises. In August 1811 the textile concern was formally wound up,[37] for Nathan had much larger fish to fry.

That they were quite as large as he later suggested seems highly unlikely. There is no record of any such transaction in

East India Company gold. And, though Nathan was undoubtedly soon engaged in large dealings in gold (his brother James sent him as much as £89,000 worth in one two-week period in August 1811[38]), there is little evidence that these had much to do with the Duke of Wellington, and none that the destination of the gold was Portugal.[39] The Rothschilds would seem to have been speculating for their own benefit.

Not until the beginning of 1814 is there any evidence of a connection between Nathan and Wellington's armies. Then, however, the evidence becomes abundant – and the connection was momentous. John Charles Herries, the British Commissary-in-Chief who arranged it, summed up its importance for the benefit of the Prime Minister and the Chancellor of the Exchequer in 1816. When the Duke's army came up from Spain into France at the turn of the year 1814, Herries said:

> It became at that time of the most urgent importance that
> a large quantity of French money should be poured into
> the Military Chest to enable the Duke of Wellington to
> prosecute his successes. Operations were undertaken for
> that object through the agency of Mr Rothschild, under
> the direction and responsibility of Mr Herries, which
> proved highly efficacious: the Chest in the South of
> France was furnished with French gold from Holland by
> shipments at Helvoetsluys so rapidly and completely that
> the Commissary General was abundantly supplied for all
> his wants without having to negotiate a bill; and from
> that time no Military Debt [the source] of so much loss
> and embarrassment [in the Peninsula] was created on the
> Continent.[40]

This memorandum not only testifies to the importance of Nathan's involvement after 1814; it also argues against any involvement by him before that date. Indeed, one of the great advantages of employing the Rothschilds, as Herries made clear in a letter to the Deputy Commissary General in June 1814, is 'that Messrs R. are not publicly supposed to be acting for the British Government'.[41] What was wanted was a private firm known to engage in large financial dealings on its own account, so that the cost of transactions would not be inflated by the desire to tap the immense resources of the government. An even more pressing need for secrecy was the fact that the French government must have no suspicion that these operations were being carried on at their very doorstep – the more so because James was based in Paris by this time. The Rothschilds had a great deal to offer, but previous close connection with the British government would not have been part of their attraction.

The transactions were large ones, and the challenge to a private firm formidable to say the least. Nathan's initial task was, according to the government's instructions, in the 'most secret and confidential manner' to collect 'in Germany, France and Holland' about £600,000 worth of French gold and silver coins within the space of two months. This was in January 1814. In March he was instructed to secure about £300,000 worth more in the next three or four weeks.[42] Clearly, Nathan was extraordinarily successful in meeting these demands. In May 1814 Herries wrote to James Drummond from Paris instructing him that the Rothschilds were entitled to the payment of £630,000 without delay: 'They are now serving us to a very extraordinary extent by their credit and if we fail to supply [them] with funds to meet these engagements the weight is greater than any individual, however rich, could be expected to support.'[43] Where had the initial capital for these transactions come from, not to mention the £100,000 worth of property Nathan had to deposit with the government as a security?[44] In 1815 the total capital of all the brothers (Mayer Amschel had died in 1812) was £136,000, Nathan's share at that time being £90,000.[45] It seems safe to assume therefore that it came from elsewhere – probably from the sums provided, albeit unwittingly, by the Elector of Hesse-Cassel.

Wherever it came from, it did the trick. The government continued to be delighted by the service they received from the Rothschilds; from Nathan, the 'Commanding General', and from his commanders in the field, Amschel at Frankfurt, James at Paris, Salomon and Carl serving where necessary, and his brother-in-law Myer Davidson at Amsterdam. Together they marshalled the sinews of war, bearing ever greater responsibilities. In August 1814, Herries instructed Nathan to arrange the subsidies due to the Austrian, Russian and Prussian governments. The payments were to be made by the Frankfurt house, and were to be reimbursed by bills drawn on London, which Herries asked be made at the longest dates possible.[46] Nor did the demand for Rothschild services slacken much for over two years.

Napoleon's defeat and exile to Elba were followed all too quickly by his return to fight again in the spring of 1815. In April of that year Herries and Nathan agreed that the latter was to be paid for all the remittances he effected, on the day preceding the post day on which he had to pay for them; they estimated that the sums involved would range between £250,000 and £300,000 per week.[47]

Associated with the Rothschilds in these ventures was Chevalier de Limburger, a tobacco merchant of Leipzig and a friend of Herries, to whose order the bills Nathan arranged on Frankfurt were to be drawn. Limburger's share of the profits was to be a quarter of those received by the Rothschilds. In April 1817 Carl wrote to James that he had been settling accounts with Limburger. According to Carl, Limburger said that 'we transacted £12 millions – 1% commission would be £120,000 & ¼ of which is £30,000.'[48] Salomon calculated rather differently, writing to Nathan on 3 September 1817: 'In my opinion our commission at 1% amounts to £160,000. Limburger's part is, then, £40,000.'[49] Whichever sum is more nearly correct, Herries was certainly right in describing the Rothschild profits as adding up, 'accounting on the smallest scale, to an ample fortune'.[50]

Nor did this represent by any means all the benefits the Rothschilds derived from their association with the British government. Other things flowed from that relationship. They rendered services to the restored Bourbons, Nathan lending LouisXVIII £200,000 to allow him to return to his kingdom in proper style. They arranged for the payment of French indemnities to the victorious powers, in that and other ways moving into a key position with other Continental powers, especially Austria.[51] In 1816, in agreement with Herries, Nathan began to bring monies belonging to the British government from Paris and invest them in public securities on the government's behalf.[52] Nor did Nathan speculate only on the government's account. His own speculations were also on a grand scale. In one transaction alone in July 1817 he sold £500,000 worth of bonds at a profit of £50,000, and one calculation makes his profit on dealings in government stocks for the whole year £200,000.[53]

Hours – indeed months and years – poring over a variety of manuscript sources do not necessarily create certainty in the historian's mind that he has emerged with an accurate picture of the past. This is not least true of financial operations. Some of the evidence is bound to be obscure, perhaps even intentionally misleading. Presumably, however, the firm's balance sheets, drawn up for the partners' eyes alone, are accurate. The story they tell is eloquent. It is also dramatic. In 1815, as has already been seen, the total capital of the Rothschild banks was £136,000, Nathan's share being £90,000. In 1818 the total capital was £1,772,000. Nathan's share at the later date was £500,000.[54] Thus had the sons of Mayer Amschel prospered, and more especially his third son.

In their calmer moments, Nathan's brothers were quite clear about their debt to him. Writing to Salomon in April 1818, Carl was in no doubt that Nathan fully deserved his larger share of the capital and profits: 'We owe everything, really everything to him.'[55] Neither were they under any illusion that Nathan's value to them lay not only in his financial genius. 'We can't thank God enough for the friends whom he gave you over there,' James wrote from Paris in 1817. Salomon quite agreed. Everything connected with England and Herries turned out well, he said.[56]

Did it turn out so well for the ultimate source of all this profit, the British government and nation? No doubt the situation was one with which the modern 'investigative reporter' (what used to be called a muck-racking journalist) would have a field day. First and foremost there is Herries himself. It was he who had associated the Chevalier de Limburger with the Rothschilds in conducting the government's business. His own association with Limburger was not, however, entirely a business one. Perhaps Herries first met Limburger, or at any rate Madame Limburger, during his student days at Leipzig. In any case, Herries had a daughter there, and Madame Limburger was her 'foster' mother.[57] This fact alone would be enough to make the reputation of a cub reporter.

And there would have been other things to dig out. For example, that the Rothschilds at least contemplated associating the younger lady in some of their lucrative ventures.[58] Ambassadors too were put in the way of profitable investments.[59] And later, in 1820, Charles Arbuthnot, a high Treasury official and a close friend of the Duke of Wellington, would borrow over £12,000 from the Rothschilds.[60]

It was, however, a very different world from today's, one in which bankers regularly called on ambassadors and foreign secretaries, and in which ambassadors at any rate returned the compliment. It was a cosy world, in which friendship could easily shade into influence, and charity into bribery. The basic question would seem to be whether the British government got value for money. Herries, for one, never had the slightest doubt. As he observed in the memorandum drawn up for Lord Liverpool and Vansittart in 1817: 'The greatest credit is due to these gentlemen for their exertions which have been devoted entirely to the public service; and the remuneration which they will receive for them (accounting upon the smallest scale to an ample fortune) will have been fairly and honorably earned.'[61]

One might perhaps think that Herries was prejudiced. He did, however, have excellent arguments to back up his case. As he said in reply to an enquiry by the Audit Office in 1820:

> At the time when the operations were executed the state of the money markets was notoriously unfavourable to British currency and was liable to be made still more so by every new and large demand for foreign money in exchange for it. The great credit and resources of Mr Rothschild, together with his skill both in effecting and disguising his transactions for the government did much to counteract this tendency.[62]

If government transactions with the Continent had to be carried on by a private bank, it is difficult to see an alternative to the Rothschilds. This would seem to be the clinching argument. The Rothschilds made a gigantic profit because they handled gigantic sums.

In any case, it could be argued that Nathan's services actually cost the government nothing. On 11 November 1817 he wrote to the Treasury Commissioners:

> About a year ago I had the honour to receive from the Commissary-in-Chief, the commission to invest in our Funds, the monies arising from the French contributions [i.e. indemnity]; and I accordingly purchased at various times Consols, and Reduced to the amount of six hundred and fifty thousand pounds, the whole at an average price of 62 per cent.
>
> Within the last month I have sold about four hundred and thirty thousand pounds of this stock, at an average price of about 82¾ per cent, leaving, at this rate, a net

profit of upwards of 20 per cent, or about one hundred
and thirty thousand pounds upon the purchase.[63]

It will be remembered that, after deducting Limburger's share of
the profits, the Rothschilds reckoned their own commission on
their transactions with the government from 1814 to 1816 at
between £90,000 and £120,000. Nathan had more than compensated for this in one fell swoop. He had also, of course, had the
free use of £650,000 for a year. Governments and bankers who
entered into such arrangements today would be severely cen-
sured, to say the least. But it was not today.

Were it today, Nathan's dramatic achievements would be
impossible – or at any rate, the drama would be of a different sort.
Even then, as the present Lord Rothschild has demonstrated in a
recent monograph the drama tended to be somewhat exaggerated. There is little in all the various versions of the story of the
Rothschilds and Waterloo – how Nathan secured early news of
the battle (in person? by carrier pigeon?), how he attempted to
inform a government that would not listen, (and/or) used the
early information to make a fortune on the stock market. The
truth would seem to be that Nathan received early news of the
battle through a highly efficient private courier service, and that
he may then have purchased Government stock, though hardly
to the extent often believed.[64] But, if there is a good deal of myth
in the Rothschild legend, what actually happened is dramatic
enough.

The scene against which these events were played was to
serve as the main backdrop of the activities and achievements of
the English Rothschilds ever since. In May 1809 Nathan, his
firm, and his young family moved to No. 2, New Court, St
Swithin's Lane, a stone's throw from the Bank of England and
the Stock Exchange.[65] It was a typical large City merchant's
house, three stories high, not counting attics and basement.
There were four windows on the ground floor, where the
business offices were housed, and two rows of five windows
each on the two stories above, where the family lived.

The family was growing. Charlotte had been born in Manchester in 1807. Lionel was born in Great St Helens in 1808.
Then, after the move to New Court, came Anthony in 1810,
Nathaniel in 1812, Mayer Amschel in 1818, and finally Louise in
1820.[66]

By the latter date the Rothschilds also had what was then a country place. It is usually described as Stamford Hill; but when Nathan sold the lease in 1835 the property was said to be eight acres, 'situate and being on the side of the road leading from Newington to Stamford Hill in the Parish of St John at Hackney'.[67] Today this would be called Stoke Newington.[68] This country retreat was acquired in 1816. In January, Nathan, though urging his brother Amschel to buy the garden at Frankfurt on which the latter had set his heart, said that for his own part he and Herries had decided that it would be unwise to buy a house or go in for any sort of ostentatious living. Herries believed that Nathan 'should not go in for luxuries because the papers would immediately commence writing against me and officials here would start questioning'. Amschel, Nathan said, needed a garden for his health (Nathan could be both kind and tactful), but *he* could do without such fripperies. As for the argument his brothers had apparently advanced, that more ostentatious living would mark their rise in society and be good for business, Nathan scoffed at that: 'All this is a lot of nonsense, because as long as we have a good business and are rich everybody will flatter us, and those who have no interest in attaining financial benefits through us begrudge us for it all.'[69] Nathan was a cold realist, and much to his brothers' disappointment, he scorned the Austrian honorific bestowed on the family in the same year.[70] They might become von Rothschild and de Rothschild, but plain Rothschild was good enough for him. (He cared no more for the barony granted in 1822, and never used the title.) He seems, however, to have overcome his reluctance to buy a house, for in May his sister Henrietta, by then Mrs Abraham Montefiore, wrote to her mother that 'Nathan has a beautiful country estate'.[71]

Nathan was a loving and indulgent father. The two older boys were sent away to school in 1815, but their parents took great care about where they were sent. The then fashionable Jewish boarding school was kept by Hyman Hurwitz at Highgate, but, Joseph Barrow Montefiore later remembered:

The parents of the richer pupils objected to Hurwitz, who was a Pole and used to wear a tall Polish hat and stride about the schoolroom with a cane ferociously stuck in his Wellington boots. They got Garcia, who was

36

previously a book-keeper at Barrow and Lousada's counting house, to establish a more select academy at Peckham, and there Lionel and Anthony Rothschild were sent . . .[72]

The whole family was concerned that the little boys be well and happily settled; and at the end of a long letter in Judendeutsch, Salomon appended a note in English to his eldest nephew: 'The good little Lionel shall take care in going to the Boarding school that he does not fall in the water. I do swim here also every morning at 6 o'Clock when time permits.'[73] The English may leave something to be desired, but the affection is clear enough.

Nathan shared his brother's affection for children. Montefiore remembered:

> In the holidays I was frequently invited to Rothschild's place at Stamford Hill where the two boys were surrounded by their father with every luxury. They had a miniature carriage with four white goats to drive about the grounds.[74]

And Nathan gave his children more than money; he also gave of himself. In 1833 a Dutch acquaintance wrote: 'Nobody realizes better than you do, dear Mr de Rothschild, the feeling of the paternal heart for our own children. Years ago I was enabled to watch you, when like the renowned King of France you let your children make their equestrian exercises on your back.'[75]

To say that Nathan gave of himself is not to say that he gave consistently and uniformly. He was not a 'modern' father. No one who lived as much as he did for his work could have been. As he wrote to his brothers:

> I am reading through your letters not just once but maybe a hundred times. You will imagine that yourself. After dinner, I have nothing to do. I do not read books, I do not play cards, I do not go to the theatre. My only pleasure is business and in this way I read Amschel's, Salomon's, Jacob's [James], and Carl's letters.[76]

This letter of course speaks of more than Nathan's love of business. It also speaks of his deep affection for his brothers. Theirs was not, however, a relationship that always ran smoothly.

Since their father's death, they had been joint partners in the family firm – not equal partners, since Nathan had a larger share than any of the others. There were times when their correspondence did not breathe affection. One example is a letter to Nathan which Salomon dictated to Davidson:

Your letters make me feel ill. It is impossible for me to send such letters to Frankfurt. I cannot for one believe that even if I were 'the learned Nathan Rothschild' the other four brothers would all be stupid boys and I would be the only wise one. Let us however forget all this. I do not wish to be upset any more than I already am. . . . I am therefore returning all these letters to you. . . . The English mail day is a regular terror for me. Every night I dream of these letters.[77]

The letter from Nathan which evoked this response has apparently not survived. But his reply, of 3 July 1814, was not conciliatory. He was, he said, thoroughly tired of the correspondence:

Therefore it is the best thing to part, and God, the good God, will give each luck, a living and a happy future. . . . I am fed up with the partnership. I know you are all clever men. And now, we have all five of us, thank God, peace.[78]

They did not part. The family firm would last their lifetimes, and well beyond. Their differences of opinion would continue. So would the correspondence, full of love and bombast. When the five brothers met, as they did periodically, others got out of the way. Yet no one doubted their devotion to one another. And it is impossible not to believe that the sentiments Salomon expressed to Metternich on Nathan's death were genuine:

Filled with immeasurable sorrow, and in the deepest despondency, I have to inform you that my brother, Nathan Meyer Rothschild, is no more . . . He has died too soon for our love and devotion, too soon to receive all those marks of respect and gratitude which were his due from his dependants, in return for the constant and tireless efforts, which he made throughout his whole life, to place their well-being on a firm and lasting foundation;

to make his house prosperous and happy; and to assure the continued prosperity and honour of his family. . . .'[79]

Even in the ill-tempered letter of 1814, Salomon told Nathan: 'You are . . . King among us.' He always would be.

Nathan was a phenomenon, the admiration of his acquaintance. As his brother-in-law Moses Montefiore (in his case through marriage to Hannah's sister Judith), wrote in 1818: 'You have beaten your antagonists so frequently that I am surprised there are any so hardy to be found in the Stock Exchange to oppose you in any considerable operation.'[80]

Nathan's contacts and influence were also continuing to grow apace. In 1816, through his brothers in Frankfurt, he became banker to Leopold of Saxe-Coburg Gotha, who in that year married Princess Charlotte of Wales, the heir to the throne.[81] It was through Leopold that he became acquainted with the confidant of that prince and of several others, the redoubtable Baron Stockmar, who would remain throughout his life a firm friend to the House of Rothschild. Stockmar would later be a friendly influence with Queen Victoria and the Prince Consort. In any case, again through Leopold, Nathan had also become the banker and financial adviser to the future Queen's father, the Duke of Kent; and when the Duke died, Nathan would continue to perform services for his widow, among other things arranging for the Duchess's supply of breakfast chocolate which was sent by way of the firm's couriers from Frankfurt.[82] Prince Leopold had proved a fruitful contact, and was likely to prove more important still. Salomon was therefore not referring to Nathan's strong monarchist feelings alone when he wrote that he imagined the news of Princess Charlotte's death in 1817 would 'throw you off your feet'.[83]

There was no need to worry, however, for there were other members of the royal family anxious to borrow from the Rothschilds. One was the King himself. In December 1823, George Harrison of the Treasury had 'the honour of transmitting and giving an account to your Majesty of the sum of one hundred and twenty-five thousand pounds, being the amount of a loan contracted for with the House of Rothschild and Sons of Frankfurt on your Majesty's Hanoverian income'.[84] Nathan had arranged it all, and Harrison felt bound to add that, 'Mr Rothschild . . . has behaved with great loyalty and honesty towards your Majesty, as it appears to Mr Harrison, in everything relating to this transaction.'[85]

There were other ways in which the Rothschilds were highly useful to the King and his government. For one thing, their European-wide network of information proved to be not only extremely reliable, but days faster than the goverment's official channels of communication. On 20 October 1826, for example, Canning from the Foreign Office could confidently assure the King that, 'The interval between this and Wednesday must probably . . . bring the confirmation from Constantinople, of the report received yesterday by the House of Rothschild, that the Porte had consented to *all* the demands of Russia at Ackermann.'[86] It is not surprising that Nathan found few diplomatic doors shut against him.

Other more conventional services continued too – to the British Government, and to other governments. Needless to say the motives of the Rothschilds were not entirely altruistic, nor the advantages to them nugatory. A brief listing of their main transactions during this period will make the point. In 1818 N. M. Rothschild issued a £5m loan for the Prussian government. In 1819 the firm contracted for a £12m loan to the British government. In 1821, in conjunction with the recently established C. M. Rothschild of Naples, N. M. Rothschild took on a loan of about £2m to the Neapolitan government. In 1822 the firm took on another £3.5m loan to the Prussian government. In the same year, they contracted for a £6,629,166 loan to the Russian government; and once more with C. M. Rothschild for another Neapolitan loan, this time for about £2.5m. And so on. In the next eight years, there were major loans to Portugal, France, Austria, Brazil, to Dom Miguel of Portugal under the guarantee of the British government, as well as further loans to the British, Prussian and Neapolitan governments. Not to mention the founding, with Moses Montefiore, of the Alliance Assurance Company in 1824.[87] It was an impressive record.

What to many was the somewhat sinister figure of John Charles Herries continued to lurk in the background of these activities. As has been seen, Herries's past was shrouded in a certain mystery, and in the 1820s he of necessity became involved in the not entirely savoury intrigues of the court of George IV.

Nathan had been worried and depressed when Herries's office of Commissary-in-Chief was wound up in 1816. His brothers thought unduly so, for he knew all the ministers personally, and in any case, it would be possible to arrange for any necessary introductions through Prince Leopold.[88] Herries, however, continued to serve the government, and in 1823 he was made Financial Secretary to the Treasury. Not only was this a strategic position as far as the Rothschilds were concerned, it also involved him closely in efforts to sort out and manage the always rather precarious finances of King George IV. Contact with that prince, brilliant and lovable as he in many ways was, had always tended to tarnish those about him, and in the 1820s the stains became even darker. The abortive attempt to divorce his Queen, which ushered in the decade, while it left no doubt that she was a harlot, had also left him looking not only a libertine but a fool. The vast corpulent hulk, inadequately restrained by corsets, did nothing to improve his public image, and he was becoming, or thought he was becoming, increasingly plagued by illness. In any event, he became ever more dependent on drugs. For both reasons he relied increasingly on doctors, and two in succession became chief royal favourite and confidant. The second of these, who began to take control in 1822, was Sir William Knighton.

Knighton from the beginning looked after much more than the King's health. On 10 April 1822, he wrote to his royal master:

> I have seen that everything has been *properly closed with* Mr Gray [of the Duchy of Cornwall Office], and I have taken the *most scrupulous* care of all that relates to your Majesty's private affairs. I have likewise *seen* Mr Rothschild, and stated to him that I was acquainted with his late money transactions relative to your Majesty. I *thought it right to involve* myself in this concern, in order to *guard your Majesty's character in this negotiation,* for upon this I shall have much to say when I have the honour of seeing your Majesty.[89]

Thus Knighton early had contact with Nathan. He would necessarily also become closely involved with Nathan's old friend, who became Financial Secretary to the Treasury the following year.

This association was to become the basis of some extraordinary allegations made about Nathan and his influence in 1828. The background briefly is this. In February 1827, the Earl of Liverpool, who had headed the government of the country since 1812, was incapacitated by a stroke. After intense negotiations, he was finally succeeded by George Canning, who formed a coalition with the former opposition, the Whigs. Canning himself, however, died in August. The King chose the former Frederick Robinson, now Lord Goderich, leader of the House of Lords in Canning's government, to take his dead chief's place. He did not, however, in the usual sense, ask Goderich to 'form a government'. Changes in the Cabinet were to be minimal, and, taking advantage of Goderich's extraordinary weakness, the King insisted on personally playing a part in such new appointments as were made. One which he arranged, and on which he insisted, was the appointment of J. C. Herries as Chancellor of the Exchequer.

That the King and Knighton intended Herries as a kind of Trojan horse seems unlikely. Very probably they had the royal finances much on their minds. The King was also strongly anti-Whig, and he wanted a conservative Tory, which Herries was, to maintain a balance in the Cabinet. The former Canningites, however, objected strongly to Herries. William Huskisson, Canning's most obvious heir and the leading member of the new government in the Commons, did his utmost to block Herries's appointment, and for the few months of the government's existence the two remained at daggers drawn. In December they had a violent row and both threatened resignation. Goderich was distraught, and at an interview early in the new year, which ended with the Prime Minister on his knees in floods of tears, the King lent him his handkerchief and dismissed him. The Duke of Wellington was thereupon asked to form a government, which, with the aid of moderate conservatives such as Sir Robert Peel, as well as the now Huskissonites, he did. The Whigs were excluded.

At the ministerial explanations when Parliament met in February, questions were raised by the Radical MP, T. P. Duncombe:

> It had been credibly affirmed, that there was a mysterious personage behind the scene, who concerted, regulated, and influenced every arrangement. 'There is,' said the hon. gentleman, 'deny it who can, a secret influence behind the throne, whose form is never seen, whose name is never breathed, who has access to all the secrets

of State, and who arranges all the sudden springs of ministerial arrangement . . .

And, Duncombe continued, waxing to his theme, there were other no less sinister influences at work:

Closely connected with this invisible, this incorporeal person, stands a more solid and substantial form, a new, and formidable power, till these days unknown in Europe; master of unbounded wealth, he boasts that he is the arbiter of peace and war, and that the credit of nations depends upon his nod; his correspondents are innumerable; his couriers outrun those of sovereign princes, and absolute sovereigns; ministers of state are in his pay. Paramount in the cabinets of continental Europe, he aspires to the domination of our own; even the great Don Miguel himself, of whom we have lately heard and seen so much, was obliged to have recourse to this individual, before he could take possession of his throne.

'Sir,' Duncombe concluded, 'that such secret influences do exist is a matter of notoriety; they are known to have been but too busy in the underplot of the recent revolution. I believe their object to be as impure as the means by which their power has been acquired, and denounce them and their agents as unknown to the British constitution, and derogatory to the honour of the Crown.' He trusted, he said, that the Duke and Sir Robert 'would not allow the finances of this great country to be controlled any longer by a Jew, or the distribution of the patronage of the Crown to be operated on by the prescriptions of a physician'.[90]

The Cruikshanks even marked the occasion with a cartoon, 'The Jew and the Doctor'. On the right-hand side a lean, masked figure in black bent over a strange medicinal pot, on the left the ample figure of Nathan descended on gossamer wings, a bag of gold clutched in each hand, making remarks in the guttural German accent which he never lost.[91]

This affair shows the extent to which Nathan's reputation had grown. The allegations, however, were mostly inaccurate or misleading. Nathan never boasted that he was the arbiter of peace and war, or that the credit of nations depended on his nod – he was not fool enough to have made such boasts, even if he had believed them. Undoubtedly, as has been seen, his couriers outran those of sovereign princes, but ministers of state were not exactly in his pay, though Herries undeniably benefited from their association. He had indeed lent money to Dom Miguel to allow him to return to Portugal in fitting style – but he had lent the £50,000 as an accommodation to the British government and under its guarantee.

Here lay the key to Nathan's relations with government. Governments made the policies, and he made it his business, and a very profitable one it was, to assist and accommodate governments in every way he could in the implementation of those policies. Nathan did not attempt to use governments, but rather to be useful to them. This was his basic principle, and that of his successors in the bank. As bankers, they aimed at profits not power.

As for the charge that Nathan or anyone else had overthrown the Goderich government, that was ridiculous, the figment of its own paranoia. The government had overthrown itself. The basic fault lay in Goderich, who had allowed the King to interfere in the first place; and in Huskisson, who was entirely aware of what was going on. It had been hopeless from the beginning.

To the charge that Nathan controlled the finances of the country, Peel, Home Secretary and leader of the House, had replied drily that he had never found that 'the other more substantial personage had interfered, in the way stated by the hon. gentleman, with the financial affairs of the country'. As Peel would have been well aware, Nathan did not interfere unless he was asked to. Then, he interfered with all the resources at his disposal, and they were considerable. At the end of 1825, he had saved the Bank of England almost singlehanded.

The economy of the country had never fully righted itself after the speculative boom, followed by a spectacular crash, of the first few years of the decade. Towards the end of 1825 a series of bank failures threatened another crisis, and the possible suspension of payment by the Bank. On 16 December a worried Prime Minister wrote to the King: 'Lord Liverpool has been unwilling to trouble your Majesty for the last few days in consequence of your Majesty's indisposition, but he feels it to be his duty to inform your Majesty that the state of affairs in the City continues to be highly critical.' He went on to say that he had 'brought to Town several of your Majesty's confidential servants in order that there may be as full a Cabinet as can easily be summoned to consider of the means which it may be necessary eventually to adopt'.

Next day, however, the financial skies suddenly and miraculously brightened, and we find the Prime Minister writing:

> Lord Liverpool has the honour to inform your Majesty that the prospect of affairs in the City is better today than it was yesterday. The demands upon the Bank have been excessive today, but they have found the means of meeting them satisfactorily.[92]

What had happened? The answer is simply stated – any boast lies in the understatement – in a letter from Nathan to his brother Carl a few days later:

> We have had no failure of any importance since last post and the money market is evidently in a healthier state. I have received some large consignments of sovereigns from Paris and paid them into the Bank and there is every appearance of the late alarm and panic being succeeded by the restoration of confidence.[93]

The Duke of Wellington, who had been in the Cabinet at the time, was right when he later remembered: 'Had it not been for the most extraordinary exertions – above all on the part of old Rothschild – the Bank must have stopped payment.'[94]

Extraordinary efforts they were, or would have been for anyone but Nathan. When called upon, the 'Commanding General' took the field again, and the mighty Rothschild battalions began to roll in the service of the British government.

The Paris bank was the collection point for the shipment of gold to London, and the orders went out to Frankfurt, Vienna and Naples to keep Paris supplied. There was no panic at headquarters; indeed the self-confidence was quite astounding. At the end of February 1826 Nathan wrote to Paris:

> I shall be much obliged by your exerting yourselves in order to make your remittances of gold as large as possible, as I have pledged my word during the next month to obtain gold to the amount of one million Sterling.[95]

Nathan did it. In September of the same year, Herries wrote to Liverpool that of the £10m in gold Nathan had promised the Bank, he had already delivered £7m.[96] It seems safe to assume that Herries would have felt pride, not guilt, for having introduced Nathan Rothschild into the inner circles of British government finance. And it would be difficult to say that he was wrong.

To argue, however, that Nathan's remarkable services to the British governments in the financial sphere gave him dominating influence with those governments is ridiculous. This became clear when he attempted to use his influence in favour of his fellow Jews.

Nathan was a good and loyal, though not a strict, Jew. Unlike their in-laws, the Moses Montefiores, the Rothschilds did not keep kosher. Years later, staying with her sister and brother-in-law at East Cliff, Hannah had to send an urgent request for information to her sons at New Court. Was the turkey they had sent down kosher-killed? The Montefiores refused to have it cooked until they knew.[97] The Rothschilds, however, did keep the main dietary laws: they did not eat pork or shellfish. They observed the great holidays, and Nathan served the Great Synagogue (the German synagogue in Duke Place, where he is buried) as *Parnass,* or Warden. He and Hannah took a keen interest in Jewish education. He seems to have been known as a soft touch for appeals in that cause, and after he died Hannah singled out the Jews' Free School as the most appropriate charity to honour his memory.[98]

The Montefiores' call on the Rothschilds in February 1829 and the discussion of Jewish Emancipation has already been noticed. Perhaps the call was made in part on behalf of the Board of Jewish Deputies, the traditional guardians of the rights of British Jews, of whom Montefiore was one. The Deputies had been encouraged by the repeal of the Test and Corporation Acts the previous year, and were further encouraged by the Government's espousal of Catholic Emancipation at this time, to make efforts for the removal of their own disabilities.

Nathan was not a Deputy, but at their meeting on 16 April 1829, he was present by special invitation and

> stated for the information of the meeting that he had consulted with the Duke of Wellington, the Lord Chancellor, and other influential persons connected with the

Government concerning the disabilities under which Jews labour, and recommended that a petition praying for relief should be prepared, in readiness to be presented to the House of Lords whenever it may be thought right.

The meeting followed this advice, and a petition was put in train.[99]

The Rothschilds continued to aid the cause. The petition, again on Nathan's advice, was to be signed only by English-born Jews (which, of course, excluded him). The Deputies decided that in the first instance it should be signed only by their own members, with two exceptions: Lionel Rothschild and I. L. Goldsmid were requested to add their signatures as well. When the petition had been drawn up and signed Nathan and Montefiore personally took it to Lord Bexley (who had, as Nicholas Vansittart, been Chancellor of the Exchequer in the Waterloo period) to ask him to present it. With some minor alterations, which the Deputies willingly accepted, Bexley agreed.[100]

Shortly thereafter, however, the efforts were abruptly halted. On 17 May 1829 it was reported to the Deputies that Bexley had seen Wellington, who had given an unfavourable reply. The Duke felt that enough passion had been generated by Catholic Emancipation and that it ought to be allowed to die down. But Bexley had got the impression that Wellington would probably be willing to support a motion in the next session.

It was certainly quite a wrong impression, and if the Duke encouraged it he was being less than candid. Wellington believed that only necessity justified change. Several million Dissenters, even more several million Irishmen, constituted such necessity. Thirty thousand Jews did not.[101] Despite Nathan's continued support, though a bill was actually introduced in 1830, it got nowhere. The cause of full civil and political rights for Jews had to wait for his son and grandson; and they fought for the cause, not as bankers, but as politicians. Financial power was not enough. Nathan's overweening influence was a product of fevered imaginations.

He was a powerful man, and he began to live more like one. In 1825 he moved his residence from New Court to a great town house at 107 Piccadilly, which had previously belonged to the

Couttses. In 1835 Stamford Hill was abandoned, and a much grander country estate was acquired at Gunnersbury Park. Here too the metropolis has since encroached, but the house continues to sit, surrounded by what is now a public park; and it is still possible to get a feeling of the spaciousness and comfort Nathan might have enjoyed. He never did, because he died before the renovation of the mansion was completed.

Nathan's children had grown up. The eldest, Charlotte, had married her cousin Anselm in 1826 and moved to Frankfurt. The three elder sons, after completing their education at German universities, were launched into banking careers. Lionel had spent some time with his father in London, and then in 1830 had gone to Paris to assist, and learn from, his Uncle James. In 1835, his apprenticeship over, he had gone to Madrid to look after the family's Spanish interests; much more important after 1831, when, as part of loan negotiations, they had acquired a monopoly of the quicksilver industry in that country. Late in the same year Lionel had taken another important step towards independence, becoming engaged to his cousin Charlotte, Carl's daughter.

The marriage, as well as a family conclave where Nathan proposed to bring his sons into the partnership, was to take place in Frankfurt in June 1836, and Nathan departed for Germany late in May. Lionel was delighted his parents had finally started their journey. The younger members of the family found Frankfurt stultifying under the influence of their pious eldest uncle Amschel; and Lionel wrote to his brother Anthony, or Billy as he was affectionately known by the younger Rothschilds, 'that I am most heartily glad that the day for my quitting beautiful Frankfurt will very soon be here'.[102]

On 11 June Lionel reported that his parents had finally arrived, with Muffy (Mayer) who had been waiting for them with his tutor at Coblenz. His father had developed a terrible boil, at the base of his spine, on the trip; but that did not prevent him immediately closeting himself with his brothers to sort out the family business. Nathan was still king. On the same day, Lionel reported in another letter to his brother Nat in London that they and Anthony were to come into the London house, and on Nathan's terms.[103]

The boil, however, got worse. An eminent German surgeon, Professor Chelius, was summoned. He was satisfied with his

48

patient's progress, but the pain was terrible. Nathan refused to have any plans changed, announcing that if he were too unwell to go to the wedding, they could have it in the hotel.[104] That was on the 13th. On the 15th he dragged himself from bed, dressed and took himself off to Carl's house for the wedding. An admiring Lionel wrote to Billy, who was cutting his banking teeth by standing in for his uncle in Paris, 'as his complaint is only one that gives pain, it required but a little resolution, of which you know Papa has enough'.[105] Other observers noted that he laughed and joked during the ceremony, and tried to hurry the rabbi along with his banter. He continued to laugh. On 9 July Lionel wrote: 'Papa underwent the operation with the greatest possible courage and all the time made jokes.'[106]

Nothing did any good. The infection got worse and spread. But Nathan's stamina remained remarkable, and his appetite for work was undiminished. Instructions continued to pour forth from his sickroom. He was particularly concerned about Anthony in Paris. His stint there was meant to be a stage in his banking education, and many of the instructions had to do with that: Anthony had to be given rope, but not enough to hang himself with.

Nathan's courage did not fail, but he was often irascible, even more often than usual. Hannah was constantly in demand, and she rarely left his bedside, night or day. Often she acted as his amanuensis, and it was from her pen that the constant instructions flowed, and the words of affection and praise. Papa wanted her to say, she wrote to Nat, that if he had seemed to express any disappointment, he didn't mean it. He was very pleased with all that Nat had done. And again, to Anthony and Nat, Papa was very, very pleased with their handling of affairs.[107]

Lionel was sitting up with his father on the night of the 25th of July, and he was called away in the middle of his letter to take instructions. He understood his father to say that they were to sell English securities and Exchequer Bills in London and Paris. He was a little sceptical about these instructions, but he didn't like to question them. When Nathan Rothschild gave an order, even his sons did not like to ask for an explanation.[108]

It was the last letter from Frankfurt. On 28 July 1836, Nathan Rothschild died.

The story has often been told how a pigeon brought the news of Nathan's death to London. Tied to the bird's leg was a paper,

49

and written on it simply, *'Il est mort.'* Or so *The Times* understood.

There was, however, perhaps an even more eloquent testimonial to the world's appreciation of Nathan. On 6 August 1836, the important event, like all others in this period, was marked by the publication of a lithograph. It portrayed a vast and empty Stock Exchange. In front of Nathan's favourite pillar stood a famous profile, in stark black silhouette. 'The Shadow of a Great Man' caught the feeling of what had been lost.[109] A void had been created at the very centre of affairs.

CHAPTER TWO

Hannah and her Children

To HAVE SUCCEEDED Nathan Rothschild would have been daunting at any age. To have done so at age twenty-eight must have been doubly daunting, not less because the other partners were only twenty-six and twenty-four. But Lionel, Anthony and Nat were not quite so isolated on their exalted eminence as it might have appeared. Nathan had not meant idly his final admonition to consult their mother in everything. Nor did they take it so.

While the remodelling of Gunnersbury was being completed, Hannah took a house at Roehampton. There she, her two younger daughters, and Charlotte, who had returned with them from Frankfurt, awaited the arrival of the latter's baby. Nathaniel, Charlotte and Anselm's first surviving son, arrived without incident on 26 October. But Hannah was in no hurry to leave the country, and even Roehampton was too far away for her sons. 'Your brothers,' she wrote to Mayer in mid-November, 'would rather we were in Town but this would not suit us.'[1]

Hannah preferred to bear her loss away from London's bustle, 'at home and grieving only'.[2] But though she spent as much time as she could at Roehampton, she could not escape London and its concerns. 'Now . . . that we are deprived of our best Friend,' she told Mayer, 'there is more responsibility upon ourselves.'[3] Hannah took her own very seriously, and in May 1837, she reported from Piccadilly: 'We are again in this bustling place. As it rather disturbs the family to be so far off towards the end of the summer I suppose we shall go to Gunnersbury which is nearly finished.'[4]

Her letters to her youngest son, pursuing his education in Germany and later at Cambridge, make clear that it was more than conventional motherly ministrations her sons desired. Her letters are full of business and politics, and her steadying hand

51

must have been most welcome. For hardly were her sons at the helm than the financial world was plunged into chaos by the rash of bank failures in America. Even before that: 'The expectation of the necessity of corn being imported has impressed many with the fear that gold must leave the country and every fluctuation in the corn market makes an equal one on the funds.' All this left the bank, particularly its heavy investments in Spanish and Portugese securities, in a highly precarious state. It was, as Hannah said, 'harrassing', but they must keep their heads: 'Patience is a great balsam and I make no doubt will cure the many complaints we have lately here.'[5] This was written in mid-November 1836, before the American disaster, but it was characteristic of her attitude – and the bank's policy – throughout. Rothschilds emerged from the crisis stronger than ever. Precisely how much Hannah contributed to all this is impossible to say with any precision. What is clear is that the young partners relied heavily on her advice and counsel. They did not underestimate this shrewd, intelligent, and worldly-wise woman, and it would be a serious mistake to do so.

But it was more than the business concerns of her older sons that occupied Hannah's attention. She had also to be father as well as mother to her younger children. The impress of her strong personality is clear upon them all.

The pattern of education of her sons had already been broadly set. As has been seen, the two eldest went to a Jewish boarding school at Peckham. Whether Nat and Mayer did is unclear. In any case, the three eldest finished their education on the Continent.

In May 1827 Goethe noted meeting Lionel and Anthony with their tutor, John Darby.[6] Besides travelling with them and meeting eminent luminaries, Darby seems to have accompanied them at their stints at university. Lionel certainly attended Göttingen. Whether he attended another university is unclear. Anthony, who was with him at Göttingen in 1827, wrote at the end of the year from Strasbourg, where he then was with Nat; and, in February 1828, knowing his mother's passion for education and its details, he informed her:

> Our studies go on in the usual way. We follow the lectures regularly at the Academy and I find a great difference between these lectures here and those at Göttingen. This university cannot be compared to that. The

professors here are not very celebrated and in most of the faculties except Medicine and Chemistry there is a great want of professors. There is only one professor who lectures on History. If any person wishes to follow a regular course of History he must remain for three or four years.[7]

Whatever its educational defects, Anthony seems to have looked back with considerable nostalgia on his days at Strasbourg. Through him, the whole family developed a passion for the local pâtés. Nor, as his letter suggests, does his time at university seem to have been without profit in other ways.

After two years of attending university lectures, Anthony went on to a more practical education in the counting house at Frankfurt. Abraham Crailsham, who was in charge of his instruction there, wrote to Nathan:

> According to your request to inform you now and then of your son's progress in the counting house I have the honour to say that I ceaselessly instruct him in all the arithmetical problems, and I am glad to perceive that he has the intellectual grasp and makes good use of what I have to teach him. In due course I shall give to the young Baron systematically the knowledge of the art of arithmetics, and I shall continue to explain to him arbitration of exchange and all of the business curriculum of the counting house . . .[8]

A year in Frankfurt was followed by a return to London for a while, where Nathan could personally supervise his son's continuing introduction to banking. But Anthony's education was by no means over. There was more European travel, especially to the sites of the other Rothschild banks. In 1832 we find Hannah writing to her son:

> Vienna must be a place of much interest as it contains so much for a scientific man. Take advantage of what may be useful to you. When again settled in a place, take some good masters for French and German, which you will need in the business you attend.[9]

The end of Anthony's education came in 1836, when he was left in charge of the Paris house at the time of Lionel's wedding and Nathan's death.

Of the older sons, Anthony's education is the most fully chronicled, but it is clear that Lionel and Nat followed a similar course. Lionel returned to London after his university career, and served his apprenticeship under his father's watchful eye at New Court. Two years there was followed by a long stint with Uncle James at Paris, beginning in 1830 and ending when he was put in charge of the bank's Spanish affairs and went to Madrid in 1835. To the young men, the process often seemed a long one. Nineteen-year-old Nat wrote in disgust from Naples in February 1831 that, as his Uncle Carl's letters of introduction had stated that he was there to finish his education, it was unlikely anyone would tell him much of interest in politics or anything else.[10] Three years later he was given his chance, being sent to Constantinople to complete a delicate financial arrangement between a recently independent Greece and the Porte. It was a traumatic baptism by fire, for his seniors repudiated the arrangements he concluded, leading to a temporary suspension of relations between Greece and the Porte[11] Nat may well have wished that his apprenticeship had been somewhat longer.

The youngest son, Mayer, was still at the university stage of his career when his father died. He had spent the previous academic year at Leipzig with his tutor, Dr Schlemmer. In the autumn of 1836 he set off for Heidelberg. Hannah, though she had a pregnant daughter under her charge, and kept a watchful eye on the affairs of New Court, did not neglect Mayer, and sage advice followed him. On 9 November she wrote:

> In your last it appears that their Mighty Highnesses the Professors are rather intolerable. I would observe every necessary etiquette and ceremony usual. But should they persevere in giving you any difficulty to attend their lectures I would immediately engage the best private masters which are to be obtained so that you do not lose your time.[12]

Hannah did not believe in ruffling feathers unnecessarily, but neither would she waste time with foolish people.

There was also gentle advice for the whole man. On 15 November she wrote:

> Yours afforded me much satisfaction. There is no news which can give me half the gratification as that of being

informed of your proper attendance to your studies and affectionate duties. The first must lead to your future advancement. The second evinces a disposition to adhere to those principles which form the mind to the protection of virtue and which, dear Mayer, will ever make you beloved. I allude to your refusal to partake of the parties which are offered to you. Papa's memory deserves to be respected, and I am sure you feel it should be.[13]

Hannah was anxious that her children should have every advantage, but they must never forget who they were or whence they had sprung. There were prices too high to pay for success.

Such considerations were much on her mind in contemplating the next stage of Mayer's education, Cambridge. She was undoubtedly more of a snob than her husband (she was, after all, an Englishwoman, born and bred), and she probably had a much juster appreciation of the importance of titles and other social distinctions. She called herself Baroness, and it was very likely her influence which prompted her sons to make application for official royal permission to use the title of Baron, which they did after their father's death. Equally, as an Englishwoman, Hannah was anxious that her sons should be able to compete for all the honours and distinctions their country could offer. But again, not on any terms. As she wrote to Mayer in October 1837:

I received your letter with much satisfaction to learn that you could become a member of an institution where our most celebrated scholars and other great characters are educated, without infringing, so as to give public offence to our religious body. I know, my dear Mayer, that you are fully impressed with the importance of a good education. I feel pleasure that you are so, for we must hope that you will achieve those benefits which others have in attaining . . . preeminence. I am also very desirous that you may avoid everything possible in infringing upon our religious duties. Do, dear Mayer, abstain from those indulgences such as riding on horseback on Saturdays etc . . . All your wants and wishes tell me now. I shall send you a Prayer Book among those which Frederick is going to send. Do not forget, dear Mayer, that there are some duties imposed to make a good man as well as a great one.[14]

Mayer was admitted a Fellow Commoner at Magdalene ('Maudlin', Hannah spelled it phonetically in her first letter – she was clearly put right immediately) on 20 October 1837. Hannah wanted a full report, urging Mayer not to 'be fatigued with the detail. Be assured I shall not.' She wished to know all about his peers: 'Are the students shy – and do they evince prejudice?' And finally: 'Shall we pay you a visit or will our company be superfluous?'[15]

The answer to the last question was that it would be. Like other undergraduates since, Mayer had no desire for the company of his mother at Cambridge. Hannah, for her part, had too much tact and good sense not to accept his explanation about the terrible burden of studies, though that seems not to have interfered with visits from his brothers. She was understanding in other ways. She did not encourage extravagance, but neither did she have any desire to keep Mayer short: 'Whenever your Tin is declining let me know also.'[16]

The answer to Hannah's first question appears to have been that, whether the students did or not, the authorities at Magdalene, or some of them, began to evince prejudice. This was probably what lay behind Mayer's migration to Trinity at the beginning of the Lent Term, 1838. In a letter apparently written at the end of the Christmas vacation, Hannah wanted to know how he

> was received on your return – and also to know if you have had any further intimation of being obliged to attend Chapel. I assure you, you have occupied my attention during this period. I feel most anxious not alone that you should attain to preeminence in your studies, but also that you might retain that proper sense of your religious duties which are incumbent on every person who has a sense of God.

She also seems to have taken legal advice, and advised Mayer that, through Sir F. French, a letter would be sent to him 'from Mr Law – Lord Lyndhurst himself'. But she also advised that he should not change his college merely from pique – 'that would be folly'.[17]

The question of compulsory Chapel attendance, the main bar to Jews at Cambridge, for, unlike Oxford, there was no religious test on matriculation, would not be settled for some years. But it was, of course, a matter of college discretion; and Mayer apparently found Trinity more understanding. This could not have been because of the Master. Christopher Wordsworth, the poet's brother, was a high and dry Tory, and one of his main concerns was to end the notorious irregularity of undergraduate attendance at Chapel. This, however, was strongly resisted by the junior members who formed a 'Society for the Prevention of Cruelty to Undergraduates'. Among other things, the Society published lists exposing the distinctly irregular Chapel attend-, ance of the Fellows. A number of liberal younger Fellows gave enthusiastic backing to the undergraduates[18] and Mayer found shelter somewhere within this protective network. At any rate, in February 1838, he invested in a second Fellow Commoner's gown, this time a Trinity gown.[19]

He spent a very happy two years at Cambridge. Not much is known about how he passed his time. Among his papers is a livery bill for boarding horses, and it is likely that, like his nephews later, he rode with the 'drag'. He also subscribed to the Camden Society in 1838.[20] And that is about all one can find out. There is no doubt, however, that Mayer looked back with nostalgia on his Cambridge years; and, as will be seen, he would fight hard, and successfully, to keep the university open to Jews.

Uncle James feared that Mayer's taste for the sporting life, further developed at Cambridge, was in danger of becoming excessive. 'Why is it,' James wrote in November 1839, 'that Rabbi Mayer does not write? Is he hunting? A young man should and has to work.'[21] Mayer in fact would never work very hard (in the bank, at any rate); but his elder brothers, who did put in long hours at New Court, were hardly behind him in their passion for sport.

Their letters to one another, besides containing much business, and often gossip, were almost always full of sport. In October 1835, Anthony wrote to Nat from Frankfurt ('this horrid place') yearning for the Puckeridge Hunt. If only, he said, he could have a few days hunting. He could not, but he asked Nat, as the next best thing, to send him a brown hunting coat with Puckeridge buttons. Some years later, Nat himself, by then married to his cousin Charlotte and a partner in the Paris bank, would lament from his place of exile: 'What magic there is in a pair of leather breeches. I have half a mind to put a pair on and gallop round the Bois de Boulogne – Old Tup would exclaim, Go it you Cockney.'[22]

The brothers were affectionately devoted to one another. 'Tup' or 'Muffy' was Mayer. Nat was 'Stag'. Anthony was 'Billy'. And Lionel, as befitted the eldest brother, was 'Rabbi', or more usually 'Rab'. The other nicknames are redolent of prowess in the field, or perhaps the bed. They seem to have been apt.

The Rothschild brothers were full-blooded young men. There were, however, distinct differences of style as well as appearance between them. All were somewhat below medium height. Nat was the most conventionally handsome, dark like all the brothers, but slimmer and with well-chiselled features. Lionel too was striking of face, but his fine head was set rather too squarely on the short powerful body. Mayer was similar in build – they were muscular versions of their father – with a face that radiated kindness, but whose looks were marred by a flattish nose. Anthony was the least distinguished in appearance; round and bluff, he looked the part of the amiable country squire he would become.

There were differences in character as well. Lionel, true to his name, was more of a 'Rab', reserved, and with a sense of humour more cynical and sardonic than ribald. He did not make a display of his feelings, and he was discreet in his private life. In March 1835, he wrote to Anthony, apparently in anticipation of the latter taking his place at Madrid, 'Bring as many nice little things for ladies as you can. You will find lots to accept them little trinkets and all sorts of things.'[23]

That, however, is the only hint one gets of amorous activities. Anthony, on the other hand, can almost be heard panting. Besides missing the Puckeridge Hunt in Frankfurt, he missed something else: 'Till now I have not seen any girls here, and I want something so bad that I do not know what to do.'[24] And Anthony's affairs were noisy and public, with women turning up both in London and Paris, intent on cashing in at the respective banks.[25]

Nat was somewhere in between. On one occasion, at least, a woman appeared demanding to be paid, but this was the exception. By and large, he was sensible and discreet. He was also more of a dandy and man about town; and the Count d'Orsay was a particular friend.[26]

Whatever the differences in their personalities, however, there was one thing on which the young Rothschilds were all agreed. As Lionel, briefly back on English soil in October 1832, wrote to Anthony, in whom his sentiment found a resounding echo, there was no place like home.[27] Thirty years in France only made Nat more aggressively 'Cockney' as the years passed. He might be a Paris banker, and the proud owner of Château Mouton, but he never ceased to long for England, returned whenever possible, and when it was not, consoled himself as best he could with *Bell's Life* and *The Times*.

For the Rothschilds (and undoubtedly for others, though for rather different reasons) it was a good deal easier to be an Englishman than an Englishwoman. The men could to a large extent determine their own destinies. Much as he lamented it, Nat chose a life of exile. Two of his sisters had little choice in the matter, and the third precipitated a family crisis by insisting on marrying not only an Englishman, but a Christian.

It was family policy, insofar as possible, for family to marry family. James had married his niece, Salomon's daughter Betty. Charlotte, Nathan and Hannah's eldest child, married Betty's brother Anselm in 1826. And in 1836 Lionel married another Charlotte, Carl's daughter, in the wedding overshadowed by Nathan's fatal illness.

In 1839, Nathan and Hannah's second daughter, Hannah Mayer, broke the pattern with a vengeance, by marrying the Hon. Henry Fitzroy, a younger son of the Earl of Southampton, and what is more, marrying him in church. She did it without her family's consent, and indeed over their opposition. They did not, however, attempt to cut her off. Her mother took her to the church door, though she would not follow her daughter through it. Nat did, and he firmly faced the family storm which immediately broke about them.

Of Nathan's four surviving brothers, it was James, the youngest, who had most nearly taken his place as head of the family. Where Nathan had pioneered in financing governments, James did the same for the new arteries of industrial growth, the railways, and as Nathan had done earlier, so now James carried the rest of the family in his wake. Nor was it only in the affairs of the bank that James gave the lead; particularly with the family in London, he attempted to exercise an authority thoroughly paternal.

Uncle James was furious over Hannah Mayer's marriage. Long letters to Nat in Judendeutsch reflect the positions of both sides in the exchange:

The fact that Hannah Mayer married made me quite ill and frankly speaking I did not have the courage up until now to write. She robbed our whole family of its pride . . . You write to me that she has found everything [in her marriage] but religion. But just that means everything. Our luck, our blessings, depend upon it. However, we shall have to forget her and cut her out of our memory . . . We just wish her happiness and in future we shall just look upon the whole matter as if she had never existed for us.

This, however, was by no means acceptable to London, and Nat wrote again, which brought another angry response from James. Nat had written 'that all she did was to marry a Christian in a Christian country'. To James, this was no justification whatever, quite the contrary. Apparently responding to another of Nat's observations, James wrote that it was not entirely a matter of money, but the remainder of his letter indicates rather the strength of his feelings than the clarity of his thought:

What sort of example would a girl be for our children who says: 'I marry against the wish of my family?' . . . Why should my children or my children's children follow my wishes if there is no punishment? Now I come to the main point: Religion. In our family we have always tried to keep up the love for, the attachment to the family . . . In this way it was more or less understood from early childhood and the children would never think of marrying outside the family. This way the fortune would stay inside the family . . .[28]

The English family, however, adhered to its own line, though possibly with some tactical manoeuvring. Anthony, who had braved in person the wrath, first of his Frankfurt and then of his Paris uncle, wrote:

I have requested Uncle James and Betty to write to you in friendly terms upon [the] subject. I said it would have a greater effect than all the quarrelsome letters in the world . . . I advise you not to receive HM for the present, so as to keep the union of the family. When all is forgotten, one can do what one likes. I told them Mamma would follow her own feelings; but it would be better if she did not invite HM for the present.[29]

60

Whether there was ever even a pretence of banishing Hannah Mayer from the family circle is unclear. If so, it did not last long.

The main effect of Hannah Mayer's marriage on her unmarried siblings was to precipitate a virtual stampede to the huppah, the little wedding-tent. As early as Lionel's wedding, budding family romances had been eagerly watched, or imagined, by the older generation. Aunt Henrietta's son, Joseph Montefiore, had got nowhere with Hannah Mayer; it was hoped that an apparent mutual attraction between two sixteen-year-olds, Louise and her cousin Mayer Carl, Carl's son, would develop into something.[30] Hannah Mayer's marriage got the process moving again in a hurry,[31] though they were not actually to be wed until 1842.

The pressure was not less on the young men. Anthony, on his mission to Frankfurt, wrote in annoyance to his brothers:

> Uncle A. was a regular bother asking me about getting married, and writing to Uncle S. that I only waited until his death to marry a Christian. . . . I told him quite short, that if Aunt Henrietta would cash up, I was ready, when he said of course he would not advise me without Louise had the same fortune as Joseph and Nathaniel. So, I said very well, and I believe he wrote to that effect – for later we left much better friends . . .[32]

Anthony and Louise Montefiore were duly married in March 1840.

The last to take the trip to the 'little tent', until Mayer was married to his cousin Juliana Cohen in 1850, was Nat, in the garden of his Uncle James's country house at Boulogne in August 1842.[33] At the same time that he married James and Betty's daughter, Nat also completed his move to the Paris bank, where he had mainly been since 1840, and began a life of exile in France. How happy were these arranged marriages? The answer is that, as with other marriages, the happiness varied. They certainly presented problems. Lionel confided to his brothers of his impending engagement to Charlotte of Frankfurt (her father Carl divided his time between that city and Naples) that he was in no hurry to leave the pleasures of Madrid: 'It makes little difference for me to go to Frankfurt a few months earlier or later, as I have no particular fancy to get married just immediately.'[34]

He seems to have managed not to get there until late in the year. Then, however, he was obviously swept off his feet.

Charlotte, still not seventeen, was a beautiful girl; and Lionel's letters after his return to Paris early in the new year are those of a man very much in love.[35]

The marriage was less than perfect. The shadow of Nathan's illness hung heavy over the festivities. Charlotte was very nervous, so much so that on the one night they managed to snatch for a honeymoon her period came on early – much to Lionel's frustration, and his brothers' amusement.[36]

The journey to London, accompanying Nathan's coffin, would not have been joyful, and this was followed by months of retirement from society. Disraeli saw them at the beginning of the next (1837) season at a concert at Parthner's. It was a dazzling aristocratic company:

> But the most picturesque group was the Rothschilds, the widow still in mourning, two sons, some sisters, and, above all the young bride, or rather wife from Frankfurt, universally admired, tall, graceful, dark, and clear, picturesquely dressed, a robe of yellow silk, a hat and feathers, with a sort of *Sévigné* beneath of magnificent pearls; quite a Murillo.[37]

But for the young wife herself, life was not so serene as it might have appeared on the surface. Hannah reported to Mayer in November 1836 that *'la Belle'* and her *'caro sposo'*, as she called the young couple, were well and still much in love: 'There is many a fond look and kiss from dimpled lips and brilliant eye.' They had their own house in Hill Street, but this did not prevent Hannah from keeping a close eye on them – rather too close for the comfort of all concerned. For, as early as the 11th of October, Louise had reported to Mayer that 'Charlotte is not yet confined, and we are getting impatient.'[38] Since they had only got married on 15 June, such impatience would seem to have been a trifle premature.

Though obviously fond of her aunt and mother-in-law, Charlotte felt slightly overpowered by her, and Lionel seems not to have been very sympathetic or sensitive to his wife's problems. Though they had a town house, they had no place of their own in the country, sharing Gunnersbury with Hannah. Charlotte evidently found this a bit much. Twelve years after their marriage, by which time Mayer had already been established for six years at Mentmore, she wrote:

You ask, dear husband, if I am going to Mentmore. As your mother wishes to go there for a few days, I have no choice but to go with her. Ever since I became your wife, I have had to do what others want, never what I would like to do. Pray that I shall be compensated in Heaven.

Having got launched, Charlotte continued to unburden herself: 'You might take the trouble to write to my mother. Once within twelve years is not too much.'[39]

To a certain extent, this was doubtless a healthy venting of frustrations, of the sort indulged in by every husband and wife on occasion. Yet there are other suggestions that Charlotte was not entirely happy. She was a highly sensitive and intelligent woman, later a great favourite of Disraeli's, and also of Gladstone's, with whom she engaged in long theological discussions. It is evident that she did not think that women were sufficiently appreciated in a male-dominated world, and by male Rothschilds in particular. She resented the fact, for example, that her husband and his family had expectantly awaited not only a child, but a male child. Two daughters, Leonora, though born with what one would have thought admirable promptitude in August 1837, and Evelina, who followed in 1839, had not satisfied them. And when Nathan (usually called Natty, and by his mother, Nathaniel) finally arrived in 1840, she noted in his volume, for she kept one on each of her children: 'He was a thin, ugly baby, but that did not signify; he was a boy, and as such most welcome to his father and the whole family. I never could prefer him to his sisters, and nursed him not so well as he ought to have been nursed.'[40]

It says much of Charlotte's intelligence and sensitivity that she was able to recognize her feelings, and admit them – which is probably why, though a sense of those early feelings had a marked effect on his personality, she later had an excellent relationship with her eldest son. For the moment, however, what is important is that these were Charlotte's feelings. The volumes on her other children are equally revealing. Leonora's arrival ended for her mother an intensely unhappy first year in England, which is sufficiently explained by the fact that she was only eighteen and away from her parents' home for the first time. At the end of the month, she took Laury, or Lally as she was sometimes called, to synagogue and returned thanks: 'I also went to the registry office and proudly wrote my darling's name in the book.' She continued to lavish every care on the little girl, especially on her education. In 1850, she notes in her daughter's volume that she wanted Laury 'to attend the classes of ancient and modern history in Bedford Square, but perhaps I had better enquire who teaches in the Queen's College – there may be better teachers in that establishment'. She finally decided on Bedford College,[41] recently founded (Queen's was only two years old); and what is particularly interesting is that though she thought formal education necessary for her eldest daughter, there is no suggestion that she even considered it for her eldest son. Probably it was only the obvious inadequacy of Natty's education by private tutors, which became painfully evident at Cambridge, that caused his brothers to be sent to King's College school (now located at Wimbledon).

It was not only that Charlotte was left more discretion in the education of her daughters than of her sons. She was indeed intensely concerned with the education of the latter as well – but the education of girls, to her mind, required more care. But for what? It became increasingly apparent that Laury was destined for their Paris cousin Alphonse. But it was evidently not only her daughter of whom Charlotte thought when she marvelled 'that a beautiful young girl . . . must esteem herself fortunate to give her fairy hand . . . to a man, who perhaps for ten or fifteen years has run the round of the world – is completely blasé, can neither admire nor love – and yet demands the entire devotion of his bride, her slavish devotion'.

But, Charlotte, continued, 'It is better so – the man whose passions are dead, whose feelings have lost all freshness, all depth, is likely to prove a safe husband, and the wife will probably find happiness in the discharge, in the fulfilment of her duties. Her disenchantment will be bitter but not lasting.'[42] It does not require a great deal of imagination to deduce whose marriage she had in mind.

Of Laury, Charlotte said that 'she attaches much importance to a certain position in the world, and would not like to descend from what she fancies to be the throne of the R's to be the bride of a humbler man.'[43] Whether or not Charlotte herself took comfort in such things is unclear, but there is every reason to think that she meant what she said about finding compensations in doing her duty as wife, mother, hostess, and lady of good works. She can be said to have settled into a happy marriage. Lionel may not have been sufficiently passionate and devoted (though he would have been surprised to be thought lacking in these respects), but he was fond of his wife, and, by his own lights at any rate, considerate of her. If he had many of the faults, he also had some of the strengths of a good husband – and Charlotte ultimately found him so.

It is only fair to add that Charlotte did not have a high opinion of the romantic qualities of any of her male relations. Of the early stages of Alphonse's courtship of Laury, she said that it was characterized by the same 'indifference shown by Mayer to Juliana . . . whether with the same intention or not, I cannot tell'.[44] Mayer's intention, of course, had been to wed Juliana, which he did in 1850, in a marriage that was extremely happy from the start. The marriage of cousins certainly created some problems, but it does not seem to have been notably less success-ful than some other methods of selection. Undoubtedly, it had the desired effect of keeping together and reinforcing the family's wealth. Nathan's daughters took fortunes of some £130,000 to their husbands. Juliana brought her cousin Mayer about £88,000.[45] By Victorian standards especially, these were dazzling dowries.

Nathan left his heirs great wealth – something in the neigh-bourhood of £1.35m. It was his wife who did most to shape the tastes that would enjoy this wealth. Hannah is usually credited with encouraging her sons in their taste for hunting, on the grounds that it was good for their health. Certainly, Nathan himself did not discourage them in this respect. Buxton wrote of Anthony that 'he is a mighty hunter; and his father lets him buy any horses he likes.'[46] As far as their mother's influence is concerned, she did not discourage this, as she did not discourage other, aristocratic pursuits. And they were all firmly convinced that it was excellent for their health.

As has been seen, however, her interests and her influence were more intellectual and artistic. Lionel, for example, attended Paris sales in the 1830s with his mother very much in mind: 'Be so good to let me know if you would like some old inlaid furniture, a secretaire or commode made in the time of Louis the 14th. Here these things are quite the rage, or if you would prefer some old Sèvres china.' And from Madrid he wrote in October 1834, that 'all my leisure time I pass in running about after pictures which are in very great numbers but few good ones.'[47] Here, he would appear to have had some success. Disraeli, in describing the family group as 'quite Murillo', may perhaps have known of the taste of Lionel and his mother for that artist. Among other of his works, Lionel was the proud possessor of 'The Good Shepherd'. In a family of avid collectors, it is not always easy to determine who bought what when. It is certain, however, that this generation were not only keenly interested, but also not without discrimination. Nat told his brothers in 1843 that he could not buy for Lionel, because 'pictures are something like ladies; everyone must please himself and select according to his taste.' His own taste in this instance was for Velasquez's 'Lady with the Fan'. In 1849, when Nat finally decided to have his pictures in England sent over to Paris, the list included twelve Hobbemas, four Ruysdaels, and nine Greuzes.[48] Few would be likely to deny that he had an eye for beauty.

It would probably be inaccurate to say that Hannah 'shaped' her sons' taste. What she rather did was to enter into it, evidence a keen interest, and thus encourage it. She wrote to Mayer, still at Cambridge, in May 1838, that she thought the house at Gunnersbury looked very well. An unspecified new room, she said, was nearly finished: 'You, dear Mayer, will know if the style is good. Having seen many of the best finished country houses, your judgement must be good.'[49]

Mayer's impression of Gunnersbury Park is unrecorded. The architect, who completely rebuilt a house constructed earlier in the century, was Sydney, the brother and very much the understudy of Sir Robert Smirke. It has been said of the latter that it was 'to a reputation for reliability rather than to brilliance in design that Smirke owed his career',[50] and the same could be said of his younger brother's work at Gunnersbury. The house is of unexceptionable neo-classical design of the then fashionable Greek variety. Neither the house, nor the rooms within it, are grand. They are, however, of pleasant proportions and comfortable. Again, it is not always easy to determine who did what, for Lionel would undertake some remodelling in the fifties. What the house and grounds do clearly reflect are the tastes of the three generations of Rothschilds who lived there. There are well-lighted walls for pictures. There are rather more conservatories and glass houses, including an Orangery, than is usual, reflecting a passion for flowers and gardening – which what is left of the gardens and the shrubberies also exhibit. Strolling through the grounds, it is still possible to understand why Disraeli, no mean judge of trees and flowers himself, was so attached to the place. It was more than just a rich man's (or woman's) house; it was also a home that breathed the taste of its owners.

Another area in which Hannah influenced her children was in their attitudes and priorities in politics. As has been seen, she took an even more intense interest in Jewish disabilities than her husband, and she continued to prod her sons. In May 1844 she wrote urging that the Jews ought to follow the recent Dissenting example of securing protection for the titles to their chapels. If they did not, she observed, they would be thought inactive and uninterested.[51] In 1845 she wrote from Paris rejoicing in the concession of municipal rights. Her joy in 'our recent advancement towards equality in rights and association' was only a little qualified by the fact that it was David Salomons whose aldermanic seat was to mark the victory. But, she advised, 'his celebrity in a good cause, we must allow him'.[52] She took an equally keen interest in the efforts of Lionel, now a member of the Board of Deputies, and of her brother-in-law Sir Moses Montefiore, their president, to take advantage of the Czar's visit to London in 1844 to secure an easing of restrictions against Jews in Russia. 'May his understanding,' she said of the Czar, 'at least improve by his travels.'[53] It would have been difficult, with such a mother, for her sons not to have taken an interest in such matters, and of course they did.

The result, and once more one suspects that their mother was at the least moving simultaneously, was to push them ever more into the Whig-Liberal camp. They had not got the lead here from their father. Nathan's closest political friends were Tories, such as Herries and Wellington. This is not to say that Nathan himself could be called a Tory in any meaningful sense of the term (which in any case was getting confused – many thought, wrongly, that Wellington himself was becoming a liberal in religious matters after 1828). Indeed, though deeply interested in the consequences of party politics, Nathan was basically neutral politically. What he wanted was stable government, and he was willing that considerable political movement should take place in order to achieve it. Thus in May 1832 he called on Wellington's close friend Charles Arbuthnot (to whom Nathan had lent a substantial sum), urging, in the interests of stability and continuity, that if the Duke took office he should concede parliamentary reform and abandon his traditional support of the conservative Continental powers.[54] In the same decade Nathan gave substantial financial assistance to a Liberal foreign policy of bolstering liberal regimes in the Iberian peninsula.[55] Peace and stability were good for Nathan's business activities, and peace and stability were therefore what he aimed at promoting.

Lionel's fundamental political reactions were probably not dissimilar to his father's, though the ultimate effect would be somewhat different. At first, he watched the parliamentary reform movement of the early thirties with some scepticism, and not a little concern. Writing from his Paris vantage point in April 1831, he remarked:

> If the Reform Bill passes it will have the same result as the revolution here. The king here wanted to take away the people's rights, which brought the revolution; in England the king gives the people more than their rights, which will have as bad consequences.

He was, however, by no means totally unsympathetic. For a few days later he wrote:

> I am pleased that the Reform Bill has had a little effect upon some of the aristocracy. It is a very good thing; some of those grand persons were really insupportable. The great difference that they always made between the different classes will soon be done away with, and the society in England will be more like that here, which is by far more agreeable.[56]

Lionel's position was far from unique. Indeed it was what is often described as the classic 'middle-class' position, founded on a desire to do away with what were considered the unreal distinctions deriving from birth, while at the same time maintaining what were held to be real and proper distinctions based on property. A corollary of this position was that, as property was a tangible evidence of talent, careers open to talent (one of the great liberal cries) by no means presupposed the removal of what were accepted as natural distinctions. Another corollary was that, in order to give talent and ability full scope, everything must be thrown open to competition – for those who could compete.

Such assumptions underlay what is widely known as

'nineteenth-century liberalism'. They dictated the main elements of the liberal programme: the removal of barriers to social and political advancement based on birth; an extension of political rights to people deemed to have sufficient property and education; and, to allow shrewdness and skill free play, the removal of protective barriers against the freedom of trade. Such was the programme subscribed to by large and powerful segments in nineteenth-century British society, and by Lionel de Rothschild and his brothers.

To call the programme 'middle-class' is somewhat misleading. It was undoubtedly espoused, among others, by those whom later generations have identified as middle-class; and it was not entirely to the interests of those who have subsequently been labelled working class. So much is true. Yet at the time of its greatest power and force, in the middle decades of the nineteenth century, it was neither conceived as a class programme, nor, according to the lights of the time, did it operate as one. Simply because we have come to take for granted – in Western society at any rate – the several sorts of freedom that it promoted, we should not underestimate their appeal for contemporaries of all classes. It would be patronizing to do so.

Powered by strong passions and ideals, the liberal programme was to prove the most important engine for change in the nineteenth century. Perhaps the most significant passions were religious ones – the frustrations of Catholics, Protestant Dissenters, and Jews. This is probably the main explanation of why the Rothschilds took themselves into the Liberal camp – as the accomplishment of the liberal programme, largely if not entirely by the party of the same name, was to be one of the main reasons why they would later remove themselves from that camp. The latter development, however, was still far in the future. Lionel's generation, and especially Lionel himself, were to find, indeed place, themselves in the vanguard of change.

What would make Lionel a Liberal, did not make him a Radical by the standards of the 1830s; and his early reactions to politics appear to have been quite as pragmatic as his father's. On 20 November 1830, he wrote that he did not think the Whig ministers would long remain in office, and advised that his father should not neglect the Duke, whom Lionel thought would soon be in office again. By April 1831, however, in the same letter in which he expressed his pleasure that the English aristocracy were being cut down to size, he urged his mother not to let Nathan lend the Duke any money. By May, 1832 he had come to the conclusion that a Wellington ministry would be bad for business.[57]

The rest of the family seem to have moved in the same direction. By the time of the general elections in December 1832, Anthony was sure that nothing would maintain the peace of Europe so well as the Grey ministry remaining in office.[58] Equally, the bank's relations with the Whig ministry, initially rather cool, began to warm perceptibly. In 1833 N. M. Rothschild, after a gap of several years in handling major financial transactions for the government, took charge of a loan guaranteed by England, France and Russia which had as its aim the firm foundation of the new Greek monarchy and the mollification of the Turks. In 1835, the bank contracted for the £15m West India loan, the purpose of which was to compensate the planters and allow the implementation of Parliament's abolition of colonial slavery the previous year. In the same year, with a £4m loan to the Portugese government, the bank did its bit to advance Whig foreign policy in the Iberian peninsula. Good relations between N. M. Rothschild and the Whig ministry would continue.[59]

Few probably would have expected the Rothschilds to forego lucrative government business because of political loyalties elsewhere. It seems not to have been until after the general elections of 1841 that the marked change in their political attitudes was noticed. Then Herries, in general advice on the financial strategy to be pursued by Peel's new government, commented on the attitude of 'Jews and brokers':

> It may be as well to bear in mind that the said gentry may not be so propitious to you as in former time. The part which Jones Loyd, Sam Gurney and the Rothschilds etc. took in the City election indicates no kind feeling towards the Conservative Party.

Herries went on to predict: 'They will not allow their feelings to stand much in the way of their own interest'; but he added the significant qualification, and here he obviously had the Rothschilds foremost in his mind, that 'they will not forgive the rejection of the bill to enable the Jews to be Common Council men'.[60]

Herries was right in stressing the primacy of religious con-

70

siderations in determining the political orientation of the Roth-schilds. One of the successful candidates in the City for whom the brothers had worked hard was that perhaps greatest of champions of religious liberty, Lord John Russell; and their brother-in-law Anselm declared himself 'delighted with the manner Lord J. Russell expressed himself in favour of our cause. I hope,' he told the London brothers, 'in a year or two to be able to congratulate one of you on a seat in Parliament.' Even Nat, though looking somewhat suspiciously on Whiggery from Paris, at the same time emphasized the crucial importance of religious issues. Upon receiving the news that the Queen had sent for Peel, he wrote: 'I trust that he will be liberally inclined towards us poor Jews, and if he emancipates us, he shall have my support.' Nat went on to say that he 'never was much of a Vig like old Tup, and I must say I am now rather more of a Tory than when I was in London. I don't like the levellers and destructives.'[61]

Such sentiments of course emphasize the broad political wisdom of the Peel of the Tamworth Manifesto: there can be little doubt that there was a constituency for the programme he enunciated in 1834. The difficulty was that the party he led was not willing to compete for that constituency, and despite some bows in the direction of tolerant Toryism, it was the intolerant element that kept reasserting itself. For someone who placed his chief emphasis on religious liberty, there was really no place but Whig-Liberalism, even if one were a little chary of some of one's allies in that broad grouping. This was clearly the conclusion of the London brothers. Tup, or Mayer's election to Brooks's on 9 May 1841,[62] as well as marking a social arrival, also signified a statement of political allegiance – one shared in their own ways by his brothers.

It is clear that from the beginning the Rothschild brothers had in mind taking their place within the political nation, what they considered their rightful place among its leaders, as members of Parliament. (As will be seen, they would have settled for either House!) The opportunity would present itself at the next general election.

Who made the first approaches about Lionel standing as one of the Liberal candidates for the City of London is uncertain. What is evident is that his candidacy was enthusiastically received in Liberal circles in the City, some thought too enthusiastically received. F. Miles wrote urging him not to allow himself to be put in nomination: 'The Whigs wish it because you would pay the whole cost of their expenses. But it is not for the money that I speak. I do not believe that you will succeed.'[63]

Lionel, however, decided to try, and at a large meeting of the Liberal electors of the City of London on 8 July 1847, he was duly endorsed as a candidate, along with the Prime Minister, Lord John Russell, James Pattison, and Sir George Larpent.[64] Money may perhaps have been one consideration. The Rothschilds were generous in support of Liberal candidates, and not only in London. But it was not money alone that made Lionel attractive, indeed, if the reports in *The Times* are an accurate guide, the candidate most enthusiastically received by the Liberal electors. He was also, and took care to be, an archetypal Liberal candidate. He was, he told the first party meeting, in favour of any reasonable extension of the franchise, whenever it could be safely done. Taxation ought to be reduced as much as possible, and any loss of revenue would soon be made up by the increase of the national wealth. He was particularly anxious to reduce the duty on tea, which pressed especially hard on the poorer classes. 'On the subject of civil and religious liberty he considered that there ought not to be any intervention by the State to restrict perfect liberty of conscience.' On the question of state grants and endowments of religious institutions, in which Russell's government had recently indulged in efforts to extend state support of education, Lionel hedged considerably. He refrained from condemning the Prime Minister's policy. 'The subject was,' he said, 'a very delicate one with him, and therefore he would not say any more at that point.' He had no hesitation whatever, however, in declaring himself an out and out free trader, anxious to support its fullest development.[65]

All this was safe and orthodox Liberalism. Nat thought it was a little too safe, advising: 'If I were you, my dear Lionel, I should go a little farther than my Lord John. You must be as liberal as possible if you wish to succeed.'[66] Lionel clearly took such advice to heart. Dissenters, who made up the most solid block of Liberal support, were extremely angry over the government's policy of supporting religious – and more particularly Anglican – schools. They were loudly and vociferously advocating the principle of voluntarism in education, and indeed in anything having to do with religion. Lionel obviously decided that it was worth cultivating such support, and on 13 July he declared to a highly enthusiastic meeting of the electors of Cripplegate Without and Cripplegate Within his 'candid opinion' against any sort of endowments whatever for any religious purpose.[67]

Whether he in fact took as rigid a position as this is doubtful. On broad principles Lionel was sound enough, but he was too pragmatic a politician to make it likely that he would have been personally inclined to take such a strict view of the matter. The point is that he was a politician, a politician with an overriding goal – Jewish Emancipation. To succeed, the cause required the support of more than the some 35,000 British Jews, and Lionel was willing to manoeuvre for that support. For obvious reasons, the best chance of success was to make the Jewish cause, not merely a Jewish cause, but an integral part of a wider Liberal programme. Lionel's every utterance during the election was aimed at doing just this. As he said at the same meeting, the religious question .

> appeared to him the great question which now agitated the public mind, and with respect to which general interest was felt.(Cheers.) It was one with regard to which he was unfortunately situated, although his views upon it coincided with those of his brother candidates beside him. (Cheers.)

In espousing rigorous voluntarism he simply carried their common principles a little further.

The important point to emphasize, however, and the point he kept hammering, was that his position was precisely that of 'his brother candidates beside him'. One of his brother candidates, of course, was the Liberal Prime Minister. The point of the election campaign was to capture, and irrevocably commit, an already well-inclined Liberal party to Jewish Emancipation. And that had been the point from the beginning. As Nat had written before Lionel had made his final decision to stand:

> I hope you will stand for the City, my dear Lionel. Should you not come in, it will be something to have been put on the list of candidates by the side of the Prime Minister by his party. It can only do good.[68]

The whole strategy demanded that it not be Lionel de Rothschild the Jew, but rather Lionel de Rothschild the Liberal who

73

stood before the electors, and he made sure that that was the case. Any attempt to make his a purely Jewish cause was firmly squelched. Thus, for example, a report that the Jewish electors intended to vote only for Lionel was indignantly denied. The Jewish electors would do their duty as Liberals and vote for all four candidates.[69] Occasionally, the fundamental importance he placed on the Jewish question shone through Lionel's speeches, but only in reminding the electors of their duty to their country, and indeed to the whole world. As Lionel told the electors of Broad Street, Langbourne, Cornhill, and Lime Street, he

> trusted the effort the electors of London were now making in favour of civil and religious liberty would be crowned with success. (Cheers.) They were now setting to the civilized world generally a great and important example; and he found from communications he received from every part of the continent that the approaching contest for the city of London was regarded with the deepest interest and attention. (Hear, hear.)[70]

Few would deny that the cause Lionel had at heart was a good one, and that he pursued it with great skill. He was an excellent politician, with a fine grasp of strategy and considerable adeptness in implementation. His efforts were crowned with success. To the argument that he would not be allowed to take his seat if he were elected, he replied in effect that that was the problem of those who tried to bar him, not his.[71] The electors seem to have taken the position that it was not theirs either. Lionel was returned third in the poll, with 6792 votes, only a couple hundred votes behind the Prime Minister, who was first.

Lionel was quite right about the intense interest taken in the contest in every part of the Continent. Among the congratulations that poured into New Court was one from Uncle Salomon in Vienna:

> May it be the beginning of the long hoped for better impulse, stirred by your example, as regards our Jewish brethren. Thus it might become truly a blessing. Everybody here takes sincere pleasure in this extraordinary honour bestowed on you and all the House of Rothschild, and I am overwhelmed with congratulations from all sides.

74

From Paris Aunt Betty waxed lyrical, albeit with mixed metaphors: 'Hope is lighting up all Europe and from every corner the echo sounds, carrying far the seed of this new era now approaching on a wider horizon.'[72]

The critical importance placed by all branches of the Rothschild family on Lionel's becoming a member of the ·British Parliament is demonstrated by events during the next year. Those who had suggested at the time of his election that there would be difficulties in the way his taking his seat had been right. In order for a member of either House to take his seat it was necessary to swear an oath on the Bible (that is, on the New as well as the Old Testament), and on 'the true faith of a Christian'. Lionel naturally did not propose to do this. The impediments therefore had to be removed. When the new Parliament assembled in December, the strategy that had lain behind Lionel's election for the City continued to bear fruit; for it was his colleague, the Prime Minister himself, who duly introduced a new Jewish Disabilities Bill. It was anticipated that the Bill would have little difficulty in getting through the Commons. The Lords were another matter, but the Rothschilds were by no means overawed by the British peerage – and they were willing to use whatever means gave a promise of success.

On 23 December, Nat wrote from Paris:

I regret much to observe that you think it necessary to use certain means to secure some votes in the House of Lords, which are not peculiarly commendable. I must say I should have preferred to have seen it otherwise; after the late *procès de corruption* which we witnessed here one fights rather shy of being a party to anything of the sort. To come however to the point, on this occasion our worthy uncle and your servant are of opinion that we must not be too scrupulous, and if it be necessary to ensure the success of the measure we must not mind a sacrifice. We cannot fix the *amount,* you must know better what is required than we do. I hope that as you say half the amount will suffice. At all events our good uncle has authorised me to write that he will take it upon himself to satisfy all the Family that whatever you do is for the best and that you may put down the *sum* to the house.[73]

Lionel had been given a blank cheque to carry the Bill.

What happened hereafter is not entirely clear. Nat advised that, 'Of course you will not cash up until the bill passes the Lords, and you must not make any bargain or care about who gets it. The thing is this in our opinion – you place so much at the disposal of the individual in question upon the bill passing and you know nothing more about it . . . All we have to do is to give the money in the event of the race being won to the lucky jockey.'[74] The identity of the hopeful jockey is not known, nor are the total sums mentioned. But they cannot have been small, as some discussions in the spring suggest.

When the Bill passed the Commons in February 1848, Nat recommended: 'You should now work the Court party. Get your friend P[rince] A[lbert] to use his influence and then perhaps it will go through.' Nat was deeply shaken by the Revolution that took place in France in the same month, and this may have conditioned his response to Lionel's next enquiry. At any rate, there were now limits to how far he would go:

> You ask me my advice respecting a loan of £15,000 to PA. I think there is not the slightest occasion to consent to it. You will find yourselves in the same position with regard to him as we are with L[ouis] P[hillipe]. If I do not mistake, my dear Brothers, he already owes you £5000 which we paid here to the Bavarian minister. I really do not think you are authorised to advance so large a sum considering the state of things, and you should in my opinion tell him so. There is not the slightest reason to make compliments with him, and I am convinced that whether you give the cash or not it will not make the slightest difference in the fate of the Jews Bill.[75]

So much for the Prince Consort. It should, however, be added that Nat was right. The refusal of the loan had no effect, not least on the Prince's attitude. 'We are very glad to observe,' Nat wrote in June, 'that you have been able to satisfy your friend PA without cashing up.'[76]

The whole affair was uncharacteristic of Rothschild methods (as far as the English Rothschilds were concerned at any rate – the rules of Continental politics were somewhat different). Bribery and corruption were no part of their stock in trade, and their reverence for English institutions, and certainly the monarchy, was great. That they were willing even to contemplate such methods is, however, an indication of the importance with which they viewed the cause of Jewish Emancipation.

Whether Hannah knew about the means under consideration is not known, but she was doing her best by other means to advance the cause. On 14 December 1847 she had written to Lionel from Woburn Abbey, where she was enjoying a brief visit to the Duke and Duchess of Bedford, that she had had 'a conversation with Lord Orford on the Bill. He is against the question and after a long debate, he said but you will gain.'[77] Clearly, the 'old lady' had lost none of her spirit. Lionel and the Bill did not, however 'gain' in this instance. The Lords threw it out in 1848, as they would do again in 1849. Nor did the fact that Lionel thereupon applied for the Chiltern Hundreds and then proceeded to smash his opponent, the former 'Young Englander' and prominent Protectionist, Lord John Manners, in a by-election in the City, 6017 to 2814, have any immediate impact on the attitude of British legislators.

Hannah would not live to see her son's triumphant assumption of his seat. In 1850, romping with her grandchildren at Gunnersbury, she suddenly collapsed. She never recovered, and on 5 September she died. Charlotte, who had had mixed feelings about her mother-in-law, mournfully recorded in her volume on Leonora: 'I had new, very pretty dresses made for my little girls, that poor Aunt might be pleased with their appearance at breakfast – she never saw them – the new dresses they wore were black.'[78]

Hannah's death left her sons a good deal richer. Her doting husband had left her an income of £20,000 per annum, as well as Gunnersbury and 107 Piccadilly. But she had endowed them with a good deal more than that – their principles, among other things.

CHAPTER THREE

Lionel and his Brothers

THERE WAS ONE MATTER on which Lionel emphatically rejected his mother's advice – on the baronetcy he became famous for refusing.[1] Hannah might well have sympathized with his reasons, however.

On 14 November 1846, Queen Victoria recorded in her Journal: 'Lord John has mentioned to me 3 baronets, whom he is anxious to make and I have consented. They are: Colonel Fergusson of Reith, Baron Lionel de Rothschild and another, whose name I cannot remember.'[2]

Russell seems not to have enquired whether Lionel was anxious to be made a baronet, and it soon became evident that the intended recipient was by no means enthusiastic about the proffered honour. A letter from his mother, written from Frankfurt, suggests the reasons. Hannah adopted her most ornate style:

> Now let me reply to your note I received on Saturday, more particularly concerning the offer of Her Majesty of the Barony [sic]. In this respect I do not think it good taste to refuse it: as your little friend [Russell] remarks: how can she bestow? The peerage cannot be bestowed at present without taking the oath, and that I suppose you would not do. A personal compliment from the highest personage should be esteemed and may lead to other advantages, but to repudiate it might create anger; and in accepting it, you do not do away with your original title. The aims may be splendid. The previous granting to the two other gentlemen, I think, has nothing to do with yours and decidedly does not reduce the compliment. This is my opinion. Excuse my candour.

Similar advice came from other members of the family. Anselm gave his opinion that it was 'a great distinction and it does not at all matter that others, not so worthy of it, were

78

favoured with it before you'. Perhaps not entirely understanding the nature of the distinction offered, he went on to observe: 'As an Englishman it becomes you much better to be an English baronet than a foreign one.' Anthony was equally pressing: 'Follow my advice and take it, and if you don't like it for yourself, accept it for one of us; these things are always better to be had when one can and don't refuse it.'[3]

Lionel rejected his family's advice, for reasons which the nature of that advice make partially clear. He was evidently concerned that the proposed baronetcy was the third offered to a Jew. Melbourne had recommended Isaac Goldsmid for the distinction in his retirement honours in 1841. Urged on by Sir Moses himself, Peel had advised the conferring of the same honour on Montefiore in 1846.

Lionel may well have resented the Goldsmid baronetcy, especially as rumours were circulating at the time that he himself would be the lucky recipient.[4] Personal pique and social rivalry within the Jewish community aside, the radical Goldsmids were almost perpetually at odds with the moderate Jewish Establishment, represented by the Board of Deputies, to which Lionel belonged.[5] Such considerations would make resentment on Lionel's part understandable. They would not of course justify it. Whig obligations to the Goldsmids in 1841 were much older than those to the newly converted Rothschilds; and the rumours that Lionel was the intended recipient would have been a reflection of the family's standing with the Jewish and general public rather than with the Whigs.

None of these considerations is likely to have affected Lionel's attitude toward Montefiore's baronetcy. Admittedly, the latter was not a Rothschild. He was, however, Lionel's uncle by marriage. Moreover, the two were in close cooperation, jointly representing the Board of Deputies in their efforts to gain the support of the British government for the cause of the Russian Jews. Of the two, Lionel's relations with the then Prime Minister were probably closer. It was Lionel, for example, who arranged Peel's letter of introduction to Count Nesselrode at the time of Montefiore's mission to Russia on behalf of the Board in 1846.[6] One of the main justifications for Montefiore's baronetcy was that, by signifying his recognition by his own country, it enhanced his power to do good. Lionel would certainly have been sympathetic to this end.

None the less, it is clear that he valued a baronetcy less because Montefiore had had one before him. At the same time, it is evident that if he was not prepared to be the third Jewish baronet, Lionel was prepared to be the first Jewish peer. Partly perhaps, as his relatives' letters suggest, he was not anxious for the lesser title because he did not wish it to overshadow his Austrian barony, feeling that only a British peerage would enhance the position he already had.

This apparently excessive concern for position, however, in itself requires some explanation. As Hannah pointed out, the refusal of a proffered honour was not the best way to conciliate the feelings of those who offered it, and Lionel could hardly have failed to realize this. One can only conclude that he was unconcerned. What is more, there is other evidence that he was ready to offend the existing powers. The following June, as Parliamentary electioneering was getting under way, Matthew Hill wrote urging him not to accept an invitation to stand for the Hythe constituency: 'Russell and myself entreat of you not to entertain the proposal which it is said has been made to you from Hythe – Sandwich.'[7] Lionel himself did not stand for Hythe, but Mayer did, to the discomfiture of the Liberal candidate already there.

Such behaviour could be put down to arrogance and pride, to *hubris*. Undoubtedly Lionel was a proud man, and one who did not undervalue himself. In July 1848 he wrote his wife that the next time she saw Disraeli she might suggest that Lionel was tired of crossing the room to talk to Disraeli, and that he would not take it amiss if the next time they met, Disraeli crossed the room to talk to him![8] None the less, there was probably more than arrogance, and little snobbery, in the position Lionel assumed. A hankering after titles was certainly not characteristic of him. As has been seen, he had not had a high opinion of the English aristocracy at the time of the Great Reform Act. He had welcomed the humbling of their pride, and himself preferred the more open society of Paris, where merit, or at least money, counted for more. Nor in later years, when a peerage seemed to be coming within his reach, would he appear to have been very excited at the prospect. When he mentioned it at all, it was with characteristic cynicism and sarcasm.

Why, then, at this time would he settle for nothing less? As often when dealing with complicated questions of motivation, it is impossible to give a categorical answer. It seems likely, however, that the stance he took was not uncalculated, but rather part of a broader strategy that had little to do with personal pique. Though by no means totally lacking in vanity, it is fair to say that the English Rothschilds never sought titles for their own sake, but rather for what they symbolized. Nathan did not seek titles at all, unless one includes that of Austrian Consul General – itself a case in point as it gave him a useful diplomatic entrée.[9] Lionel's son Natty would make sure that the peerage, when it came, would be given a much wider than merely personal significance. Lionel himself was acutely conscious of the implications of his achievements for Jews generally, as indeed were the whole family. His brother Anthony's wife is another example. Though for personal reasons, Louise was, as she recorded in 1850, 'less zealous and warm in favour of the representative', she remained 'as deeply interested in the cause as ever'. Nor was this a mere form of words. Her diary shows that the representation of London was a constant topic of conversation, speculation, and planning within their circle. As she recorded of a dinner party at their town house in Grosvenor Place in December 1847, 'Disi' (as she called him)

> spoke of the Jews' life in his strange Tancredian strain, saying we must ask for our rights and privileges, not for concessions and liberty of conscience. I wonder whether he will have the courage to speak to the House in the same manner.[10]

The Rothschilds never sympathized with Disraeli's arguments for Jewish Emancipation. The 'Tancredian strain' in which he did indeed argue for it later in the same month was not in the least to their liking, however convenient it may have been for an aspiring leader of the Tory Party who happened to have been born a Jew. They dismissed his sophisms that Jews were entitled to special privileges because of their special relationship with Christianity (having made possible the Atonement by killing Christ, among other things!) for the arrant nonsense they were.[11] Their own line was, however, in its own way no less high. To them, as in liberal theory generally, liberty of conscience was not a privilege but a right. As such, it should not be asked for as a boon – nor did they ever do so. It seems likely that at the same time that they were capturing the Liberal Party for the cause, they also felt it necessary to make the point that they were no mere Liberal hangers-on and dependents.

Certainly, they could hardly have made it better. Lionel's refusal of the baronetcy put Russell and his government in an embarrassing position, from which he finally deigned to remove them by allowing Anthony his wish of taking the title in his stead. The point was emphasized by Lionel's triumph in the following year's election – which proved, if anyone had ever doubted it, that the Rothschilds were at least as important to the Liberals in London as the Liberals were to them – and by their independence in the matter of the Hythe election. It had been forcibly demonstrated that the Rothschilds did not grovel for titles – or for anything else. Doubtless making the point would have been psychologically satisfying, but it was more than a matter of self-gratification.

It was an important point to have made, for the Rothschilds and for English Jews generally. The Rothschilds had no objection to being called, as they increasingly were, kings of the Jews. Nathan had loved power. So did Lionel, and he had no desire to hide that power. He aimed at more, however, than mere self-aggrandizement. He was his mother's, as well as his father's son.

The struggle to put the final capstone on Jewish Emancipation by securing the recognition of their right to sit in their country's legislature was a long, hard slog, exhausting almost in the mere repetition. The difficulties reflect the symbolic importance of the issue. This was the last great stand of a Toryism that had had to concede first the theory of an Anglican, then of a Protestant, and finally of a Christian nation. In no case had the theory approximated to reality, but it had perpetuated – and was meant to perpetuate – prejudices which their opponents felt bound to extirpate. The battle may have been largely a symbolic one, but it was a battle that had to be won.

This is why the opponents of Jewish Emancipation fought so hard against it, and why Lionel's dogged determination was so important. Not one, but two bills were lost in 1848. The Lords threw out another in 1849, which, as has been seen, was followed by Lionel's resignation of his seat and triumphant return in a by-election. As Middlesex had once spoken for Wilkes and the rights of the electorate, so the City of London now spoke for Rothschild and his cause.

By this time the Liberal leaders appear to have become

somewhat embarrassed by the continuing popular pressure.[12] Lionel and his supporters in the City had no intention of lessening the pressure, however, indeed in the summer of 1850 it was increased. On 25 July a large meeting of the electors of the City of London at London Tavern decided that Lionel should claim the seat to which he had been elected, and next day the short, square figure of the duly elected Member appeared at the Table in a tense House of Commons. The Clerk rose to tender the oaths according to the usual form. In a voice clear, but taut with emotion, Lionel demanded to be sworn on the Old Testament. This provoked a chorus of dissent from the Tory benches, led by Sir Robert Inglis, that hardy perennial opponent of Dissenters, Catholics and Jews; and the Speaker called on Lionel to withdraw. With slow and solemn dignity, he retraced his steps down the House.[13]

A spirited debate followed, rehearsing once again the hoary arguments for a Christian nation guaranteed by a Christian constitution, on the one hand, and complete religious liberty, on the other. Inglis professed to find it impossible to believe that some in the house were actually contemplating the admission to their number of a person not prepared to signify his adherence to 'our Common Redeemer'. Loud cheering from the Government benches, and three divisions assured him that that was precisely the case. For good measure, Lionel was recalled to the Table to explain that he wished to take the oaths on the Old Testament, 'because that form is the most binding on my conscience'. That point having been clarified, it was decided to let him take the oaths as he requested.

On 29 July therefore Lionel once again presented himself and the Speaker informed him of the decision of the House. There was no difficulty with the Oaths of Allegiance and Supremacy. These he took without scruple, though covering his head in the usual Jewish form and with a mere 'So help me God' rather than the traditional Christian formula. That formula was, however, an integral part of the Oath of Abjuration. It was necessary to renounce any loyalty to the Stuart dynasty 'upon the true faith of a Christian', and in those words alone. Phrase by phrase, Lionel repeated the oath after the Clerk – until he came to the last. 'I omit these words as not binding on my conscience,' he said, and clamping his hat firmly on his head he concluded the oath as before. He had the pen actually in his hand to sign his name on the roll when the Speaker ordered him to withdraw. Though there were shouts of encouragement from the Government benches, Lionel had decided that the best policy lay in correct behaviour. With quiet dignity, he withdrew himself once more from the House.

Lionel and the family were prepared for yet another appeal to the electors of London, but much to their relief, that did not prove necessary.[14] An Opposition motion that his refusal to take a legal oath rendered his seat vacant was defeated. Neither, however, was the House prepared to say that he could take his seat without the oaths prescribed by law, and indeed a resolution was passed that he could not. Most Parliamentary supporters of Jewish Emancipation, not least Lionel himself, took the position that the law must be changed. The problem was how this was to be accomplished, for, not for the first time or the last, the two Houses were at odds. There was a constitutional deadlock.

It continued in the following year, when yet another bill was thrown out by the Lords. This time there was a more radical challenge. David Salomons, who had been returned in a by-election at Greenwich, decided to circumvent procedure and take his seat without the formality of the oaths. He did so on a Friday late in July, voted, and actually retained his seat until Monday evening. Louise was in the House to hear 'a most interesting, exciting debate. D. Salomons spoke admirably and the Jews have no reason to be ashamed of their first oratorical display.'[15]

Louise would clearly have been prepared for the cause to triumph without her brother-in-law. It was not to be. Salomons was ejected from the House, prosecuted, and most important of all, rejected by the electors of Greenwich at the general election of 1852. But London remained loyal to Lionel. It was a closer run thing than before. A strong Conservative candidate was at the top of the poll. The vote for all the Liberals was reduced, and Lionel was the last of the successful candidates, with 4748 votes. Still, it was not a bad showing for a Member who had been prevented from taking his seat for five long years. Louise had lamented in her diary that she was unable to share Anthony's intense excitement about the coming elections, but on the day of the triumph, 'I felt excited, *malgré moi*.'[16]

The House of Lords, however, were unmoved. 1853, 1854, 1855, 1856, and 1857 saw the defeat of efforts to get round the impasse. But, if London's loyalty had waned somewhat in 1852, it waxed again in 1857. In the general election in March of that year, Lionel was returned second in the poll, with 6398 votes. When, following the defeat of the 1857 bill, he once more resigned and offered himself anew to the judgment of his constituents, he was returned unopposed. London's loyalty was neither unnoticed nor without influence. In May, following the apparently triumphant vindication of his government by the electorate, Lord Palmerston wrote to the Queen of its plans for the future:

> Viscount Palmerston begs to state that the Cabinet have well considered the question as to whether it would be advisable in the present session of Parliament to propose any measure for the admission of Jews to Parliament, and if such a measure were to be introduced whether it would be best that it should be proposed by an independent Member or by a member of the Government. It has been thought that it is due to the City of London with reference to the election of Baron Lionel de Rothschild, to give Parliament early in this session an opportunity of again considering the question of the admission of Jews, and that such a proposal would have the best chance of success by being proposed by the Government . . .[17]

The City of London had always been one of the most important constituencies in the country. Before 1832 it had been rivalled in size and influence only by the great county constituency of Yorkshire. Since 1832 it had had more rivals for size, but it had not lost the prestige that accrued to the commercial and financial as well as the political capital of the land. No government wished to remain too long at odds with London. The leaders of the Conservative Party were no exception to this rule. Disraeli had his own reasons for wishing Emancipation well, and both he and Derby, as leaders of the party whose majority was blocking Emancipation in the Lords, were concerned about the continuing deadlock between the two Houses. The Lords were a useful instrument to the Conservatives, as long as they did not block too much, too long. Neither the Lords nor Conservative interest benefited from acrimonious confrontation with the House of Commons backed by the electorate. There was therefore considerable reason for both sides to seek a way around the impasse. When Palmerston's government was ousted for not standing up to France over the Orsini incident in 1858, the minority Conservative government which took its place did everything to facilitate a settlement. It took the form of a compromise which allowed each House individually to determine the formula for admission to its precincts.

Three days after the necessary Act was passed, Lionel, flanked by his old supporters Russell and Abel Smith, walked up the House of Commons to the Table. There he declared his objection to the Christian formula that remained a part of the oath laid down in the recent Act, and then withdrew. Russell thereupon moved that the new Member might take the oath without the objectionable words, 'on the true faith of a Christian'. This passed with only token opposition. Once more supported by Russell and Abel Smith, Lionel returned to the Table, and, with his hat on his head in Jewish fashion, took the sanitized oath. Pausing briefly to shake the hand of the Leader of the House, Disraeli, he proceeded to a seat on the Opposition benches.

Previous writers on the subject have found it vastly amusing that although for some sixteen years Lionel was a Member, he never opened his mouth in debate. This, however, is to miss the point. Though quite adequate on a platform in a straightforward and factual way, Lionel had never aspired to oratory. The great cause to which he had devoted himself did not require it. It was won the moment he settled himself on the front bench below the gangway on the Opposition side, not far from a place long occupied in comfort by his brother-in-law Henry Fitzroy. Fitzroy was there because he had been born a Christian. Across the House, its Leader was there because he had been baptized one. Much more important than anything Lionel could ever have said were those seven words that for eleven long years he refused to utter.

The contrast with the brilliant friend with whom Lionel stopped to shake hands on his way to his seat is one that struck people at the time, and has ever since. When Lionel died, his son Alfred wrote Disraeli that his father had always looked upon him as his closest friend.[18] The feeling was probably reciprocated. Certainly Lionel was one of Disraeli's intimate friends. It is arguable that some younger men, particularly Monty Corry, were closer to him, but after the death of his own, the Rothschilds were the nearest Disraeli had to family. Their homes were open to him at any and all times; he had only to suggest himself for a quiet meal or a breath of country air, which he did very often. Particularly favoured were 148 Piccadilly, which Lionel had acquired in 1841, and Gunnersbury Park, which he took over after his mother's death. In the former, Disraeli often stopped for a chat on his way to and from the House, and in both he could always be sure of a warm welcome and a good meal.

Just how the intimacy developed is unclear. It may well have come through Nat, whose friendship with D'Orsay, Bulwer and others of that rather raffish and dandified circle would have given him a mutual acquaintance with Disraeli. At any rate, he was known to the family generally by the mid-forties. Hannah had somewhat mixed reactions to *Coningsby*. She found Disraeli's treatment of the good qualities of Sidonia's race and his arguments for their emancipation 'rather abrupt', as she put it. Nor could she 'perfectly comprehend his meaning about the government of the country'. Few have. Nevertheless she wrote him a note 'expressing our admiration of his spiritual production'.[19] The following year she wrote to Charlotte from Paris that she hoped their 'party at Brighton was convivial and Mr D'Israeli's wit and talent were as sparkling and exhilarating as the best champagne'.[20]

No one would ever have so characterized Lionel's wit. Shrewd, incisive and dry were the words to describe him; and the confident assertion made by almost every authority that Sidonia's creator took Lionel as his model must be treated with extreme scepticism. Apart from anything else, though certainly acquainted, Lionel and Disraeli were not intimate at the time the book was written. As late as 1847, the latter was still addressing the former as 'My dear Baron',[21] not 'My dear Lionel' as he would later become. There can be little doubt that the fabulous financier with his mysterious international connections was Rothschild-inspired (though not by any particular Rothschild). That is as far as one can safely go.

Though extremely fond of Disraeli, the Rothschilds were by no means without mixed feelings about him. Most mixed were Louise's feelings. Intensely shy and outwardly sweet and passive, Louise made the mistake of leaving a journal that shows her to have been consumed with jealousy and insecurity. One of four children of Nathan's sister Henrietta and Montefiore's brother Abraham, who had died relatively young, Louise had not come to the family so well endowed with worldly goods as her sisters-in-law. She was also a plain girl, and the combination probably made her painfully shy and unsure of herself. Though far from unintelligent – both Thackeray and Matthew Arnold not only enjoyed her hospitality, but her company – she fancied herself dull and uninteresting, and as a consequence was apt to see slights where none were intended. That is to say, she assumed that other people shared her assessment of herself – and resented it!

Someone as aggressively brilliant and witty as Disraeli was not, therefore, likely to appear to advantage in her eyes. Nor did he. As she remarked of one meeting with him in 1850: 'Disi was less condescending than usual; therefore I liked him better'; this after the ritual remark about there being 'something inspiring in the presence of clever men, but one feels *lamentably stupid* by comparison'.[22] Mrs Disraeli, by contrast, she found 'an odd mixture of *good sense* and *non sense*, of amusing humour and gaiety and no less amusing absurdity; but I must like her, for she is, I am sure, *really true*'.[23]

Louise also recognized, and was repelled by, Disraeli's lack of principle. Dining at 148 Piccadilly in January 1853, shortly after the first Derby-Disraeli minority government had been forced to resign, she sat next to the latter, 'who looked perfectly wretched':

> Had Disraeli even wished to carry out any great principle, or to bring forward some truly useful measures, he would not be so cast down . . . but his own elevation having been his only aim, he has nothing now to sweeten the bitter cup of ill success.[24]

She had been particularly disillusioned when, after the brilliant pyrotechnics of December 1847, Disraeli had remained largely silent about Jewish Emancipation thereafter. Having gone to the House of Commons to hear the speeches in February 1849, she praised Russell's and called Gladstone's speech a 'fine, silvery toned one. . . . Disi was silent. Mrs Disi was right when she spoke of the changes that friendships undergo; last year he was our warmest champion and now!'[25]

Disraeli's attitude did not, in fact, seriously affect his friendship with the family. Its other members seem to have been more tolerant of the shifts which his aspiration to the leadership of his party required. But if they tolerated those shifts, they recognized them for what they were; and they gained him no credit in their eyes. Lionel was particularly cynical about Disraeli's claims of steady support in 1858. As he wrote to his wife on 13 July: 'Dizzy said again today that it was by the greatest chance possible that we had got the division for us instead of against us on the second reading of our Bill – he worked all he could for us – so he said - ' A few days later Lionel wrote that he had seen Disraeli again:

> I told him that we were very anxious to have the royal assent to the Bill in time to enable me to take my seat this year. But you know what a humbug he is: he talked of what is customary without promising anything.

Lionel took everything Disraeli told him with a large pinch of salt, and he was only amused at the Disraelis' parading of wounded feelings: 'Mrs Dizzy dined at Mayer's and told them the old story again, saying how much Dizzy had done for us and how angry he was once because we would not believe it.' But they did not believe it.

Despite this, and other strong and continuing political differences, however, the friendship continued unabated. Partly no doubt this was a matter of expediency on the Rothschilds' part. Their success depended in large measure on contacts and information; Disraeli provided both. But it was more than a question of utility: there was also genuine friendship and esteem. With the possible exception of Louise, they loved him. And it is clear that, though it is not always easy for us to understand his charm, he was an extremely lovable person.

His relationship with the Rothschilds provides at least some clues why. For one thing, it is evident that he got on remarkably well with children and young people. Sending an invitation for lunch and the opportunity to view a military parade from Grosvenor Gate, he wrote on one occasion to Charlotte, 'bring the beauteous children'.[26] An excellent way to most parents' hearts is through their children, and the Rothschilds adored theirs. So did Disraeli. True, Louise, not surprisingly, found him 'extremely affected' with her daughters, Connie and Annie.[27] Perhaps, however, children stand affectation better than their elders, and even enjoy it. Lionel's seem to have done. An exchange about 1850 is revealing of both sides. Evelina wrote to her mother:

> Yesterday Mr and Mrs Dizzy met Leopold in the Park and they asked him where you were? 'Mamma is gone to Frankfurt to see her father who is indisposed', was Prince Goldfinche's reply. Mr Dizzy asked him if he was sorry when you left. 'Certainly and I cried a long time.' 'Pooh, what nonsense, you don't mean it.' Leopold thought he was in earnest and answered: 'But would you not cry if your wife was to run away and leave you behind.'[28]

Leo's remark was perhaps more perceptive of the Disraelis' relationship than he realized, but they were clearly amused by it and passed it on.

The rest of the children adored Disraeli as well. Though Natty, with undergraduate rectitude, would sometimes censure Disraeli for lack of principle, he was clearly one of his young men. Disraeli would make Natty his executor. After Mary Anne died, Alfred took the lonely widower into his bachelor quarters in Seamore Place. Mayer and Juliana's daughter, Hannah, was equally captivated by Disraeli's charm. Juliana wrote on one occasion from Mentmore that, as the Liberal and sarcastic Robert Lowes were coming, she dared 'not ask the Dizzys, to Hannah's great regret, as she considers Mr Disraeli a most amiable and an indulgent spectator judging by his applause of the tableaux last year'.[29] When Hannah married Lord Rosebery in 1878, it was Disraeli whom she asked to stand in her dead father's stead and give her away.

There is something attractive about distinguished statesmen who stop to pass the time of day with small boys in the park and clap loudly at little girls' dramatic performances. It was probably this kind of charm, rather than his formidable wit, that explains Disraeli's hold on so many of his contemporaries. Like Charles James Fox, another politician sometimes derided for lack of principle, Disraeli had a genius for friendship.

But there was another reason why the man who took such ferocious pride in his Jewish ancestry was drawn to Judaism's greatest and most powerful contemporary representatives – or rather why they were drawn to him. Louise put her finger on that reason: 'I cannot help feeling . . . when I listen to him a sort of pride in the thought that he belongs to us – that he is one of Israel's sons.'[30]

The Baroness Lionel, for her part, could take Disraeli on, charm, wit, intellect and all. She was one of that circle of women to whom he made elaborate, ritualized and completely platonic love. 'I would,' he wrote grandly from the Cabinet, Downing Street, in November 1867, 'also send you my love, but I gave it to you long ago.'[31] And on 25th February 1868, in response to a query who was to be Prime Minister (though here Lionel was included as well), 'Your devoted Dizzy – to be communicated by Lord Stanley at the House today'.[32] Fed on books, politics and social chit chat, their friendship would go on as long as he lived.

Though Louise fought hard against it, Charlotte was the earliest, and probably most consuming, object of her sister-in-law's jealousy. She was all those things Louise was not, as the latter painfully noted in her journal. On 18 January 1849, after they had attended a wedding: 'Charlotte Lionel was *much admired* by all the guests and she certainly looked strikingly handsome. I went home early, tired, nervous and out of sorts.'[33]

Again on 1 April 1851, after she had dined in company at 148 Piccadilly: 'Charlotte amiable and unaffected. She is an accomplished hostess and understands thoroughly making her house agreeable, which I do not at all.'[34]

And finally, after a meeting of a committee of Jewish ladies formed to promote emigration of the poor, in May 1853:

> Charlotte spoke against our plan of sending out the six young girls by government and carried her *opposition*. She spoke extremely well but was not quite gentle and conciliatory enough – is it possible to combine strength, firmness and courage with modesty and kindly demeanour towards those who differ with us . . .[35]

To her sister-in-law at any rate Charlotte was consistently conciliatory, good humoured, and more than that, solicitous, with good effect in the end. She also managed to remain neutral in the quarrels between the other branches of the family, though that was by no means easy. In the formation of the Aberdeen Coalition in December 1852, Hannah Mayer's husband Henry Fitzroy found himself passed over for Secretary of the Admiralty, another member of their circle, Ralph Bernal Osborne, getting the job instead. (Fitzroy became Under Secretary at the

Home Office.) This caused considerable bad feeling for a while, and Louise recorded in her journal: 'HM is furious they say with Mr Osborne and intends never speaking to him again which Charlotte says she can *quite* understand, and yet she could *not* understand my feelings towards Juliana.'[36]

It was another sort of competition, the marriage stakes, from which Louise's animosity to Juliana arose. Juliana herself had been the prize. Mayer of course had taken the prize; and the loser had been Louise's brother, Joseph Montefiore. Louise felt that the Rothschilds, and especially Lionel as head of the family, had thrust Joseph aside to get Juliana and her handsome portion for Mayer. She never forgave any of them, writing on 3 March 1850:

> All is at last arranged between Mayer and Juliana and I hope we shall now be quiet. I am *as usual* pleased that she is Mayer's and not Joseph's bride and angry at the manner the Rs have behaved towards Joseph.

And a week later: 'I am angry about all the matrimonial news – nearly as vexed as Mamma, though, thanks to my secretiveness, I can hide it.'[36]

She was quite successful in hiding her animosity to Lionel, much less so that towards Juliana, and this would considerably complicate family relations. There is an old story that the Rothschilds all settled in the Vale of Aylesbury, only a few miles apart, so that if no one else would call on them, they could call on one another. There is more than one reason to doubt this story, but the best perhaps lies in Louise's sentiments at the prospect of her and Anthony following Mayer and Juliana to the Vale and settling a couple of miles away from Mentmore, at Aston Clinton:

> A country residence with or near those I like would be delightful, but at AC I should only have the society of those I care little about.[37]

It did not augur well for the future, and the auguries would be confirmed.

There were several reasons which drew the Rothschilds to the Vale of Aylesbury and Bucks. The first would seem to have been their passion for hunting and the necessity of combining it with an active business life in the City. With the coming of the railways, it was a quick run from Euston to Cheddington. In

1858, for example, Lionel could plan to run down to Mentmore for a gallop and be back in London in time for the House.[38] A leisurely day's hunting was easily arranged.

What made the Rothschilds shift their attention from the fox to the stag is not clear. They may have acquired the taste in France, where staghunting was popular, or it may have been its aristocratic and indeed royal connotations in Britain, where the taste for it was shared by Lord Derby and the Queen herself. Nat, passionately interested from his place of exile in Paris, hinted at this sort of social competition, sharpened by the closeness of the Royal Buckhounds at Windsor. 'Ride like trumps and do not let the Queen's people fancy we are all tailors,' he urged his brothers in November 1840.[39]

Whatever the origins of their preference, it was with a pack of staghounds that they made their appearance in the Vale in 1839. After experiencing some difficulty, they finally found a huntsman and a home for them at Tring Park, which Lionel would buy some thirty years later but where they now rented stables and kennels.[40] They also found a warm welcome from the sporting gentry in the neighbourhood, the Dashwoods of West Wycombe among others being desirous that the Staghounds might meet in their neighbourhood again.[41] The pack was a popular addition to the Bucks scene from the beginning.

But there were difficulties with rented accommodations. Among other things, the hounds got out and turned their attention to the tame deer in the park at Tring. The Rothschilds therefore began to look for more permanent quarters for horses, hounds and deer (for the latter were kept for the purpose, the victim being carted to the site of the hunt and turned out for the chase). In 1842 Mayer, the official Master and presiding genius, found a suitable place, purchasing a small estate of several farms located in the parishes of Mentmore and Wing, from a Captain Harcourt.[42]

It was from this base that the far-flung Rothschild domains in the Vale would grow. Growth was probably intended from the beginning; in any event, it was not long before it became evident that the family desired not only a place in the country, but landed estates. By November of 1843 Mayer was transmogrified in Nat's bantering correspondence into 'the Squire of Mentmore', and early in the next year the Squire was looking into buying property at Tring.[43] The pattern of land-owning in the Vale, dominated by a large number of small properties which given time might be consolidated into substantial estates, was clearly another of its attractions. A letter from Lionel in Frankfurt in 1844 about the purchase of the Creslow farm, famous for the fat cattle it had sent up to Smithfield from early in the century, shows that the family had looked into the situation with considerable thoroughness:

> The lawyer's letter about Creslow is very jesuitical, as you say. Cannot you find out from Lady Stafford before you make an offer if they would sell? I believe that this Rowland has been there for a good many years. I should think that the rent is the same as what he at first paid. If so I should not mind having it as 33 years purchase would pay me 3% p.a. There are so many little places around it which might be bought worth the money, that the whole together might be made to pay a fair rate of interest.[44]

It was by such methods that the Rothschilds put together their estates. They were lucky, however, and the process of estate building was given an unexpected fillip by the financial difficulties of two old families, the Dashwoods and more spectacularly the Dukes of Buckingham. The sales of the Duke's property in 1848 and the death of Sir John Dashwood King in 1849 brought a great deal of land on to the market, and the Rothschilds were the main beneficiaries, either in the first instance or from subsequent purchases by their assiduous Aylesbury agent, James James. Thus Sir Anthony acquired the great bulk of the Aston Clinton estate, while Lionel bought various properties in Aylesbury, Bierton and Hulcott, and the Halton estate from the Dashwoods. The result, among others, was to make them almost overnight electoral powers in the large rural borough of Aylesbury. In the by-election of 1848 the largest single influence in the borough was that of the Duke of Buckingham; in the by-election two years later it was the Rothschilds.[45]

The estates on which this electoral influence was based were large ones. In 1883 Lionel's heir owned almost 10,000 acres in Bucks, Mayer's about 5500.[46] They were landed magnates, and their great wealth made them even greater electoral magnates. Even before these marked augmentations of their position, Mayer had established himself as a local figure. 'The Baron' (in Bucks this almost always meant Mayer) had been a prominent participant in Aylesbury steeplechasing from 1841. Then, on 13 November 1845 came 'the first public meet of Baron Rothschild's hounds, when a fine stag was uncarted on Mr John Gurney's land on Bierton Hill, Aylesbury. There was a large field.' The stag-hunt, open to anyone who paid a modest subscription and enjoyed by many devotees, the novelist Anthony Trollope among them, became a well-known institution in the Vale. And, as *Local Occurrences* went on to record, in February 1847 Baron Mayer de Rothschild became the High Sheriff of Bucks for that year.[47]

'The Squire of Mentmore' was acting like one, and at the time of his marriage in 1850 he decided to mark his arrival in county society in the traditional manner, by building a great house to serve both as the centre and the symbol of his power and influence. Few such ventures have been more successful in achieving their object. As his grandson-in-law rightly observed, Mayer created

> an enduring monument in Mentmore and its village; an amazing creation of a great house in a wide park and noble gardens, transmuted, as if by the hand of a genie, from its first state of rolling pastures sloping up to the crest of a foothill of the Chilterns, and dotted with fattening bullocks.[48]

Like great eighteenth-century houses in intent, Mentmore and its environs also resembled them in conception and execution. House, gardens and park were meant as one composition, intended not only to blend with nature, but to enhance it. Few can doubt that the intention was realized, and brilliantly so. Situated on its slight eminence, Mentmore commands magnificent views of the Chilterns, but it is also itself a pleasure to view, whether from a distance with its towers peeping above the surrounding trees, or from the end of the avenue of *Wellingtonia* which has the house as its centre and focus.

But if Mentmore was eighteenth-century in the grandeur of its conception, it was also a very Victorian achievement, which was only appropriate, for the Rothschilds gloried in their age and its accomplishments. On her first visit to the Great Exhibition of 1851, Louise could only think of 'how proud and pleased poor Aunt would have been to have witnessed such a day of triumph for English intelligence, art, order and loyalty'.[49] Hannah, who preferred 'the amusement of scenes and the bustle of changes' involved in rail journeys to the more sedate pleasures of travel by carriage,[50] would undoubtedly have been proud and pleased. Her sons demonstrated similar feelings in the most tangible way, unhesitatingly putting themselves down for £50,000 of the £180,000 guarantee fund required in July 1850 to allow the Great Exhibition to go forward.[51] So it is not surprising that Mayer commissioned Joseph Paxton, the architect of the Crystal Palace, to design his house.

The latest authority has called Mentmore 'in many ways the finest of Paxton's works as an architect, and now that the Crystal Palace is gone, the most complete *oeuvre*'.[52] Though it would seem to be going rather too far to describe it, as Paxton did his conception in 1850, as 'a gentleman's house to be covered wholly with glass',[53] it was only natural that the imaginative use of that material is its most distinguishing characteristic. The plan of the house is basically simple, the main apartments forming one hollow square, with another slightly larger one at a lower level, and to the north of the main block, occupied by service quarters. A conservatory constitutes a south wing to the main block, making a third side of a large entrance court. The main entrance is in the form of a *porte-cochère*. From that one passes through a sub-hall lined with Caen stone and paved with Sicilian and Rogue Royal marbles to the great hall, 48 feet deep, 40 feet wide, and 40 feet high. This was dominated by the magnificent Rubens fireplace. It was, however, very innovative in its design; for the great hall was in fact the interior court of the hollow square, but roofed in glass. A grand staircase of Sicilian marble rose from the hall to a landing, where it branched into two. At the first-floor level, the hall is surrounded by corridors and 'an open arcade of great beauty and richness', with balustrades of alabaster and green marbles. At the entrance side is more of Paxton's favourite material, that side being made up of archways containing great sheets of polished plate glass. Beyond the great hall lay the main dining room, with the drawing room to the left and the library to the right. A cross-communicating corridor gave access to the morning room and conservatory on the left and a small dining room on the right. The principal interiors were in several styles: François I, Louis XIV, Louis XV and Louis XVI.

The effect of all this, and of the exquisite and growing collections of French antique furniture, paintings and Sèvres

NATHAN ROTHSCHILD
Unashamed devotee of the God of Trade

HANNAH ROTHSCHILD
A woman of beauty, poise and charm

which it housed, was the intended one of great opulence and magnificence. But thought was also given to modern comfort and convenience. A heating chamber in the service block served a central hot-water system, and provision was made for ventilation. The house not only looked, but was, light and airy.

The style of the house was Jacobean. This seems to have been Mayer's decision. It was a style perfectly suited to the extensive use of glass in which Paxton specialized, and the decision to model it on Wollaton Hall appears to have been Paxton's. The effect of the four-square, towered house, built of Ancaster stone throughout, copper casements gleaming with plate glass, is undoubtedly a most pleasant and effective one.[54]

Mayer took a keen and active interest in the building of the house. He was by no means a passive spectator, as a letter from Paxton in 1855, justifying what had obviously been found a rather stiff bill of £38,000 demonstrates:

In conclusion, I am sure you will do me the justice to admit that as far as alterations are concerned, they are entirely in accordance of your own creating [sic] and in accordance with your own desire, and that although I of course consented to these alterations I have given you to understand that they would be an expensive operation and that I have not suggested any expensive addition or alteration of my own accord.

The alterations Paxton detailed were the adding of the conservatory, the taking down and rebuilding of the porch, and extensive alterations to the northwest front.[55] Mayer was an exacting client, with distinct tastes of his own, and the changes he insisted on were hardly minor ones. It is unclear what the third involved, but the first two had a profound impact on the total effect.

A letter from A. Barker, who collected for Mayer, shows not only the circumstances which made possible the extraordinarily fine collections, but also suggests Mayer's rôle in bringing them together:

The fine collection of precious objects you have, have been obtained in consequence of the disasters of the ex-royal family of France and the misfortunes of others connected with them and if not purchased at the time they presented themselves could never have been

97

obtained and I am sure you will remember how often we have consulted as to how you would like each room decorated.[56]

The golden opportunities that offered themselves required an agent on the spot, with taste, wide discretionary powers, and a great deal of money behind him. Barker was clearly such an agent, and he served his employer well.

Doubtless on occasion it was necessary to take the bad with the good. None the less, it is evident that Mayer knew what he wanted, and that by and large he got it. Few with a taste for French furniture and porcelain in their greatest periods would not envy Mayer his collections.

The magnificence of Mentmore prompted the great Baron James to emulation. Paxton was employed, and Ferrières was the result. For the rest of the family to compete in the building of country houses was not easy thereafter (though Ferdinand would later manage it at Waddesdon). Anthony at Aston Clinton did not even try. What he actually did was to enlarge an existing house, once the seat of Viscount Lake, and to enlarge it not once but twice in the space of less than ten years. Despite the fact that Paxton was again at least nominally in charge, though his assistant Stokes probably did most of the work, architectural historians do not find the result to have been a happy one. As the most recent authority has it, Aston Clinton House, now demolished, was judged 'a most extraordinary rambling structure, two storeys high, and showing its origin clearly from the rear: two dissimilar wings joined by a conservatory at the rear and a shallower block at the front'. The critical dissection of the house goes on from there.[57] Undoubtedly, it was no architectural masterpiece, but to the untrained eye it does not appear to have been totally unpleasing, a neo-classical creation of the Italianate variety until recently exemplified in two lodges that survived at the main entrance. The situation of the house, nestling at the base of the Chilterns, was certainly pleasant, and the park and gardens, on which Anthony who was a keen gardener lavished great attention, greatly enhanced it, with some particularly fine conifers and evergreen shrubs.

Whatever its merits, however, Louise did not see them. Her reaction on an early visit to the neighbourhood was that Mentmore 'will be magnificent. Halton looked very pretty and Aston

Clinton much the same.' What she meant is made evident by a later reaction, after the family had settled in. On 23 August 1853 she wrote:

> the season is over and we are quietly established in our own little country house – a ten years' dream is realised and am I happy at its realisation? But was a dream ever realised? Never . . . Aston Clinton is not *the* country house that I dreamt of . . . The tranquility of the country is pleasant however to me and I feel that in time I may grow attached to this little place which I thought at first sight, the ugliest on earth.[58]

She kept her discontents and insecurities largely to herself, or at any rate kept them from her husband. For his part, he settled in happily to the life of farmer and landlord, and if the glory of Mentmore ever caused him pangs of jealousy he never let on.

As far as country places went, Lionel and Charlotte remained contented with Gunnersbury, to which they made only a few relatively minor alterations. Though Louise felt threatened by it (she wrote of 'the stately carriage drive to the stately mansion'[59]), it could hardly compete with Mentmore. But the Lionels seem not to have minded. Its six hundred odd acres provided ample room for a breath of country air and the gardening and farming pursuits they also enjoyed.

Theirs was an urban splendour. In the late 1850s Lionel purchased 147 Piccadilly and for four years, from 1859 to 1863, a giant reconstruction took place which merged it with 148 to create a grand new mansion, next to the Duke of Wellington's Apsley House at 149. In the meantime, he rented a house in some ways even grander, Kingston House in Knightsbridge, near where the Albert Hall would later be built. Macaulay recorded his impressions on going to dinner there in 1859:

> Yesterday I dined with Baron Rothschild. What a paradise he lives in. I had no notion of the beauty and extent of the gardens behind Kingston House. A palace ought to be built there. It would be the most magnificent and delightful town residence existing. When I said this to the Baron, he acknowledged it, but said that he was only a tenant, and that to purchase the fee simple would be a serious matter. Three hundred thousand pounds had

been offered and refused for these eight or ten acres.

The dinner was a curiosity, seeing that pork in all its forms, was excluded. There was however some compensation as you will see from the bill of fare which I enclose. Send it back that I may show it to Lady Trevelyan. Surely this is the land flowing with milk and honey. I do not believe Solomon in all his glory ever dined on Ortolans farcis à la Talleyrand. I may observe in passing that the little birds were accompanied by some Johannisberg which was beyond all praise.[60]

Lionel and his brothers lived in a grand and opulent style. They were large landowners. They were even greater political magnates. Richard Bethell, a future Liberal Lord Chancellor, owed his seat at Aylesbury to them.[61] Anthony's election to Brooks's in 1853, thus joining Mayer who had been a member for a decade, was partly in recognition of their enhanced political importance.[62] The brothers were, as Anthony put it in his rather crude way 'liberal as well in word as in tin'; and, as he rightly observed, it was at Brooks's and the Reform, of which all three were members, that most of the arrangements were made to put the latter commodity at the service of those anxious to spread the Liberal word on the hustings.[63] At the 1859 general election, Mayer himself stood again for Hythe, and this time he won, being returned without a contest. 'Tin' may well have had something to do with this too; for, as Dod's Electoral Facts had delicately put it a few years before, the borough had long been considered as permanently attached to the 'monied interest'.[64] Mayer thus became the second Jew to sit in the House, and, as Cecil Roth has pointed out, it was on the occasion of his taking his seat that the form adopted for Lionel's admission the previous year was regularized and made a matter of course for all Jewish MPs thereafter.[65] As became Liberal MPs, the grandees of their party, Russell, Landsdowne, and Granville, graced their tables. So did Thackeray and J. T. Delane of The Times. Nor had their position in the world of finance in any sense waned. In February 1856 Palmerston congratulated the Queen on the fact that the Rothschilds had undertaken a large government loan:

It is satisfactory to have as a proof that the revenues of the country are not exhausted, that it being known that Messrs Rothschild were about to offer for the loan of five millions, a sum no less than twenty-eight millions was offered to them by parties wishing to have shares in the loan, and upwards of three millions was actually paid into their hands yesterday as deposits by those wishing to be contractors.[66]

Clearly, the fact that the Rothschilds had undertaken it had something to do with the loan's success.

Indeed by 1860 all those factors existed which Lord Granville would urge nine years later in support of Gladstone's recommendation of a peerage for Lionel. The Rothschilds represented, he said:

> a class whose influence is great by their wealth, their intelligence, their literary connexions, and their numerous seats in the House of Commons. It may be wise to attach them to the aristocracy rather than to drive them into the democratic camp.[67]

Yet, despite all their power and magnificence, the Rothschilds were not yet quite accepted into English society. They were still somehow alien. Their closest circle of friends, those who were the habitués of their dinner tables as opposed to their occasional ornaments, reflected this. Disraeli was a converted Jew, Bernal Osborne of Jewish descent. C. P. Villiers was certainly of impeccable English roots, but his long advocacy of Corn Law repeal had left him with a reputation for being something of a crank, even after his principles had triumphed. Delane undoubtedly had his own special reasons, not unconnected with his profession, for being a regular diner at Rothschild houses.

There was a perception of something a little exotic about the Rothschilds. On 10 April 1856 Queen Victoria had a drawing room, at which 122 young ladies were presented to make their bow to the Queen and society. The Queen recorded in her Journal: 'Nobody very striking excepting Mlle. de Rothschild, Baron Lionel's daughter, who is extremely handsome.'[68]

If there was anything more striking about Laury than her beauty, generally admitted to be breathtaking, it was her aggressive and unyielding Englishness. For half a century and more, the Baroness Alphonse, as she became in 1857, would be as uncompromising and adamant an exile as her Uncle Nat had been before her – an Englishwoman in Paris. A 'Mlle' she never was. Nor could anyone have been much more English than her father, whom ten years before the Queen would have made a baronet. Yet there is no doubt that the Queen's was a common perception.

In fact, however, the final process of integration was already underway. In October 1859 Natty de Rothschild, as he called himself, had gone up to Trinity.

CHAPTER FOUR

Cambridge and 'Society'

SINCE EARLY IN the nineteenth century, education has been the quickest, surest, and most effective way to acceptance in the upper reaches of English society. Thus while there were at least four 'middle-class' Prime Ministers (five if one includes Canning) during that century, only one, Disraeli, did not come by way of the old public schools and universities. Addington, Peel and Gladstone were all Oxford men, having previously attended Winchester, Harrow and Eton respectively. There were many reasons why Disraeli was deeply distrusted, but one was that he had not shared those youthful friendships and experiences that served as a bond among the great majority of his political peers. He certainly thought so, and keenly felt the lack, as his novels bear evidence by their idealization of life at school and university.

Of Lionel and his brothers, only Mayer had approximated to such an education, and of the three, he was undoubtedly the one most fully welcomed in the privileged purlieus normally entered only by birth and inheritance. His early election to Brooks's is one example; the relative ease with which he joined county society in Bucks another. As landowner, sportsman, High Sheriff, in all the capacities of a country gentleman, he moved easily on the Bucks scene from the beginning.

Or so it seemed. In fact, there was a strong under-current of prejudice against the Rothschilds, particularly among those who might have been considered their peers. This is clearly reflected in the reaction to their political activities. Lord Carrington, a leader of the so-called 'old Whigs' in the Aylesbury constituency, at first violently opposed the Rothschilds' appearance on the scene there, dubbing them, in a rather peculiar turn of phrase, 'the Red Sea'. Presumably he referred to not being engulfed thereby. He certainly said some very strong things to that effect, though he never descended to the level of bad taste of one of his allies, Acton Tindal, who swore that *he* would never submit to the 'circumcision' of the Liberal Party at Aylesbury![1]

All this changed fairly quickly, however. Less than a decade later, when a vacancy in the county representation occurred on the death of the first Lord Chesham in 1863, Lionel was in the thick of the negotiations at Lord Carrington's London house in Whitehall. 'Charlie' Carrington, still an undergraduate at Trinity, was the only Liberal candidate seriously considered, but, much to his own relief, he had the excellent excuse for not standing that he was not yet of age! 'They will not be able to find a man,' Lionel wrote to another Trinity undergraduate, his son Leo, 'so you may tell your friend Charlie that at the next general election he will be obliged to come forward.'[2]

There was more than one reason why Lionel was now welcome at Lord Carrington's house. Apart from anything else, by this time it was abundantly clear that anyone interested in the representation of Bucks would find it difficult to ignore him. But it did no harm that Charlie was a close friend of all three of his sons, and that they and their sisters were frequent visitors for hunting and house parties at Gayhurst, the Carringtons' house near Newport Pagnell. That Lionel much cared whether he was received by the Carringtons or not seems unlikely. He was not a social snob, and he valued a good deal more the sort of benefits to be derived from acquaintance with the father of another of Leo's Cambridge friends, Lord Hyde. Anxious for information in the tense summer of 1869, Lionel instructed Leo to delay his departure from Paris until Hyde's father, Lord Clarendon, arrived. Clarendon would know 'what is going on and will tell you the truth'.[3] But, whatever the advantages one sought, Cambridge and the privileged circles to which it gave access was bound to be helpful. The friendships made there rendered Rothschild influence more subtle, more pervasive, and thus infinitely more potent than naked financial power, great though that was, would ever have done.

That this was an objective clearly perceived and consciously pursued, is highly unlikely. Like other hallmarks of the Establishment, in the modern sense of that word, education at one of the ancient universities was something to which people of wealth and a certain position naturally aspired. Such an education was the high road to a career in politics or one of the learned professions, to those activities that marked and distinguished the upper classes. This is why for the first three quarters of the nineteenth century, until religious tests were effectively abolished, nonconformists of all sorts battled against them. It was doubtless why Mayer had gone up to Trinity, and why he was anxious to keep the doors open for other Jews.

The case of his cousin Arthur Cohen gave him the opportunity to do battle for the cause. Though lack of a test for matriculation made Cambridge a university nonconformists could aspire to, compulsory chapel attendance would have made residence there impossible had there not been a disposition, as in Mayer's case, to bend the rules somewhat. No college was inclined to do so for Cohen when he wished to go up in the Michaelmas term of 1849.

Mayer turned to his friends. Abel Smith, who was at the same time fighting Lionel's battles in the House of Commons, wrote to the Master of his own old college, Christ's. The reply, what Abel Smith called 'Cartmell's confession', was not favourable. The Master said, in effect, that he had nothing against Jews. Some of his best friends were Jews. But there was the matter of chapel attendance. Cohen had said that he was willing to attend chapel. 'But it would be most repugnant to my feelings and contrary to my notions of what is right, to exact from Mr Cohen an outward compliance with a form of worship the basis and spirit of which he entirely disclaims and disbelieves.'[4]

Mayer then wrote to the Prince Consort, who had been Chancellor of the University since 1847. He particularly wanted the Prince to exert pressure on the Master of Magdalene, who was also Dean of Windsor. Mayer wrote:

> As there are several instances, beside that of the writer, of members of the Jewish persuasion having passed through the University, and as there is nothing in the statutes to warrant preliminary inquisition into the religious belief of applicants for admission, Baron Mayer Rothschild ventures to submit to His Royal Highness that, irrespective of individual hardship, it is not expedient and desirable, on public grounds, that a precedent should now, for the first time be established for pointed exclusion of the members of one religious community from the benefits of a Cambridge University education.[5]

This would seem to have done the trick; at any rate, in November Cohen wrote happily from Cambridge: 'Of the religious strictness of Magdalene you will be able to form a correct opinion, when you hear that the Dean yesterday called me to his rooms and, informing me that on Wednesday and Friday the Chapel only lasts 10 minutes, advised me to attend on these days instead of the other days, and at the same time communicated to me that my attendance on Sacrament Sundays would not be required.'[6]

Cohen went on to observe that the men were divisible into 'reading men' and 'non reading men'. Non-reading men were heavily in the majority at Magdalene. '*Candour* also obliges me to say that I am afraid the character of our "fast men" is deteriorating and becoming vulgar' but perhaps it was sour grapes that caused him to add, 'and that Christ College will soon surpass us even in this department of men.'

Cohen further sub-divided his contemporaries:

There is the 'fast man', he prepares himself in the morning for the 'drag' in the afternoon; and return[s] home just in time for Hall, with yellow gloves, splashed top-boots and whip in his hand.

There is the quiet and proud 'dandy'! He rises at 12 o'clock, passes two hours at his toilette and, exquisitely dressed, takes a walk up and down the King's Parade, making use of his lorgnette in a most impudent manner. After this promenade he goes to his rooms and dines with some companions, for a dinner in Hall would be too vulgar for his 'refined taste', and its bustle and hurry might be injurious to his *delicate* health.

And there in yonder garret, dingy and dull, sits the 'reading man'; he works the whole day, except during Chapel, which he regularly attends from two to four, when he takes an awfully fast walk – six miles an hour. He writes daily about 80 problems and dreams of 'triangles, squares, Cicero, Socrates'.

Cohen's conclusion might be guessed: 'These men I have represented are the extremes of Cambridge men, and I myself am going the middle way.'

Whatever way Cohen went, it proved to be the road to success. In his final year, 1853, he was President of the Union, as well as third Wrangler (that is, he was placed third in the Mathematical tripos). He did not take his degree, however, until 1858, following the abolition of the religious test for the BA by the Cambridge University Act of 1856. By that time he was already launched on what was to be a highly distinguished career at the Bar. He served as a legal adviser to several Royal Commissions, as well as representing Britain at the International Court of Justice at the Hague. He became an MP, and in 1905 was made a Privy Councillor. Cohen would always evidence a strong loyalty both to his religion and to his university. The former he served as President of the Jewish Board of Deputies, the latter as University Counsel from 1879 to 1914.

The Cambridge Cohen described was, with one significant exception, much the same as the one in which Natty arrived in the Michaelmas term of 1859. The exception was that a religious test was no longer required for the BA. Otherwise little had changed. The life of a sporting man was still apt to centre around the 'drag', then as now based on Trinity, in which the field follows a scent that has been laid rather than an actual quarry. On the academic side, mathematics was still dominant and effectively unchallenged. As Natty ruefully observed, 'To get on here one must be wedded to Mathematics and think of nothing else.'[7]

He was right. Cambridge had still not got over Sir Isaac Newton, and a majority of the Senate held that mathematics was the only proper discipline for a young mind. Other subjects had, it is true, made some headway. In 1854, for example, it was conceded that one could sit for the Classical Tripos without the ordinary degree in Mathematics, but only on the condition of strengthening the mathematical content of the Previous Examination, popularly known as the 'Little Go'. One was perfectly free to excel in other fields at Cambridge, as long as one was willing first to excel in mathematics. That remained the hard fact of life in the autumn of 1859.[8]

Change was still going on, and indeed was gestating at this very time. In December a Syndicate, or committee, appointed to consider changes in the Moral and Natural Sciences Triposes made its report. In February 1860 this was accepted by the Senate. Natty reported the results to his parents:

Today the Senate passed three Graces, two of which will affect the system of education considerably. For the future, anyone can graduate if he takes honours in his Little Go and in the Moral and [sic – actually or] Natural Sciences triposes. Moral Sciences include Moral Philosophy, Political Economy, Modern History, General Jurisprudence and the laws of England; the Natural Sciences, Human and Comparative Anatomy, Physiology, Chemistry, Botany, Geology and Mineralogy, excluding the mathematical part of Crystallography.[9]

There may well have been a certain plaintiveness in Natty's letter; for there is good reason to believe that he might have distinguished himself in either of these areas, especially as it was possible to specialize further within them.[10]

It was not to be. One great obstacle would have remained, for what he called honours in the 'Little Go' required not only the ordinary subjects for that exam, one of the Gospels in Greek, a Latin and Greek classic, Paley's *Evidences of Christianity*, the first three books of Euclid, and arithmetic; but also the 'Additional Subjects' for those aspiring to honours other than mathematical, that is, the fourth and sixth books of Euclid, elementary algebra, and elementary mechanics.[11] Since the 'Little Go' was normally taken at the end of the fifth term, this meant that the best part of two academic years of a non-mathematician's university life had to be devoted to mathematics, willy nilly. To many, and Natty may have been among them, it seemed more sensible to read mathematics and be done with it.

In any event, Natty's preferences had little to do with the matter. Both his parents were not only deeply devoted to their children and intensely proud of them, Lionel and Charlotte were also determined that their 'chicks', as Lionel called them, should excel in everything; and academic distinctions were not among those least prized. As Charlotte had written some years earlier, in the case of Alfred, 'The classical languages and mathematical he must study, for I am anxious he should visit Cambridge and distinguish himself there.'[11] The traditional way to distinguish oneself at Cambridge was as a mathematician, as Arthur Cohen had done, and that was enough for Natty's proud parents. The result was to be disastrous.

Natty's failure might have been foreseen from a remarkably perceptive report by his first tutor in 1850:

Not mathematical, but he must practice arithmetic. Fine talents for history and miscellaneous information. He has a good memory . . . He has no talents for music. Not mechanical. Fine taste for the drama and for astronomy. He has good talents for learning languages, and can appreciate their beauties. This remark applies *more* to foreign languages than to the classics.[13]

It was not a formula for success in mid-nineteenth century Cambridge.

Natty was the sort of man for whom the University reformers were working, a modern man keenly interested in his own time; and one can discern in the ten-year-old the outlines of the mature intellect. Like his grandfather, who could keep a whole day's complicated dealings on the Stock Exchange in his head and repeat them for his clerk on his return to New Court,[14] Natty had a phenomenal memory. As Disraeli would later remark: 'When I want to know a date in history I always ask Natty.'[15]

His mother, anxiously recording his progress, would continue to observe similar characteristics, his concern for the present and the practical, for example. As she notes in 1855:

Natty like his excellent father takes interest in a variety of things and pursuits; in business and in politics, in curiosities of every sort, in farming, in the cultivation of fruit, flowers and vegetables. He reads diligently, and likes both history and poetry. He is studying botany . . .[16]

The last interest continued to be a consuming one, as she recorded the next year: 'and as in the fields and gardens it can alone be studied in all its branches, and with real pleasure, the pursuit of it takes my son out into the open air and gives him wholesome and invigorating exercise'.[17]

It is easy to imagine a Cambridge in which such a man would have flourished. In a reformed Cambridge. In an unreformed Cambridge, where he could have followed his own bents. In almost any Cambridge but the half-reformed one in which he found himself.

The battalion of private tutors by whom he had been prepared had not accomplished much in the way of overcoming his deficiencies. These were apparent from the time of his arrival in Cambridge, and he complained bitterly about them. His evident difficulties must have influenced his parents' decision to send Alfred and Leo to King's, and Natty was clearly anxious that his siblings should profit by the mistakes made in his own education.[18]

For himself, there was little he could do but soldier on as best he could. It was distinctly unpleasant. He dutifully went to College 'lectures', which were more like schoolroom exercises: in algebra, for example, they spent the hour doing problems which were handed in at the end. He worked equally hard with his coach, the rough equivalent of the modern supervisor, who like the latter was responsible for most of the real education which took place, but unlike him was privately employed. He also read hard, reporting of Todhunter on trigonometry that it was interesting and easy, 'that is for a book on mathematics'.[19] Nor was mathematics his only difficulty. He also, and not surprisingly, intensely disliked the required large dose of Paley in the form of *Evidences of Christianity:* 'the most absurd conglomeration of words I ever broke my head over, so that there is *no* danger of my being converted as many up here have prophesied'.[20]

Sadly, it all availed him little. Before the 'Little Go' his hopes went up and down, but he finally got through. His hopes were less after that, though his efforts did not slacken. The Tripos was normally sat after the tenth term. On 24 March 1862 Natty wrote his parents that he must devote every night to mathematics until Passover. But the signs were not good. Students often spent the long summer vacation on a reading holiday with a coach in the Lakes or some other attractive spot, as Natty himself had done at Scarborough in the summer of 1860. For the summer before his final term, his tutor and the Master would not sanction such a method of study for Natty: 'The only arrangement Lightfoot and Whewell will agree to for the Long Vacation is the residence of a Master of Arts in King's Parade with me.'[21]

The prognostications did not get any better. His coach reckoned that 'if I remained up here and read *very* hard I might just *scrape* . . . through.' By the autumn, the advice was that he was certain to be 'plucked' – to fail.[22] Natty left Cambridge at the end of the Michaelmas term of 1862, and did not return for his examination.

Especially with all the fond hopes that had ridden upon him, it could have been a crushing experience. But Natty was not the crushable sort. He had developed his defences, and they were effective.

In 1849 his mother had written of him:

> He is really amiable, that is to say mild, gentle, kind to all around him and most affectionately devoted to his father, and brothers and sisters, but he lacks cordiality and frankness. He is reserved and shy, and not generous; in fact he is the only one of my children fond of money for the sake of hoarding it.[23]

The last opinion, she would later revise, finding him always careful with his money, but not mean.

His tutor's observations in 1850 generally reinforced Charlotte's assessment and expanded it. 'He has not much self-esteem, but he is fond of praise.' And again: 'No fighter. He can conceal his thoughts and feelings, and is rather sly.'[24]

Of these latter remarks, the second perhaps proves the first, for to put Natty down as 'no fighter' was a serious error. It was admittedly not a brilliantly aggressive sort of fight that Natty showed; rather the quiet adamantine sort that Grant would show a few years later before Petersburg, the sort that often wins the war.

As has been suggested earlier, it does not require great sophistication in psychology to suspect that his mother's resentment against the male sex, which strongly coloured her early attitudes towards her eldest son, had something to do with his shyness and lack of self-esteem. Doubtless his ability to conceal his thoughts and feelings was part of a protective response. He did his best to please and live up to expectations, but if he could not, he lowered his defensive curtain and brazened it out.

The result was a certain dryness and crustiness of manner that would become truly formidable in later years, and a sardonic turn of phrase that was formidable from the beginning. How much of this was reaction to his parents, and how much emulation, is difficult to say. One of his mother's most consistent observations about Natty was how he doted on his father, and there was undoubtedly much in Natty strongly reminiscent of Lionel writ large. But however much of his personality he may have owed to his parents, the defences it provided were turned as effectively toward them, and their overpowering solicitude, as toward other threats.

Checked in his academic ambitions, Natty sensibly developed other compensating interests. For one thing, he became a keen follower of the 'drag'. His parents strongly objected that this would interfere with his work. He replied to their letter on 6 November 1860:

> The part which interests me most is the *complete* misconception you have of what is conducive to my work and health here. Last year I followed your advice and took no tiring exercise of any kind. My work did not improve; on the contrary grew gradually worse and my condition and health suffered materially as my feeble efforts in the hunting field during the vacation showed. I have found by experience that in order to get on here at all it is *absolutely* necessary to take 2 hours at *least* of violent exercise per diem, so that if I do not go with the drag I must do something else in the same way. But as riding after hounds for a short time suits my taste better than being knocked down at football by Rob Lang or Sir G Young, or than rowing in a bad boat or following the footdrag, I intend to follow the horse drag unless I have your positive commands to the contrary, and all the more particularly as I see all those who read hard take far more exercise than I do.[25]

Lionel and Charlotte gave way before this onslaught.

One might have thought they would already have learned their lesson from an earlier experience. For Natty's interests were by no means confined to the hunting field, and he had already become active in the Amateur Dramatic Club as a stage manager. This too had brought its protest from home, which he answered with irrefutable undergraduate logic:

> The ADC takes up some time, but I have found I do not work one bit more if I do nothing but work and only destroy my health and make life up here a curse and a plague, in addition to which I have very little to do with the theatricals whilst some of the actors will be in for their Little Go at the time and three or four are likely to take high honours. I came up here unprepared and cannot expect to

do much. If I am never seen, people will expect more and at the end of the time set me down for a greater fool than I am.[26]

The argument that if he worked too hard, too much would be expected of him, obviously floored his parents. Natty went on to become a member of the Committee of the ADC and to take an active part in its management.

He was evidently popular and successful, and not by throwing his money around. Guests at his rooms at 2, King's Parade were regaled with such simple delicacies as carrot soup and roast turkey from the College kitchens, washed down with lots of sherry. It was left to Lionel to soften up his College tutor, Lightfoot, with gifts of Johannisberg '46 and Sauterne '47. Nor did Natty spend much on his sporting activities. The horses, he hastened to assure his parents, were hired.[27] These were not, of course, the activities of an impecunious scholar. Natty was moving in the circles of the rich and the well-born, but without any special ostentation. He did not attempt to buy acceptance, but he achieved it. In the Michaelmas term of 1860, much to his own satisfaction, he was admitted to the exclusive Athenaeum, in company with Arthur Guest and the Duke of St Albans.[28]

His friendship with St Albans led directly to an even more exalted one. Early in the Lent term of 1861, he wrote to his parents: 'I happened to be in St Albans's rooms on Saturday last, having been selected to ask the young Duke what kind of Masonic preferment he would like, when Grey announced HRH the Prince.' Natty was about to leave, but was told to stay, and, though not formally introduced, 'was addressed by my own name so that I suppose an introduction was considered unnecessary'.

Natty was not especially impressed on his first meeting with the future Edward VII:

I fancy the little spirit he ever had is quite broken, as his remarks are commonplace and very slow . . . He is excessively fond of the chase but Windsor does not approve of the national sport and allows him but one horse, and does not even find horseflesh for his equerries. He is very fond of riddles and strong cigars and will I suppose eventually settle down into a well-disciplined German Prince with all the narrow views of his father's family. He is excessively polite and that is certainly his redeeming quality. If he followed the bent of his own inclination, it strikes me he would take to gambling and certainly keep away from the law lectures he is obliged to go to now.[29]

Natty would also notice, as others did, a love of rough horseplay usually associated with those much younger than the Prince, and a general immaturity. He did not find attractive the Prince's habit of bowling at the legs of his competitors in cricket, and the bad grace with which he lost at cards.[30] Nevertheless, for those parts of the academic years of 1860-1 and 1861-2 that the Prince of Wales spent at Cambridge, Natty was one of the intimate little circle in which he moved, and Natty became in time quite fond of him.

The Prince was immediately taken with the 'drag', and after his first viewing of it sent Natty, who was in charge of laying out the course, 'word through St Albans to select three drags for next week near home and such that he may be able to see the whole without taking a fence'. Later, during the Easter term, Natty served as judge and handicapper at the university races near Fulbourne, where 'the Prince of Wales was present and acted as a scarecrow on the Proctors, who left us alone and did not interrupt the proceedings'. Then there were parties up the river to Byron's Pool, on one of which St Albans' sister, Lady Diana, 'shocked her mother and brother by smoking one of the Prince's cigarettes'. And there were large dinners in the Master's Lodge and cricket parties at Madingley.[31]

The intimacy continued when they returned for the Michaelmas term in the autumn. Natty was present at a dinner party at Madingley where the Prince talked of his desire to join his regiment, the one with which he had done duty that summer at the Curragh, which was being sent out to reinforce Canada against the threat of an arming Union. 'They talked,' Natty reported, 'of our annexing Maine and Portland, but I could not make out what generals and admirals were to do all these wonders.' He and Alfred, who had come up that term, also frequently joined the Madingley party in hunting with the harriers. They followed with keen and sympathetic interest the course of the Prince Consort's illness, and were hunting with the Prince of Wales on the day he was summoned to Windsor to attend at his father's deathbed. Natty warned his parents that 'it is perhaps better to say as little as possible about the festivities here last week.' Charles Kingsley, then Regius Professor of History, had told him that when he was last at Windsor, 'the Queen had attributed the Prince Consort's illness to a cold caught here'. [32] Among the messages of condolence the Prince received at Windsor were letters from his two Cambridge friends, home for the holidays at Gunnersbury Park. [33]

The friendship formed during their Cambridge days would continue to bind the Prince and the Rothschild brothers for the rest of their lives. Natty was not enough of a courtier to become a member of the Prince's most intimate circle of friends, nor had he any desire to do so. Alfred, however, whose bachelor lifestyle made him in many ways more congenial to the Prince, was certainly among that number, and their cousin and brother-in-law Ferdinand, who married Evelina in 1865, was an even closer friend.

Natty and Alfred had not particularly courted the Prince's friendship. It arose rather from the fact that they were a part, indeed at the very centre, of that Cambridge set with whom it was judged suitable for him to associate. Their friendship with the Prince of Wales was not the cause of their social success at Cambridge, but rather the result of it. Still, it undoubtedly did them no harm, then or in the future; and the same can be said of many of the friendships they made at Cambridge.

Alfred in a sense sailed into Cambridge on Natty's coat-tails, with a ready-made circle of friends and activities. The Athenaeum threw open its doors to Natty's younger brother. So did the ADC, where he enjoyed a considerable success as an actor. But his parents' academic ambitions were not to be realized in him either. In the summer of 1862, after only a year at Cambridge, Alfred became extremely ill, though it is unclear exactly what his complaint was. His parents were distraught. Lionel had his study at Kingston House converted into a sickroom, and there he and Charlotte watched over Alfred, even taking their meals with him, until he recovered. After this illness, which seems to have lasted over much of July and August, it was apparently judged inadvisable for Alfred to continue his university career. At any rate he did not.

Leo too proved a disappointment. It was not for lack of Lionel's pushing. He clearly could not restrain himself from exhortations, and they were constant and unceasing, but to no avail. Lionel and Charlotte seem to have learned one thing: Leo was destined for classical rather than mathematical honours. His desire for them, however, was rather less than his parents'. He had heard enough about Leo's dinners and his parties, Lionel wrote about a month after Leo had gone up in the Michaelmas term of 1863; he would like to hear about his lectures and his essays.[34] Leo was full of optimism in his replies, and seems to have won the good opinion of his coach, Natty's friend Richard Jebb, but he clearly did not apply himself, except to sport and the ADC. Lionel hoped to see Leo in 'Class 1 and very high up', he wrote in October 1864, but the signs were not good. In October 1865 there were reports from Oxford, where Leo had spent the previous summer, that his coach had found him very quick, but that he needed to work harder.

That was the general opinion. In February 1866 Lionel received a letter from Leo's Cambridge coach that his pupil seemed unable to make his supervisions; perhaps he was unwell? Was Leo unwell, Lionel wanted to know, or was he dining out rather too often? In fact he was, and in Town as well as in Cambridge. His brothers managed to shield him a good deal, but sometimes they were caught out. 'Who is to pay Alfy if the horse loses?', Lionel scribbled on the bottom of Alfred's note offering services at Epsom. 'I must say I never heard of young students backing horses.'[35]

The result was inevitable, and not as bad as it might have been. Leo got a third, though it was a bare third. Natty had gone to give support during the harrowing ordeal, and he wrote from Cambridge urging his parents to try to be pleased that Leo had at least got honours.[36] Lionel did his best. 'Your examiners,' he wrote, 'were quite right in saying you were a good hand at guessing.'[37]

The success of the Rothschild brothers at Cambridge had been a social, not an academic one. Interestingly, anti-semitism seems not to have posed a great problem – at any rate, one of which they were aware. True, the problem of chapel attendance had not disappeared. Natty was confronted with it immediately on his arrival; for whatever might seem to have been implied in the Act of 1856, chapel was still a matter for the individual colleges, and Trinity expected its undergraduates to attend. Lionel and Natty's tutor, however, made strong representations to the Master, and Whewell finally agreed that, if the Dean was prepared to excuse him, he would acquiesce.[38] Once more, Natty seems to have prepared the way for his brothers, for there is no indication that chapel attendance ever became an issue for either of them. All three brothers appear to have become fond of Whewell, and he of them, though they did not find the frequent dinners at the Lodge especially amusing.

Thereafter, the only time that Natty seems to have been made unpleasantly aware of being a Jew was on the occasion of a debate at the Union. He wrote to his parents that he had gone prepared to speak in what he thought was a debate on the growing power of the lower classes, but the main speaker turned it into an attack on the House of Commons:

> My blood boiled with rage when he quoted as the solitary instance of the too great power of the House of Commons the passing of the Jew Bill. I had hoped that the day was gone by for all distinctions of this kind and if I had spoken at once, I might have aroused religious passions not so easy to quell as to arouse.

He finally, and probably sensibly, decided not to speak at all. Two of his close friends at Trinity, Sir George Young and William Everett, son of a former American Minister to the Court of St James, answered the attack, and Natty kept quiet. There is no indication in his correspondence that he was ever provoked again. Coolness and caution would appear to have paid off.

Coolness and caution would always be among Natty's prominent characteristics, in business and in politics. His feelings might be strong, but he kept them tightly in check. At this stage in his career, Natty was a passionate Liberal. As his mother had early noted, he was keenly interested in politics and his letters home were full of them. One, on the occasion of Gladstone's Budget speech of 1861, will serve as an example:

> I was very pleased to see that the City people were pleased with the extension of Free Trade. I was immensely struck by the wonderful eloquence of the Chancellor of the Exchequer and comparing it with the recollections of Dizzy's last budget oration thought it infinitely superior . . . Even if the eloquence had not been so great, it is a greater speech regarded as a financial statement. I

did not expect to see much done for the lower classes by the present budget and on the whole it is very satisfactory. At the same time one cannot feel quite at one's ease when the expenditure of the country increases at the rate of 17 per cent. I hope though that now reforms will be adopted in the Dockyards and in all Government offices. And as soon as our quondam allies become united to us by ties not of Christian but of mercantile love, they will I hope disarm and allow us to do something similar. If the Government make use of Bright for India just as they have used Cobden for the Budget, they will reconcile the whole liberal party and even if obliged to go to the country on the Reform Bill must gain considerably by so doing.

The views expressed in this letter are not exceptional. Though perhaps unusually shrewd and well-informed for a man just beginning his fifth term at Cambridge, they were typical of a fairly advanced Liberal, with their emphasis on free trade, economy in government, and a pacific foreign policy. In the latter respect, it should be noted that the focus of foreign policy in the sixties was on Europe, and that there were no outstanding questions in the Middle East or Asia. In those areas the Rothschilds had always been strong Palmerstonians. As Lionel had said at the general election of 1857: 'To use a commercial expression, he had always been ready to endorse blindly his full confidence in the foreign policy of the noble viscount.'[39] In the sixties, Natty, at any rate, sometimes found Palmerston's policy toward the Continental powers too full of bluster and bully for his taste. But if he did not then fully share his father's Palmerstonian outlook, which he probably did in essence, he would soon adopt it. This would be important for the future. For the time being what one notices most about his youthful political opinions are their shrewdness and intelligence. Though Disraeli would doubtless have been wounded by the unflattering contrast with Gladstone which his young friend drew, it was quite accurate in this instance. And if Natty's hopes for the Cobden-Chevalier treaty, which lowered tariff barriers with France, were never fully realized, neither were they silly.

Leo too was a precocious politician. At the time of the 1865 general election, Lionel was suffering from the rheumatic complaints that were to dog his later life. Leo, still an undergraduate, took his father's place on the hustings. The dramatic qualities of the performance of the young thespian, soon to be elected to the Garrick, may have been remarkable, but again the ideas were not. Leo too stressed peace, economy, retrenchment and reform. He too was concerned about the condition of the lower classes. The solution was for the government to lessen the burdens of taxation upon them, and by leaving more money in everyone's pockets to encourage a general prosperity that would benefit all. This was what Liberalism stood for. In Leo's mind, there was but one answer to the question of 'whether you would rather be ruled by Palmerston, Russell and Gladstone or Derby, Disraeli and Malmesbury'.[40]

In ordinary circumstances, one might have expected Natty to have taken his father's place on the London hustings, but Natty was fighting his own election at Aylesbury. Having joined the bank on coming down from Cambridge two years before, Natty was now advancing the family's electoral interest in Bucks. He stayed with Sir Anthony at Aston Clinton, and he worked hard. But the twenty-five-year-old candidate clearly had his own ideas. He reported to his parents of the last day's canvassing:

> We drove over to Missenden and were met by a large party who promenaded me through the town and over the hills and far away like a tame bear, friend and foe we called upon alike. I made up my mind before starting that at 4 o'clock I would leave off and when the time came I told them in distinct terms that I intended to go home as I wished to keep well for the nomination day. Luckily they all were of the same opinion as myself and had had walking enough themselves.[41]

It sounds very much like the kind of gruff straightforwardness for which Natty would become famous. People did not always find it engaging, but it seems to have done him no harm with the Aylesbury electorate. He might not waste words, but he said what they wanted to hear, and that is what counted in this election. The Liberal party in Aylesbury was still not united at the top. Acton Tindal, he who had opposed the surgical operation on the party, was still an enemy. On this occasion, he brought down a former Member, who had the added advantage of being the brother of another prominent Bucks Liberal, Sir Harry Verney of nearby Claydon. Frederick Calvert (Sir Harry had been born Calvert and had taken the name Verney on inheriting the estates) thus had several advantages. But he also had one great disadvantage. He refused to give an unequivocal pledge to support the total abolition of Church Rates. When the same question was put to Natty, he gave a simple, one-line reply in the affirmative. This was all that the Dissenters who made up the backbone of the party at Aylesbury required. Calvert was forced to retire in confusion, and Natty was returned unopposed.[42] The family would hold the seat, transformed and expanded into Mid-Bucks in 1885, for over half a century, and it would become one of those looked upon as virtually a feudal fief. In the first instance, however, it was not only Rothschild money and Rothschild influence, but also Rothschild principles that counted in establishing that hold.

Whatever the explanation of Natty's election, this, the third family seat, did nothing to detract from a growing awareness of Rothschild power and influence. It was this awareness that lay behind the rumours, beginning at least as early as January 1863,[43] that Lionel was about to be made a peer. When in 1868, after the Second Reform Act, his friend Disraeli became Prime Minister, the gossip reached such proportions as to terrify the Liberals. Lionel himself treated it with a mixture of amusement and contempt. On 9 March he reported to his wife that C. P. Villiers had come to him from Lady Palmerston's, where everyone was talking about the current rumours:

> Our friend is famously intrigued about the paragraph in the papers respecting my being raised to the peerage. Just like everything else, the Liberals would like to carry out everything themselves. I always hear what he has to say and don't contradict him. He could not understand or could they at Lady P's that I would accept anything from the present Government. They all fancy Dis is under great obligations to us. So the best thing is to hold my tongue and let him think what they like. It is only amusing to hear all this nonsense.[44]

The Liberals, however, clearly took it seriously, and Gladstone did not waste much time after he returned to power in proposing Lionel for a peerage. In 1869 the Queen would not hear of a 'Jew peer', and the Government was forced to give the plan up for the time being.[45]

The Queen's view, however, was becoming increasingly untypical. 'Society', led by her own children, was taking the Rothschilds to its bosom. It was the younger Rothschilds in the first instance, but they took their elders with them. Perhaps the greatest coup took place just a few days before Lionel wrote to Charlotte about the rumoured peerage, the visit of the Prince of Wales to Mentmore on 6 March 1868. Lionel was unable to get up much enthusiasm about it, it is true; and after a few perfunctory lines in a letter to his wife, passed on to 'more serious matters'.[46] Natty, though he made rather more effort for his mother's benefit, also left something to be desired as a chronicler of the event. But everyone else was agog, and full of minute details of what took place.

The Prince's party left Euston at 9.00 am, in the Duke of Sutherland's private saloon carriage. He was accompanied by Colonel Kingscote, Lord Alfred Paget, whom Mayer thought had been sent by the Queen to give a report, Natty, and three other members of their Cambridge set, Fitzmaurice, A. Ellis, and Henry Bourke. They were met at Cheddington by Mayer, Sir Anthony, and all of Mayer's carriages. Juliana awaited them at Mentmore, according to Ferdy, 'clad in velvets and in sables, driven out of her mind for fear of the draughts'. Juliana herself reported that

> Hannah did the honours by receiving HRH at the door as Mayer and I do not share Mrs. Dizzy's opinion that a royal visit cures illness, and therefore did not venture into the draughts on the occasion. He came to me in the White Drawing room.

According to her descendants, it is the draughtiest room at Mentmore.

Ferdy had noticed that in the hubbub and confusion before the Prince's arrival, only Hannah had maintained her composure. As he passed with the Prince through the great hall, he noticed something else:

> The maids had been strictly forbidden to show themselves in the gallery, but the temptation proved too strong, so they all lied flat down on the floor and peeped down through the bannisters and thus gazed at HRH.

It was perhaps as well that Juliana seems to have remained unaware of this diversion.

In the drawing room, the Prince was all admiration, and desired to see the rest of the house's treasures. They also chatted about his recent visit to the Baron and Baroness James at Boulogne. After a brief tour through the downstairs rooms, breakfast was announced at 10.15. Juliana was struck by the evident enthusiasm with which her guest attacked his food:

> I must say that he did ample justice to that repast and made me envy him his appetite and digestion. He is very chatty and pleasant and amused me by his youthful enthusiasm about some strawberries. My gardener was very pleased at having some pots covered with ripe fruit and several baskets full quite ripe for the occasion. He had been cultivating them for the Judges' visit, so I told the Prince that they had loyally ripened nearly a week in advance for him, and he said with boyish glee, 'Well they are the first I have seen and quite excellent and I am very glad to have a *hold* over the Judges.'

Ferdy was also struck by the strawberries, and by the exquisite Sèvres that held them. All of Mayer's choicest stands and dishes were displayed on the dining table, 'and all covered and filled with magnificently red strawberries which at this early season presented a novel and most inviting aspect'. Natty, for his part, provided confirmation of the Prince's appetite: 'There was ample time for partaking of all the delicacies in and out of season and HRH ate as if he did not mean to go hunting.' Natty also noticed the dramatic effect of the sun illuminating the entrance and great halls – Paxton would have been gratified – and, typical of his own tastes, noted that they 'were resplendent with flowers'.

It was the Stag Hunt that provided the occasion for the Prince's visit, and Mayer had taken pains to make sure that he would enjoy himself. Secrecy had been scrupulously maintained by the Rothschilds; but word of the visit had leaked to the papers, and a crowd had assembled at Wingrave, where the party was driven to mount their horses. Mayer, however, had taken further precautions, sending 'the deer van on to Aston Abbots, so that when the hounds were laid on in that magnificent meadow on Aston Abbots hill, there was no crowd at all'. The deer had been released well before their arrival, going off over the heart of the Vale, and providing a fine chase of almost two hours, much enjoyed by those who followed him. 'The Prince,' Natty reported, 'went very well and considering that the pace was terrific and the best riders fell on every side, he was very lucky to escape without any accident at all.'

The party returned to Mentmore at four o'clock, and 'the Prince dressed as expeditiously as his Mamma, and ate a capital meal before he started at five.' This, according to Juliana. Natty, who returned to London with him on the Scotch Express specially flagged down at Cheddington, was also amazed at his zest for life and his stamina, reporting that when the Prince arrived in Town, 'he went off to pay visits where I know not'. The Prince, Natty said, 'was delighted with his run, with the country he rode over, and with his reception'. He could also inform his mother that 'both Uncle Mayer and Juliana were highly delighted with the Royal Visit and the field very much gratified at the run of the season'. Clearly, the visit had been a success from everyone's point of view. It is probably not surprising that Natty found the party he attended that night at the Gladstones' rather 'dull'.[47]

It was not of course only Rothschild men who made the family popular in Society. Natty reported to his mother, in Paris attending her elder daughter who had just had a child, that the Prince was most solicitous about Laury. The reason for the Prince's interest is not far to seek. His friend Ferdy Rothschild shared, among other tastes, the Prince's taste in women. Eddie Hamilton recorded the following conversation at Waddesdon many years later:

> Talking of beauty Ferdy R. said he had no difficulty in singling out the most beautiful women he had ever seen – they were the Baroness Alphonse de Rothschild, the Empress of Austria, Mrs Langtry and Mrs Sands.[48]

The Prince early sought, and received through Alfred, Laury's photograph, returning two of himself by the same intermediary.[49] The flirtation never went beyond this formal and quite harmless level, but it was doubtless enjoyed by both. Laury was ferociously English and an ardent royalist. On a visit to Paris in 1861, her sister Evelina, Evy as she was usually known, found Laury in deep mourning for the Duchess of Kent. She was much abused in Paris for going around looking like a crow, but, Evy observed, 'she will be an English woman wherever she is. Quite right!'[50]

Ferdy did not mention his wife among the most beautiful women he had ever seen, but it would not have been inappropriate. Her mother found Evy's fair beauty 'completely English'. It did not go without appreciation. Charlotte recorded, obviously with some pride, that Evy was much admired and followed by idlers on the street. At the age of thirteen, she had already received her first proposal of marriage, from one Frederick Glass, whom Charlotte described as 'a mechanic, a civil engineer, a half-educated person', who had seen her the previous year at the Crystal Palace.[51]

Charlotte had observed of Laury that she attached much importance to position in the world, and that she 'would not like to descend from what she fancies to be the throne of the R's to be the bride of a humbler man'.[52] Of course, she did not have to. Alphonse was grand enough for anyone, and though he turned out to be very much the jaded roué sort of husband Charlotte had imagined, Laury seems to have been happy enough.

From all one can gather of her short life, Evy placed a good deal less emphasis than her elder sister on the vanities of the world. Her letters show her to have been an intelligent young woman, with a well-developed sense of humour. She was, however, destined for a marriage no less exalted than her elder sister's, and one that would probably have been a good deal more conventionally happy. During the short time it lasted, it appears to have been an extremely happy one.

Ferdy was the second surviving son of Lionel's sister Charlotte and Anselm. The latter had moved to Vienna after the Revolution of 1848 and taken his own father's place as head of the family bank there. Charlotte died in 1859, and a couple of years later Ferdy, who had been deeply attached to his mother, took up what was to become a permanent residence in the land of her birth.

For reasons that are not entirely clear, Natty never cared for Ferdy, and, though their relationship was cordial enough on the surface, Ferdy returned Natty's dislike with interest. Natty seems to have found his cousin somewhat pretentious and pushing. He reported to Leo of an early meeting on the hunting field that, though 'the Anglo-Austrian rode well in front during the view and obviously thought himself highly proficient, the hunt didn't see much of Ferdy thereafter'.[53] Ferdy, for his part, would later complain to Rosebery that Natty had tried to stir up trouble with his Uncle Lionel by complaining about Ferdy's hunting attire! The pettiness of the issue in this case is matched only by the pettiness of Ferdy's letter.[54]

Ferdy emerges through his letters in later life as a man more than a little querulous and fussy. Natty, for his part, was one of those people of whom it is sometimes said that they do not suffer fools gladly. He seems to have put Ferdy down as a fool, and though he certainly did not go out of his way to be offensive, neither did he put himself out to be ingratiating. Ferdy was quick to take offence, and Natty did not take great pains not to give it. They simply did not get along.

In fairness to Ferdy, however, it seems likely that a long and lonely life as a widower tended to accentuate his less attractive characteristics. What is more, there were those who found him a most congenial companion even in later life. The Prince of Wales was one. Leo and Alfred were others. Natty may have been too hard to please.

Evy was a less complicated personality, and not so censorious in her judgements. She viewed the rest of the family and their circle with good-humoured amusement, and she was quite content with her own lot. Uncle James's great new house at Ferrières, she found 'too magnificent'. It was not as green as 'our little Gunnersbury', which she found distinctly to its disadvantage, and her final judgment was that, though they had imitated Mentmore in everything, 'they will never have those beautiful Buckinghamshire views'.[55]

The Disraelis, of whom she was very fond, she also found highly diverting. While staying at Gayhurst, she had been seated next to Lord Carrington at dinner. They had gossiped about the Dizzys; and she reported home with great glee Carrington's story of Disraeli appearing at a meeting at Aylesbury in high grey gaiters, looking for all the world like a farmer.[56]

One of Disraeli's opinions, however, Evy seems to have shared without reservation. They had been staying together at a house party at Mentmore. Lord Stanley was also there, and so was Ferdy. Disraeli had found the latter a 'most fascinating youth'.[57] Evy married Ferdy on 7 July 1865, in a grand wedding in the remodelled house in Piccadilly.

They set off on a Continental honeymoon, ending at Schillersdorf, Anselm's great Silesian estate. Evy reported home contentedly that Ferdy was 'a dear old duck' and did everything to make her happy. Like all the Rothschilds, they scrupulously observed the Day of Atonement. Ferdy's elder brother had gone to Vienna for the holidays, but as Ferdy did not wish to leave her, 'we have been saying our prayers at Schillersdorf'. There was a synagogue only two miles from the estate, but the 'absence of cleanliness in this country' made it impossible to go there. She found ordinary Polish peasants as rude and feckless as she found Polish Jews, and she was not much more impressed with the local nobility. A visiting Prussian count had asked her whether they had a million pound banknote framed and hung at New Court, and other stupid questions. Silesia, she concluded, was not England.[58]

They returned home in December, and moved into their town house in what was becoming almost a Rothschild precinct in Piccadilly; they were No. 143. Evy settled into the life of a Society hostess, entertaining herself and helping her mother to entertain. One afternoon's activity may perhaps serve as an example. Evy was helping her mother with a party they planned to give for the Disraelis at Gunnersbury. Of their acquaintance in Town, Evy wrote suggesting that they invite Mrs Norton, the Duke of Wellington, the Egertons, Lord Henry Lennox, John Hay, Charlie Carrington, and Charles Grosvenor. While she had been writing, she had been interrupted by calls from Lady Molesworth and Arthur Ellis, come to say goodbye before he set off for Russia with the Prince of Wales. Delane of *The Times* had only just left.[59]

The following summer there was a round of country house visiting, and then she and Ferdy went for a holiday at Scarborough. Just after the middle of September, Ferdy left for Vienna, to lend a hand at the bank in the chaotic situation created by Austria's defeat in the Austro-Prussian War that summer. Evy went home to await the arrival of the baby she expected in December. On 3 December Lionel wrote to Leo that his mother had gone to be with Evy, who was feeling a little uncomfortable. The baby wasn't expected for a day or two, by which time Laury, who had been delayed by a visit from the Prince of Wales, would have arrived from Paris.[60] On 4 December Evelina died in childbirth.

Several weeks later a desolate Ferdy wrote in response to a birthday greeting from Leo that 'henceforth my life can merely be wrought with sorrow and with anguish and with bitter longings'. He went on:

Mine is a loss which years cannot repair, nor any accidental circumstances relieve. Ever since my childhood I was attached to her. The older I became, the more we met, the deeper I loved her and in later years she had so grown into my heart that my only wishes, cares, joys, affections, whatever sentiments in fact a man can possess were directly or indirectly wound up with her existence. I can find no consolation in the future. It may partly come from the past, in the recollection of those bygone days, when she lived, when we were so intensely happy.[61]

In her memory he established the Evelina Hospital for Sick Children in London. He would never marry again.

The awful gloom which descended with Evy's death helped to obscure the circumstances surrounding another important family event, Natty's marriage in Frankfurt on 17 April 1867 to Emma, daughter of his father's sister Louise and his mother's brother Mayer Carl (or Charles as he was called by his English relatives). But there is another explanation for the mystery which enshrouds the events leading up to the wedding. Emma's own later version was that she had been intended for Nat's son, James Edouard of Paris, but that she and Natty had fallen in love and completely disrupted the family arrangements. The lack of any reference to their engagement in an extensive family correspondence suggests that something was amiss, and entries in Connie's diary further substantiate Emma's account of what took place. Despite the disruptions caused by the Austro-Prussia War, Louise and her daughters managed their usual annual visit to England. On 25 September 1866 Connie notes having gone to Gunnersbury: 'No secret about Natty and Emmy . . . Hope they will be very happy.' And on the day of their wedding: 'Another young happy creature full of life and vigour given herself to the man of her own choice, to the man of her heart.'

Evy's death would be enough explanation of why Lionel and Charlotte did not go to Frankfurt for the wedding, but it does not explain an extremely guarded and equivocal letter of congratulation that Juliana at Newmarket wrote to Leo at Frankfurt:

I am sure you know me too well to misjudge anything I write and I trust to your kindness to convey to your dear parents in the most welcome terms, the assurances of my heart-felt participation in all their joys and sorrows.[63]

Lionel and Charlotte were in seclusion at Gunnersbury.

They did, however, send gifts, according to Natty, pearls 'like pigeons' eggs' and a ruby tiara.[64] Leo, Alfred and Laury were all at Frankfurt to support their brother, and though Uncle Charles's remarkably rapid acquisition of pro-Prussian feelings – or so it seemed to his nephews – kept him in Berlin until the eve of the wedding, all went off well. Leo wrote home to his parents that 'a wedding is always trying to one's feelings', but he urged that they would soon be gaining a daughter. Alfred wrote simply that Natty was 'radiantly happy'.[65]

On their return to London the young couple settled at 6 Buckingham Gate. Leo, just down from Cambridge with his third class degree, went off for a summer on the Continent, followed by a long trip to Russia with Ferdy. Alfred had taken up the life of a bachelor clubman, and was an active member of the Marlborough House set, one of the Prince's favourite partners at late-night games of whist. The Nattys were on the more sedate outskirts of that circle, though in fact Natty went alone with Alfred to a concert the Prince gave at Marlborough House on 10 March 1868 in honour of his wedding anniversary. Emma was still recovering from the birth of their eldest child, Walter, the month before.

Lionel looked with indulgent amusement on the social success of his children. As always, he was preoccupied with more serious matters. He was entering the period of his greatest power and influence in the world of high politics and high finance.

CHARLOTTE (AND HER CHILDREN)

She kept a diary for each child, revealing as much about her own personality
as about the doings of her offspring.

BARON LIONEL NATHAN DE ROTHSCHILD.
Member of Parliament for the City of London.

BARON LIONEL NATHAN DE ROTHSCHILD
A proud man, greatly concerned with his social position

CHAPTER FIVE

High Finance and High Politics

LIONEL WAS NOT the financial virtuoso his father had been. Nathan had raised merchant banking, and N. M. Rothschild in particular, to a pinnacle of prestige and influence in the land. He had made them a major force in an exploding national and international economy. He had rendered them a power courted by all governments, and perhaps feared by some. And he had done this, in part, by making foreign securities a regular and accepted part of the portfolios of ordinary investors. There did not seem to be much left for Lionel to do.

True, Nathan had been almost exclusively a banker and financial adviser to governments. In his day Rothschilds played no important role in the private sector of the economy. This would come in Lionel's day, when the firm would take a leading part, particularly in the development of railways. But they were French, Belgian and other foreign railways rather than British ones, and the moving force was Uncle James of Paris. Lionel was a worthy, indeed an indispensable, lieutenant, but he was not the initiator.

Lionel built on the foundations his father and uncle laid, strengthening and consolidating the structure they had begun. Nathan had been brilliant and daring. Lionel was cool, cautious and shrewd. Nathan had achieved his successes by taking chances. Lionel did not take many chances, but he had a steady head and good nerves. He did not panic easily, which in the world after 1840 was an important quality for those who had something to conserve. He also had a good eye for opportunities when they presented themselves, and he did not hesitate to seize them. Under his leadership, N. M. Rothschild & Sons not only averted some disastrous reverses in the world of finance and politics, it reached the zenith of its power and influence. Lionel left his family as well as his bank a great deal richer and more powerful than he had found them, their position assured and their prestige solid and secure. He built on good foundations, but it was a mighty edifice he reared upon them.

By the time of Nathan's death, the main functions of the bank had already been firmly established. They were those ordinarily associated with merchant banking in the nineteenth century. Rothschilds provided their governmental and other customers with the facilities for the transfer of money and credit. In this connection, they bought and sold bullion and bills of exchange, as well as providing drafts on the Rothschild houses abroad. Their other main area of activity was in what today would be called investment banking. Here they served as advisers on and issuers of government loans and stock and bond flotations. The ordinary pattern was for Rothschilds to contract for a loan or stock issue. They advised on the initial price, usually below par value, and would undertake to dispose of the issue at this price. Usually part of it would be sold to other firms and private customers, with Rothschilds retaining the rest. They received a commission of one or two percent on the par value of the whole issue, making what they could out of speculation with the portion they retained. In managing these and their other capital assets Rothschilds also therefore played a prominent role on the Stock Exchange. Briefly, then, these were the activities over which Lionel presided.

In the later 1830s Rothschilds had been substantially involved in American finance, more involved probably than they would have wished. Their involvement had been one of Nathan's last initiatives. In negotiations that came to a climax in 1834 Rothschilds replaced Barings as the official bankers of the United States in Europe.[1] In effect, this meant that they acted as bankers for the State Department, though the main value was perhaps in prestige. Barings had become entangled in the struggle between President Jackson and the Bank of the United States, and Rothschilds had seized the opportunity. But they in their turn became involved in the disputes. The Bank's charter was not renewed in 1836, and reliance was placed instead on the Jacksonians' favourite instrument of state banks. The Bank, however, continued its activities under a Pennsylvania charter. The continuing struggles were one of the factors that lay behind the financial crises of 1837 and 1839. The Rothschilds remained loyal to the Bank of the United States. In the crisis of 1839 they accepted its bills when most other banks refused them,[2] as well as organizing a £900,000 loan to tide it over its difficulties.[3] But in 1841 the Bank of the United States finally failed. This was only one of many anxieties that arose out of the bank's American business during these years. Rothschilds were perhaps not too sorry when the US government's official account went back to Barings in 1843.[4]

It was a favourite aphorism of Uncle Amschel's that 'Governments are like teeth: if you lose them, you must get them back again'.[5] But the principle was never applied in this case. The crisis of 1837 had convinced the Rothschilds that it was necessary to have a trusted agent on the spot, and August Belmont was sent out for the purpose. Thereafter the great bulk of their American business was done through him. There was talk in the late 1840s and again in the early 1860s of establishing a Rothschild house in the United States with one of James's sons as its head. Such talk caused Belmont considerable annoyance. The Rothschilds, for their part, were frequently annoyed and dissatisfied with him. Apparently, however, because of James's reluctance to allow his sons to stray so far from his paternal guidance, nothing ever came of the plans for an American house, and Belmont continued to act as their main agent.[6] The chief exception was in California, where their cousins the Davidsons usually acted for them in the purchase of gold ores,[7] a commodity in which they had developed a special new interest. Otherwise, however, it was Belmont who made the running. The resulting business was often substantial and lucrative, but it would seem in retrospect that a great opportunity was lost.

Yet whatever the difficulties and lost opportunities of Lionel's early years as head of the London house, it prospered. Its Spanish investments, particularly the quicksilver monopoly, proved their worth and would continue to produce an excellent return for several more decades. The financing of the Belgian state railways, where the family got its start in this line of activity, was also lucrative; and during these years they were the main bankers to the Belgian state, now ruled over by their old friend Leopold, with their even closer friend Baron Stockmar at his elbow. The result was a healthy balance for the London house. Their uncles were impressed with their profits. For the time being, however, Lionel was not prepared to press for a larger share of the total profits of the five banks. When the partnership was renewed for another five years at Frankfurt in 1844, he was quite satisfied simply to 'thank God for what we have and may we have to divide as much the next time we meet'.[8]

Part of the reason for this continued success no doubt was that Lionel continued to be adept, as his father had been before him, at cultivating important personages. He did not do it for its own sake, or for the social cachet that might accrue, and he found those who did slightly ludicrous. Some years later he was more than a little amused, though philosophic, about James's excitement over an invitation from the Emperor Napoleon III. 'What a funny fellow our worthy Uncle is,' he wrote to his wife, 'and how little things influence him. Everywhere people like attention.'[9]

Lionel himself valued it less than most, but this did not prevent him being assiduous in his attentions to royalty when he thought they might be useful. In June 1841 Queen Victoria wrote to her Uncle Leopold of the Belgians, who was a little fearful that she was committing too much to correspondence that might be seen by prying eyes: 'My letters to Brussels and Paris are *quite safe,* and all those to Germany which are of any *real* consequence I always send through Rothschild which is perfectly *safe* and very quick.'[10] Lionel was eager to provide such services and to make them as convenient as possible. Very much the courtier, he wrote to the Queen's confidante and former governess shortly thereafter:

> Baron Rothschild presents his compliments to the Baroness Lehzen and in answer to her note which he received only last night, begs to say, that Tuesdays and Fridays are the regular days for forwarding letters to Frankfurt – but any other day they can be sent via Paris and will arrive at their destination in nearly the same time. A special messenger can be sent any day.[11]

Though quite prepared to provide quiet services behind the scenes, Lionel, despite his refusal of the baronetcy, was far from completely spurning tangible signs of royal favour and patronage. Indeed on occasion he actively pursued them. Here long years of attention to that loyal servant and confidant of all the House of Coburg, Baron Stockmar, proved helpful. Writing to Prince Albert of the royal couple's forthcoming trip to Germany in 1845, Stockmar asked:

Will you allow me to take this opportunity to present a request from the House of Rothschild, which it might be well to grant. This House requests that the honour be accorded to it to be allowed to act as bankers in Germany to supply any need for money which Her Majesty might have on this journey. Rightly, letters of credit for the Queen are not allowed. However, if Your Highness before your departure would allow Lionel von Rothschild to be called, the simplest and best way might be arranged for the necessities of this journey. Nor will this involve any bad reflection. People like to say the Queen is associated with them, and the advantages of her relationship can't be achieved without notice.[12]

This simple and straightforward request of Stockmar's was granted. The Rothschilds became bankers to the Queen. In terms of prestige, it was primarily the Frankfurt Rothschilds who benefitted, but much of the business was transacted through the London house, and since the relationship continued after the journey had taken place this was of some importance. Monies destined for Germany were paid through the bank. It seems also to have served as a channel for loans to the Prince Consort; and Lionel had contemplated the possibility that another loan might become a counter in the game to win Jewish Emancipation. A further advantage was that the relationship kept the Rothschilds close to the royal circle, which apart from anything else meant that they were in touch with an important source of information. On 12 May 1846 Anselm wrote from Frankfurt that Stockmar had passed through on his way to Brussels and London: 'He is still as friendly for our House as ever he was and promised me solemnly that as soon as he will know something about the American and Corn Bill question, you my dear Lionel, will be the first person to be informed of it.'[13] In a business where much depended on early and accurate information, the advantages of such a source were not slight.

Any precise assessment of its importance is impossible. Nor is it much easier to make a precise judgment about the propriety of such relationships. Today we tend to look askance at too intimate a connection between great figures of politics, on the one hand, and finance, on the other. There are excellent grounds for doing so. Nonetheless, close relationships continue to exist for the good reason that cooperation between the two spheres of activity is often necessary. The same was true in the mid-nineteenth century, though perhaps for somewhat different reasons. In that period, apart from the essential financial assistance they could provide, banking houses such as the Rothschilds played other, scarcely less important roles. In the flow of information, for example, the advantages were far from being all on one side. The Rothschild sources of intelligence were often quicker and better than the government's. Not only that, the great banking houses of Europe, and more especially one with the far-flung connections of the Rothschilds, served as a highly useful channel of informal communication between governments. Through its devious routes, initiatives could be floated and compromises arranged in a way difficult if not impossible at the level of formal diplomatic relations. The Rothschilds were part, and an increasingly important part, of a complicated web of finance, politics and diplomacy. It is essential to keep in mind the whole web, and difficult to unravel the individual strands.

In the mid-forties, however, though the effect would soon be to refocus their interest on politics, the concentration of Rothschild attention was in the private sphere. This was the great era of French railway building, and the Rothschilds were at the centre of the activity. In 1845 the Paris and London houses organized an issue of £6m to launch the Chemin de Fer du Nord, and another of £8m for the Lyon, Paris, Lille, Valenciennes line.[14]

Not unnaturally, in view of its importance in linking London and Paris, the Northern line was the one with which the English Rothschilds were most closely connected, and they took an active part in running its affairs. In the middle of July 1846, Anthony wrote from Paris that, though a serious accident had caused a falling off in the railway's takings, 'I don't care much as it will give time to our employees to learn their business'.[15] The partners' correspondence during this period shows that they devoted a good deal of time to sending out engineers, consulting English authorities such as George Stephenson, and other matters involved in getting the line off to a good start. The English partners viewed the results of their varied activities with considerable complacency. Late in the summer, taking the cure at Wildbad, Mayer and James discussed a loan to improve the harbour at Dover, which they thought would be beneficial to their railway. Mayer wrote:

The more I see, I am convinced the more, there is no place like our old New Court. Where would the rubbishy French shares be, if we did not support them? I think we may give ourselves a few airs and be as great men as others.[16]

The next couple of years would provide some basis for complacency at New Court, and the London bank would indeed again become exalted among the houses of Rothschild. The reasons, it is true, were not quite the same as they appeared to Mayer in the late summer of 1846. For the years that followed, as well as being those in which Lionel took the lead in the cause of Jewish Emancipation, would also be years of great political crisis and turmoil, years which seriously shook society generally, not least the world of finance. During these years the London house would remain an island of relative calmness and a source of succour to the other houses. Part of the explanation lay in the stability of the English political system, which saved the country from the violence which racked Western Europe. No revolutionary mobs raged through New Court. The terrors for an international banker, whose fate was intimately connected with the success of ventures all over the Continent and with regimes that were tumbling like ninepins, were of a different sort. These times of all others called for steady nerves and a cool head, and it was well that Lionel had both.

In the most important crisis in the British Isles, the Irish Potato Famine, the Rothschilds played a prominent role in the efforts to deal with the suffering. The British Relief Association was launched in December 1846 in Lionel's room at New Court, with the bank subscribing £1000. The committee, whose efforts continued to be centred at the bank, ultimately raised £500,000; and *The Times* rightly paid tribute to the fact that 'throughout the period of extreme pressure Baron Lionel was indefatigable in his exertions'. These private efforts were followed by Rothschilds and Barings joining to float a loan of £8m to fund the government's attempts to deal with the needs of the starving population.[17]

But, whatever the immediate tragedy for millions of sufferers and the long-term implications, the Irish Famine did not shake the world at the time. Its effects were important in precipitating the repeal of the Corn Laws and disrupting British political parties, but they were not cataclysmic. The Revolutions of 1848 were altogether different, and the reports that began to pour into New Court early in the year were such as might have struck terror into the heart of the most steely-nerved prince of finance.

From Paris, where it all started at the end of February, Nat wrote just after their good friend and ally Louis Philippe abdicated:

> We are in the midst of the worst revolution that ever happened. You may perhaps see us shortly after this reaches. Our ladies and children left us at three o'clock for Havre and London and, please God, they will reach you safe and sound.[18]

Louise's journal reflects the seriousness with which the news was received in London: 'If our house can only weather the storm, I shall be quite content and shall not care for any losses, however severe.'[19]

James decided to stay in Paris; and Nat after a brief trip to England soon returned. The Provisional Government proved to be moderate. Louise was able to report after another visit late in April that Nat 'is in much better spirits and no longer thinks there will be a *sanguinary revolution* – our *purses alone* will bleed'.[20] What primarily worried the Rothschilds was the fate of their heavy investments in French railways. But Nat positively welcomed the possibility of a state takeover. 'I wish to God it was already settled,' he had written on 10 April, 'and we had the *rentes* instead of the shares – one security is available and the other is not.'[21]

Nationalization did not in fact occur, and thanks largely to infusions from London neither was there a liquidity crisis. But the French alarms were by no means over. In June there was the threat of an even bloodier revolution by the great mass of unemployed workmen left to their own resources by the Provisional Government's closing of the National Workshops. James's son Gustave wrote:

> I cannot tell you how black everything is indeed and nobody can say what is to happen tomorrow – to be pilfered, to be scorched – all walls are covered with lists where to plunder and we are mentioned as having 600,000,000 francs.

'All we can do is to trust in God'[22] – and, as it proved, General Cavaignac, whose troops in the bloody June Days put down disorder and paved the way for a resurgence of conservatism in France.

Paris was not the only Rothschild house that suffered. At the end of March, Anselm wrote from Frankfurt that Uncle Amschel's windows had been smashed, and that 'here as elsewhere the mob is master'.[23] In June, Alphonse, who was visiting Frankfurt, observed of the members of the liberal and nationalist Assembly who attended a dinner given by Amschel, that they were 'most enraged republicans, uncombed and with beards, the very idea of it would make our fiercest democrats shudder'. He went on to describe the dinner table 'beautifully set to entertain the Barbés of our time, who arrive in stained suits and dirty boots'.[24] The members of the Frankfurt Assembly, mostly middle-class professionals, would seem to have looked more dangerous than they actually were. In any case, the letter forwarded by Paris is unlikely to have reassured the London house.

In Naples too panic prevailed. 'Dear good Lionel', wrote Adolphe. 'Do bring back our English correspondents, else my poor father will be driven to despair. I do not know what to do.'[25] Worst hit of all the houses was Vienna, where Salomon had tied himself closely to Metternich's regime. Metternich was forced to flee, and Salomon was not far behind. Anselm, who had gone to look into matters there in April, did not panic, but he stated the simple truth when he reported back to Frankfurt that they could hope for no succour from Vienna or Paris: 'We depend entirely on London and on our own resources.'[26]

London was forthcoming, but to say that Lionel received the acclaim and gratitude of the rest of the family for his efforts would not be accurate. Assistance was given on Lionel's terms and according to his assessment of the overall situation and the needs of all the houses. This did not always please his uncles. Amschel was particularly demanding. On 15 May Lionel sent the following firm reply to one of those demands:

> We received today your letter of the 10th. Answering your request that we should send you silver and draw on Paris for it, we are sorry not to oblige you, because we have no remittances to Paris. Even if we had to remit to Paris, we have to say that our Paris uncle needs money

himself. Therefore you, dear Uncle, must send us remittances in bills or gold if you want silver.

Amschel returned the letter with a furious memorandum scribbled across the bottom of it, claiming to have made generous advances to London in the past, accusing them of ingratitude, and ending: 'You are really good, dear nephews; however, you are not always thinking sufficiently while you are writing.'[27]

Lionel, who was no more intimidated by his uncles than he was by anyone else, remained unmoved. Anthony, who went to Frankfurt the following month to look into the situation in person, confirmed his brother's judgment. Indeed, he recommended:

> As regards the silver *follow my advice and put it a little dearer*. They make so much that they can afford to pay a little dearer . . . They made up their accounts and they have 26 millions, taking everything as low as they can.[28]

It was necessary for Lionel to resist the panics, or wiles, of his relatives as well as those of others.

In the end, however, the soundness of his judgment had to be recognized even by them, or at any rate by the one who counted most, Uncle James. On 19 September 1850 Nat wrote from Paris:

> Our good uncle communicated to me his plan for the increase in the amount of money we take out of the House. He proposes that the rate of interest on the capital for us should be raised, how much will be seen when we meet at Frankfurt; that the interest remain at 3% for the other partners but in the event of the other houses making as much as you London gentlemen, that they should on the division of the profit have the difference of the rates of interest before the profit is divided amongst the five partners.[29]

The primacy of the London house was recognized. No more eloquent tribute was possible to the abilities of its head. Lionel had proved himself in the most trying times.

London's leading role would continue in the decade that followed. In 1851 the lion's share of the Austrian government loan, £2.25m was reserved for subscription there, with Frankfurt taking the remaining £1.25m.[30] It was also the London house, this time in cooperation with Paris, that assumed the responsibility for the rehabilitation of the fortunes of the Vienna house.[31] London remained a rock of stability and a refuge in troubled times.

Unfortunately, the partners' correspondence for the period between 1852 and the early 1860s is either lost or inaccessible,[32] but a mere list of the loans and stock issues during this period suggest the scope and volume of activity.[33] In 1852 the bank contracted for a Brazilian government loan of almost £1.5m. In 1853 Rothschilds organized the conversion of the Belgian state debt. In 1854 they undertook an issue of £2.5m in bonds for the Eastern Railway of France. In 1855 there was a great £16m loan to the British government, as well as a large part of an even bigger French government loan. The primary explanation of these loans was the cost of financing the Crimean War; and in the same year Rothschilds undertook a loan of £5m to the Turkish government. Jointly guaranteed by the British and French governments, this loan was so successful that it had to be allocated to would-be subscribers at the proportion of 20% of the amount applied for. The next year came another almost £9m loan to the British Government, and yet another of £5m the spectacular success of which Palmerston boasted about to Queen Victoria.

The interest of the London house in foreign railways also continued. In the same year, 1856, the bank played a substantial part with the other houses in the launching of the Imperial Lombardo Venetian and Central Italian Railway Company. In 1858 it undertook by itself an issue of £1.8m to finance the Bahia and San Francisco Railway Company of Brazil, and in the same year a loan of over £1.5m to the Brazilian government to provide a third of the capital of the Dom Pedro Segundo Railway Company. In 1859, this time in conjunction with P. Cazenove & Co., it took part in a £2m issue for the San Paulo Railway Company. 1859 also saw another large state loan of £6m to the Austrian government, and the renewal of a Brazilian state loan. A new loan of £1.25m to the same government in 1860 completes the main stock and loan issues of N. M. Rothschild & Sons for the decade.

Aside from the scale of activity, perhaps the most significant thing to note is the bank's increasing involvement with the government and government policy. Partly no doubt this was a matter of contacts and influence. This would seem to have played a role in the family's acquisition of another lucrative venture during this period. On 3 September 1849 Lionel wrote to his brothers from Wildbad:

> Billy writes something about a change in the system of the Mint. You may be sure that it is my plan, and what I have told J. A. Smith and Lord John repeatedly and that it will be adopted. I hope the ministers will have courage enough to make the alterations and that we shall be able to get it – it would be a capital business . . .[34]

It was probably these discussions that ultimately led to Rothschild's acquisition of the lease of the Royal Mint Refinery in February 1852. Under this and subsequent agreements the same year, they were empowered to refine gold and silver, and to present their bars directly to the Mint and the Bank of England for acceptance at the official rate.[35] It was this concession which lay behind Rothschild activity in California and other places where the precious ores were discovered.

If Lionel had taken part in general discussions which ultimately led to his family's acquisition of a lucrative business, they acquired it only because of the advantageous terms they were able to offer. This was equally true of the large loans to the British government they contracted for during this period, all of which were put up for public tender. The British government needed money. The Rothschilds provided it on the best terms available.

In view of the arguments first advanced by J. A. Hobson that financial power – and he singled out the Rothschilds by name – was the directing force in political action, it is important to attempt to get a clear view of their relationship with government on this, the eve of some of their more spectacular involvements in foreign policy. It is true that Hobson's arguments were directed particularly to a later period, the so-called Age of Imperialism in the last quarter of the century. But not only was Hobson's analysis appropriated whole by Lenin, thus endowing it with a timeless and universal application for those sympathetic to Marxist historiography, it is also necessary to bear in mind that Rothschild relationships with government had a long history. They had not grown up overnight, and their history is of considerable significance in understanding the later period.

In the three decades after 1860, the Rothschilds' best-known involvement in foreign and imperial policy was in the Middle East. Their name will always be linked with the purchase of the Suez Canal shares and the growing British involvement in Egypt. It is therefore important to be clear about the origins of their financial involvement in the area, and it must be emphasized that the objects to be advanced at the time this involvement began were the British government's, not primarily the Rothschilds'. They made a great deal of money, it is true, but they made it by rendering it possible for British governments to do what they had already decided to do. No one ever has, or could, argue that the Crimean War was a Rothschild policy, nor was the 1855 loan to Turkey that grew out of that war. Once more the Rothschilds were simply providing the financial wherewithal to promote what had become a prime object of British foreign policy, a Turkey as strong and stable as possible, to serve as a barrier against what was seen as a growing Russian threat to vital British interests in the Middle East. At this time, and indeed later, Rothschild involvement was undertaken not primarily for their convenience, but for that of the British government.

It is true that as time went on, and the Rothschilds, at the instance of successive governments, became more deeply involved in the area, they became identified with the policy they were financing. That is to say, they became advocates of continuity of policy, and did their utmost to prevent abrupt reversals. There was, however, more than one reason for this identification, and even in the later period the simplistic view of great financiers attempting to lay down the law to servile politicians simply will not do. The Rothschilds moved in several spheres, and at more than one level. They were, among other things, politicians in their own right. By the last decades of the century, partly for reasons examined in earlier chapters, they had become fully accepted members of that relatively tight little circle where political questions were canvassed and solutions advanced.

To say that the Rothschilds ever became a dominating influence in the shaping of foreign and imperial policy would be going much too far. They did, however, become respected advisers of successive governments. Perhaps even more significant, they became important auxiliaries in the gathering and dissemination of information and the implementation of policy once arrived at. Part of the reason for the prominent role the Rothschilds came to assume has already been suggested. Their international network for gathering intelligence was, it is not too much to say, unrivalled. This, however, had been true for a long time, recognized by Foreign Secretaries as early as Canning. What changed was the growing willingness of the official world from the 1860s onwards to make use of this network – not only to secure intelligence, but also to float initiatives and lay the groundwork for formal agreements later.

The advantages were clear enough. Alphonse spelled them out in 1870 in suggesting that the London and Paris houses act as intermediaries between the British and French governments in bringing about a mediatory role for the former in the Franco-Prussian War:

> I need not tell you that I have offered our cooperation to the Ministers should they ask for it. We are on very fair terms with all, to act as agents, be it on their or on your part, of official communications which either of the two governments would like to forward to feel their way, without giving it the meaning of an official communication.[31]

By then British governments had for some time been favourably disposed to take advantage of the Rothschilds' services.

There were distinct limits to the role they were expected to play, and no one had a clearer appreciation of those limits than the Rothschilds themselves. Natty, in his blunt matter-of-fact way, would later comment to Disraeli of one of the more important links in the Rothschilds' international network, the German banker Gerson von Bleichröder, that 'he has become arrogant and forgets that he is very often merely "a ballon d'essai" '.[37]

Neither Lionel nor Natty ever made a similar mistake: self-importance of this sort was not one of their failings. A shrewd and cynical view of the world protected them from such errors of judgment. Interestingly, a wave of anti-semitism in Germany, which Bleichröder's much boasted of friends in high places showed a distressing reluctance to repudiate, was the occasion of the remark. Natty agreed with Disraeli that Bleichröder and his arrogant attitude was one of the causes of the Jewish persecution. There is no indication, however, that analogous considerations dictated Rothschild circumspection. They were certainly not unaware of anti-semitism, and they were keenly sensitive to the dangers to politicians themselves of appearing to have too close associations with bankers in general, and the Rothschilds in particular. But it would appear to have been business rather than Jewish considerations that dictated the Rothschild attitude. They were quite clear that, as bankers, their role was primarily one of usefulness to governments; and this applied to all the various services they might be able to offer. Though they would dabble heavily in diplomacy, they never viewed themselves as more than auxiliaries to the official policy makers. Simple self-interest plainly indicated such a policy on their parts. Following it had made them rich, and would make them richer. It was both easier and safer to make sure of being in line with official policy from the beginning rather than to attempt to change it later.

Again and again in the years that followed, the application of these principles in Rothschild dealings can be clearly observed. Their attitude, however, was more than one of mere self-interest. The services they rendered were not only because they thought such services would do them good, but also because they considered them to be their patriotic duty. For they were Englishmen, and not only Englishmen but increasingly part of the small governing class which considered it a responsibility as well as a privilege to rule.

One result was to bring new attitudes, new assumptions and new sources of influence. Part of the means by which this transformation was wrought have been examined in the last chapter. At Cambridge the Rothschilds had become more than accepted by English 'Society', they had become part of it. Natty and his brothers graced its drawing rooms and trod its corridors of power with the ease and assurance of those to the manner born. In a country and an age where power was still remarkably concentrated, friendships counted for much. Those made during, and growing out of, the Cambridge years would be of lasting importance. But it was not those friendships which first brought the Rothschilds into the innermost sanctums of power. Rather it was their friendship with another one-time outsider, Disraeli.

During the sixties and seventies the nature of that friendship changed slowly and subtly, but profoundly. It was not because the friendship had not been close before. It had been, but it became much closer. Indeed, it reached a degree of intimacy it would have been difficult to surpass. There were several reasons. As Disraeli became more powerful, and more secure in his power, the Rothschilds became more useful to him, and he to them. There seems never to have been any question of financial dependence. In 1847 they lent him some government stock certificates, presumably as security for a loan.[38] They also put some good investments in his way, as for example some shares of the Northern railway. But there seems not to have been much more in it than that. The scorn with which Lionel dismissed the notion of any financial dependence suggests that he was aware how unwise it would have been. On the one recorded occasion when Disraeli discussed a loan with Lionel, he was told that Rothschilds did not lend to their friends.[39] But they could offer other things perhaps even more enticing to one who loved power. They could offer alternative means of influencing policy; and if not money for himself, money to achieve great diplomatic coups. And they could offer information of all sorts, a commodity no less useful to politicians than to financiers.

The Rothschilds were always delighted to have any politician's news, but another thing that may have affected their relationship with Disraeli in the sixties was the fact that, as a politician, he was becoming more acceptable in their eyes. As has been seen, they had not accorded him the unbounded admiration yielded by almost every historian for his stand on Jewish Emancipation. They found Disraeli's ardour in their cause a good deal less than they desired. The differences between them did not interrupt their friendship, but neither were they likely to have made it closer. In the sixties the differences began to disappear.

On 7 July 1867, towards the end of the debates in the House of Commons on the Second Reform Bill, Lionel received two callers in Piccadilly in quick succession. C. P. Villiers came bearing news from the Liberal camp, followed by Disraeli bringing intelligence from the government side. Lionel wrote to his wife in Paris: 'Dizzy, and well he may be, is much pleased that the Reform Bill will soon be passed and that his name is associated with it.'[40]

The Rothschilds were still not labouring under any illusions about Disraeli's devotion to principle. Not long after he had become Prime Minister the following February, in succession to his ailing former chief Lord Derby, Natty wrote to his mother, once more called to Paris by family concerns: 'From what I can hear, the Liberal party is not likely to be more united about the Irish Church than they were last year about Reform and by fair means or foul, Dizzy will tide over this session.'[40] Lionel, writing on the same day, took an equally cool view of the situation. He would make no predictions until 'Dizzy's programme is published. He may propose Liberal measures, and he then will be supported by the public who always are fond of a man of talent.'[41]

In the event, Disraeli did not support 'Liberal measures'. He was undercut by Gladstone with his proposal for the disestablishment and partial disendowment of the Irish Church. The Rothschilds, the essence of whose Liberalism was 'Civil and Religious Liberty' and reducing the power of the Anglican Church, supported Gladstone. Such issues, however, were passing; and other issues, which for the Rothschilds came to assume the first priority, were coming to the fore.

Disraeli had already been the means of bringing the Rothschilds into the heart of the delicate game of diplomacy. The Foreign Secretary in the Derby-Disraeli government of 1866-8 was the former's son, but the latter's protégé, Lord Stanley. Stanley came to rely heavily on the Rothschilds. The great issue of foreign policy in this period was the Austro-Prussian War and its aftermath. Like almost everyone else, Napoleon III had not expected the overwhelming Prussian victory; and the French Emperor felt that his prestige would not permit such a dramatic shift in the European balance without some compensation for France. His search for compensation created a highly dangerous and volatile situation.

For the time being, war was averted and Napoleon completely outmanoeuvred by Bismarck; but there were some tense times. After canvassing a number of possibilities, the French Emperor finally hit on Luxembourg as suitable compensation. Bismarck seemed to encourage him in this object, knowing full well that German sentiment would not permit it. When this became evident in the spring of 1867, the threat of war was very real. A way had to be found to allow Napoleon to withdraw with dignity. The solution arrived at was a declaration of Luxembourg's neutrality guaranteed by all the great powers, and it was agreed on at a conference in London early in May which Stanley chaired.

There had been one critical hitch, the guarantee, on which Prussia absolutely insisted, and which Stanley was extremely reluctant to give. On 7 May he decided to do so; but he recorded in his diary of the meeting that day: 'I had, for form's sake,

145

reserved my consent till the next meeting, but made it be understood that I would give way, only wishing to place on record that I do so in deference to the unanimous decision of the government.'[42] One of the ways it was made understood was in a telegram from Rothschilds to Bleichröder in Berlin. On the same day, Lionel wrote to Bleichröder:

> We wired you today that we accept your drafts ['tratten'] which means that our government is inclined to accept the conference under the conditions as suggested. Your friend will like it but please don't mention our name and tell nobody that we give you political news.[43]

Bismarck may have got the news from other sources, but he can hardly have got it earlier. Judging by the freedom with which Rothschilds would use Bleichröder's communications, the injunction to secrecy was probably not seriously intended. It may well have been added simply to underline the importance of the information being relayed.

Rumours of war would continue, and Stanley would continue to rely heavily on the Rothschilds. On 9 September, he wrote to the Queen:

> Lord Stanley, with his humble duty, submits to Your Majesty the enclosed extract from a letter addressed to the Chancellor of the Exchequer by Baron Rothschild, whose information as to what is passing on the Continent is generally quite as early and quite as accurate as that which can be obtained through different channels.[44]

It might seem an extraordinary admission for a Foreign Secretary, but the information given was undoubtedly comprehensive and accurate. The French, Lionel reported, could count on no Austrian support for any action against Prussia. There was considerable anti-Prussian feeling in the rest of Germany as well, but there too it could not be turned to French advantage. Nothing was more likely to unite German sentiment than aggressive moves by the French. Lionel believed that the French Emperor grasped the logic of this situation, and he was confident that peace would be maintained.

Lionel was right in his short-term prediction, and the uniting of Germany in the Franco-Prussian War three years later fully confirmed his broader analysis. The sources he cited were

Mayer, who had just returned from Paris, his own conversations with highly placed persons, and letters from different German watering places. Among the writers of the latter, as correspondence in the Rothschild Archives shows, were C. P. Villiers and Lionel's sister Louise. As well, of course, there would have been the daily correspondence from the Paris, Vienna and Frankfurt houses, and the almost as frequent letters from Bleichröder in Berlin. It was a varied and complex network on which Lionel could draw, and Disraeli was fully justified in requesting his analysis of events – which he had done. In that part of Lionel's reply which was not included in the extract sent to the Queen, he had apologized that the time of year prevented him from making as full a reply as he would have wished:

> When all the great men are away, it is very natural that the little people should follow their good example. Our friends also have been travelling about and have not written to us as regularly as they usually do. I am therefore not able to answer your kind letter as I should like.[45]

He had not done badly.

Ironically, the return of their political friends to power late in 1868 meant that the Rothschilds were further removed from its levers. Liberal nervousness about Disraeli's intimacy with the Rothschilds lay behind Gladstone's strenuous efforts to get Lionel a peerage the next year, and they remained in close touch with the Prime Minister and the Foreign Secretary. The Rothschilds could not be ignored, but they were not privy to the secrets of this government as they had been to those of its predecessor.

Belief in Rothschild power and influence certainly did not wane. It is true that it was not the government that was believed to be the focus of this influence, but an institution ususally thought only slightly less powerful, *The Times*. During the summer of 1870, while bellicose opinion in France and Bismarckian diplomacy prepared the way for war, *The Times* was highly critical of the more obvious of the two, French sabre-rattling. The English Rothschilds, as Alphonse complained from Paris, were held responsible. 'The Times articles,' he wrote on 1 August, 'produce a very great effect here and your relations with M. Delane are exploited against you, as if we had the slightest influence with that independent journal.' On 24 August, after a

French newspaper had once more identified *The Times* as 'the journal of "M. de Rothschild" ', the Paris house felt it necessary to issue a public denial of any connection between the family and that newspaper.[46]

In October 1870, after the French armies had been crushed by the Prussians, *The Times* advocated British mediation to achieve the retention by France of Alsace and Lorraine, but with those provinces neutralized under a British guarantee. This time it was the turn of the Queen's secretary to be critical. As Colonel Ponsonby wrote to her:

> This does not seem a very likely mode of leading to peace, but the suggestion will produce some feeling on the Continent. The Times is said to be still much influenced by the Rothschilds.[47]

Had it been possible for British intervention to have achieved the retention of Alsace-Lorraine by France, there would certainly be cause to doubt the wisdom of Ponsonby's opposition to it. In fact, lacking an army that would render intervention credible, Gladstone's government was forced to face the fact that it was helpless to influence the situation in any way. It had no choice but to be a passive onlooker.

What influence, if any, the Rothschilds had with *The Times* is not easy to establish. Their intimacy with Delane is beyond doubt. If there was a more frequent visitor to their houses in town and country than Disraeli, it was the editor of *The Times*. Whether or not he was passing on the Rothschilds' opinions to the world at large, he was certainly passing on the government's opinions to the Rothschilds. Two of his letters to Lionel during this period enclose letters from Granville. How much use they were is questionable. The first, of 7 July, in what can only be called a toadying fashion, declared the Foreign Secretary's entire concurrence with the views expressed by *The Times*. He then went on to express the opinion that neither France nor Prussia actually wanted war, but only 'a diplomatic success in the game of brag'. The second, of 3 November, bringing news of a twenty-five days armistice and negotiations for a permanent peace, was probably of greater value.[48]

It also appears that there was broad concurrence between the views expressed by *The Times* and those held by the London Rothschilds. Ferdy, writing from Paris early in August, was highly critical of French sabre-rattling. He also found the French Rothschilds *'plus Catholique que le Pape'*.[49] But if the London Rothschilds were unsympathetic to French bellicosity, even when indulged in by their own relatives, they were no more sympathetic to the crude Prussian views of the head of the Frankfurt house. On 27 August, for example, Mayer Carl wrote:

> The French must be humiliated, which is the only way for us to be preserved from further wars, and I have no doubt that the French must give up Alsace and Lorraine, a great part of their fleet and at least one hundred million sterling as war contribution.[50]

Such draconian terms did not find favour in London. Urged on by his Paris relatives, Lionel did call on Gladstone to discuss the possibility of British mediation, but the inevitable result of these efforts seems to have been conveyed well before Ponsonby's letter in October. On 7 September Alphonse expressed his thanks for 'your kind letters and we learn with deep regret that England is not prepared to intervene'.[51]

All this hardly adds up to convincing evidence that the position of *The Times* was inspired by the Rothschilds. The only hard evidence which exists that they were attempting to inspire anything in that newspaper during this period has to do with a quite different matter. They did their best to see that *Lothair* and the new edition of the rest of Disraeli's novels, with the famous preface, were given prominent attention in *The Times*.[52] Beyond this, all that the evidence for 1870 clearly demonstrates is yet another dimension in the Rothschilds' extraordinary information network. The editor of *The Times* was part of the Rothschild network, as they were of his. But it is hard to see in their common views anything very exceptional, much less sinister. They began by being critical of the French, and ended up being frightened of the Germans. In this, they did no more than parallel official opinion. As far as mediation was concerned, in suggesting that, Lionel was suggesting only what the government would have done if it could. 1870 clearly demonstrated the extent to which the several Rothschild branches had identified with their respective homelands. The French Rothschilds were good Frenchmen; the German Rothschilds, good Germans; the English Rothschilds, like good Englishmen, worked for peace and the balance of power. Their line was a patriotic one, and it is hard to see much more in it than that.

All that can be said of the Rothschild relationship with *The Times,* now and later, is that they were on intimate terms with its editor (as they would be with his successor, Buckle), saw him frequently, and were constantly exchanging views and information with him. It would be surprising if one had not had some influence on the other, but who influenced whom, and to what degree, it is impossible to say. One thing which can be said with confidence is that there was no question of financial dependence. This was a subject on which the family were, and would remain, extremely sensitive. In a letter to his Paris relatives in January 1908, Natty alluded to efforts to facilitate *The Times's* conversion to a public company in which he and his brothers had expressed a willingness to take part. But he took care to explain himself further the next week: 'I did not mean to convey to you that we had found all the money The Times newspaper was in want of. . . only that we had offered to find a very small amount of money.' Natty clearly wanted to avoid the slightest suspicion that the family had any notion of acquiring a significant financial interest in the paper.[53]

In what can only be described as the gigantic financial operations which made possible the conclusion of peace between France and the new German Empire in 1871, Lionel's role was central and dominating. It was in the partners' room at New Court that all the complicated strands came together. The French Rothschilds acted for their government, but it was Lionel who managed the conversion of their London assets into the English currency which the Prussians had agreed to accept in payment of the war indemnity. It was also Lionel who organized the two huge loans of 1871 and 1872, in which, mainly in conjunction with Barings, some £239m in stock were issued. N. M. Rothschild & Sons headed a group of bankers and financiers who guaranteed to maintain the stability of foreign exchanges while these immense sums were transferred to Germany, chiefly by bills of exchange. Ayer's conclusion that 'the work and anxiety involved in this vast undertaking would have prostrated any man of inferior calibre' does not seem excessive.[54]

That the Rothschilds did extremely well out of these and other ventures during this period is beyond question. In 1872 Lionel proposed that each of the houses withdraw £700,000 from capital, the total amount to be shared among the partners. As the Naples house had been wound up in the early sixties, after that city had ceased to be the capital of an independent state following its incorporation into the new Italy, four houses, or £2.8m were involved. The Paris house was in complete agreement. All the houses were so prosperous, they wrote to Anselm in Vienna, that such a capital withdrawal would not be felt. Anselm agreed.[55] If serving the interest of the European state system was doing good, the Rothschilds were doing well by doing it.

In January 1875, after dining with the Rothschilds, Disraeli wrote to Lady Bradford that he had found Lionel extremely unwell. He feared the worst: 'This would be a great death, for his brains are as large as his fortune and he does everything.'[56] In fact, Lionel had four more years of active, if painful, life ahead of him. A severe rheumatic condition largely deprived him of the use of his legs, but his intellect and business acumen remained as keen as ever. It was at the end of this same year that Lionel's most famous deal left him a great deal richer, and won his friend the Prime Minister the admiration of Europe after the coup over the purchase of the Suez Canal shares.

In the interval between Disraeli's fall from power at the end of 1868 and his return to office in 1874, he had grown closer than ever to the Rothschilds. The great change was his wife's death, which shifted an immense emotional dependence on to his small circle of friends. In July 1873 the pathetic widower wrote to Charlotte from Hughenden, suggesting that Lionel might like to make him the present of a portrait: 'My lost, or my absent friends are assembling around me in my solitude, and it pains me that the countenance of one of my dearest should be wanting.'[57] It was about the same time that Disraeli suggesting himself to dine became a matter of course. 'Might we come to dine with you today?' he wrote on 5 October 1875, probably referring to himself and Monty Corry. 'If inconvenient, which it might be, I will try and call to see Lionel in the evening.'[58]

This suggested dinner is the nearest in date which I have found to the period of intense activity over the purchase of the Suez Canal shares, which began in mid-November. It underlines a degree of intimacy that makes nonsense of the dramatic story which has become part of folklore. It is safe to say that the whole of the story will never be known. It was clearly never meant to be. 'I can but approve, my dear Natty, of your refusal to put down in writing what had been agreed upon by your late father and Disraeli at the time when the English government purchased the Canal shares', Alphonse wrote in July 1883. 'Nothing could have been discussed during those conversations that might be of retrospective interest.'[59]

It is one of Alphonse's droller observations. But, if every detail can never be known, the main facts can be. They have been ferreted out by the present Lord Rothschild in a monograph that effectively demolishes some of the more fanciful flourishes of the traditional version, though leaving the basic romance of the tale intact.[60] It is a dramatic story, and well and fully told there.

The salient facts are briefly put. The Suez Canal had been opened in 1869. Its opening revolutionized the strategic situation of the British Empire. As the shortest and easiest route to India, it became literally the lifeline of the Empire. But because of the reluctance of previous British governments to contemplate such a revolution, Britain had no more interest in the Canal than any other European power, and rather less indeed than the French. Disraeli was anxious to establish such an interest, one so substantial and evident as to justify in the eyes of the world the preponderating influence in the Canal that Britain's vital strategic interests dictated she must have. In November 1875 the financial necessities of a virtually bankrupt Khedive put such an opportunity within his grasp. The some forty-four percent of the ordinary shares of the Suez Canal Company held by the Egyptian ruler constituted the sort of evident interest he required. All he needed was quick access to £4m. The Rothschilds advanced it, being paid back some five months later, with a net profit to themselves of almost £100,000 by way of a 2½% commission and £53,000 in interest.[61]

No one, save Disraeli and his government, has ever called the Rothschild profit modest. There have been those, beginning with Gladstone and other leading Opposition spokesmen, who have decried it as exorbitant. Lionel himself contended it was reasonable. Monty Corry called upon him and got a full statement of his side of the case during the Parliamentary debates the following spring.[62] Lionel pointed out, in the first place, that considerable risks were involved. He had been called upon to pay out £4m in four instalments over the course of a month. Had the Khedive insisted in being paid entirely in gold, the money market might have been considerably disrupted, not to mention other extraneous factors that could have upset it. Under such circumstances the Rothschilds might have found themselves paying in money that was a good deal more expensive than they had originally bargained for.

Leaving aside the fluctuations of the money market, Lionel observed that, at the best of times, the removal of several million pounds for several months from the firm's reserves in itself involved risks. For example, a foreign government that ordinarily did business with the Rothschilds might have required a large amount of ready money, which the firm could not have provided, and taken its business elsewhere. 'But,' Lionel went on, 'even if no such contingency should arise, the "standing out" of so large a sum must be taken to cripple the resources and opportunities of a house of business accustomed to make rapid and great profits.'

Lionel did not claim to be involved in a charitable enterprise. The government had required the Rothschilds' services, and he had provided them for what he calculated to be a fair price. He denied that the risk of Parliament not backing the government and voting the money had influenced him in the least. That was a matter for the ministers. He did, however, contend that the case was unprecedented. Government had never before gone to a private firm for this sort of advance. Could the government have gone elsewhere, to the Bank of England, for example? There were various difficulties. But the greatest was that that semi-public institution could only have acted with semi-public discussion: 'It is a point . . .which could only have been determined by the full Board, at the obvious sacrifice of dispatch and secrecy.'

Lionel had put his finger on the critical consideration in the whole transaction. In order to accomplish the great object in foreign policy Disraeli had in mind, he needed a great deal of money, he needed it quickly, and he needed it quietly.

It was a tall order. 'Four millions sterling! and almost immediately. There was only one firm that could do it – Rothschilds.' Disraeli's breathless report to the Queen was essentially justified. True, it was not quite so breathtaking as later fable would have it. Lionel had rather longer than the time it took to consume a muscatel grape (Monty Corry's famous version) to make up his mind. And he had longer than the twenty-four hours Disraeli suggested to the Prince of Wales at the time. But even a week or two to reach a decision and marshall his resources was not a vast time. It was enough for Lionel, not only because he had great resources behind him, but also because he knew how to bring them into play most effectively, and rightly judged that they could be brought into play in this instance.

Disraeli also told the Prince of Wales that one of the difficulties the English Rothschilds had to contend with 'was that they could not appeal to their strongest ally, their own family in Paris, for Alphonse is *si francese* that he would have betrayed the whole scheme instantly'. Disraeli was right that the English Rothschilds had taken no one, including their relatives, into their confidence beforehand. Once agreement had been reached, however, their international network was brought into action, with the Paris Rothschilds taking a substantial share in the operation. The government had called upon the Rothschilds, and they had responded quietly, efficiently and effectively.[63] There was, as Disraeli said, only one firm that could have done it. The Rothschilds had provided a first-rate service, and they had been well paid for it. The government had got what it wanted, and the Rothschilds had got what they wanted.

The Liberal Opposition was highly critical of Disraeli's coup and those who had played a part in it, and the sharp criticism, particularly by Gladstone and Robert Lowe, undoubtedly put a strain on the Rothschilds' traditional political allegiance. But there were other reasons why their Liberalism cooled during this period. In 1860, Natty, with perhaps more than normal undergraduate wisdom, had observed that he always thought 'one of the chief reasons of Dizzy's unstatesmanlike reputation was his great want of patriotism'.[64] This came after a decade in which Palmerstonian Liberalism had upheld traditional British interests, while Disraeli had flirted with the peace party during the Crimean War. In the 1870s the situation was entirely reversed. Now Disraeli maintained the traditional interests, while Gladstone questioned them in a manner which many, the Rothschilds among them, thought quite insane.

Once more the main focus of interest was the Middle East and Russian designs on Turkey. Disraeli set himself to resist those designs and did all he could to bolster the Turks. Gladstone came out in violent opposition to that policy. After the infamous atrocities perpetrated by Turkish troops in the spring of 1876 in the course of putting down a Bulgarian revolt, he threw in his lot with a great public campaign to repudiate the Turks and all their actions. Since the Russians took advantage of the situation to advance their own interests by backing the Bulgarians, the upholders of the traditional British line in the area considered Gladstone's position both foolish and unpatriotic. There was, in fact, much good sense in his position. He argued, for example, that the best way to block Russian penetration in the area was to allow Bulgarian nationalism free play, which proved to be the case. Whether his opponents would have recognized the good sense in his position under the best of circumstances is perhaps doubtful, but any chance that they might have done so was effectively removed by a much more prominent element in the position of Gladstone and others active in the Atrocities agitation, the argument that because the Turks and their regime were immoral it could not be in Britain's interests to support them. His opponents had no doubt that this was utter nonsense.

The Rothschilds took this latter view. They fully backed Disraeli and his policy throughout, from his early efforts to prevent war by diplomatic pressure, through his attempts to avert Turkey's defeat, and when that came, his final successful effort to force Russia to accept a compromise peace at the Congress of Berlin. The warm terms of their approval are suggested by a letter Lionel wrote to Disraeli at the end of March 1877, when one of the latter's intermediate initiatives appeared to have borne fruit. Lionel wrote

> to tell you how truly I rejoice at the success of a patriotic and just policy. Owing to your great firmness and statesmanlike views we have arrived at a point where we may confidently expect to congratulate you on the prospects of a general peace.

This proved somewhat premature. But Lionel's approval was no less warm, and his optimism better justified, in a letter he wrote to the Prime Minister at the Congress in June 1878.[65]

Needless to say, Rothschild support consisted of more than mere words of praise. Their matchless information network continued to keep the Prime Minister informed. Diplomats such as the Russian Ambassador Schuvalov, Shou as he was affectionately called by them and others, were probably fed with information Disraeli wished them to have. Bleichröder, as before, certainly was. The Prime Minister continued to come to them for information, and they continued to get it for him, from their relatives and elsewhere. Reporting to the Queen on the results of one such request for information, from Vienna in August 1877, Disraeli observed of the Rothschilds:

> That house is extremely hostile to the present Russian policy, and have refused to assist the Czar in his present exigency. They are intimately connected with Austria and the Austrian Imperial family.[66]

In fact, their most recent financial dealings would have pointed in the other direction. In 1870, 1871, 1872, 1873, and 1875 they had been associated with Paris in Russian loans involving a total issue of £69m. Their loans in the Austro-Hungarian Empire in the same period were something in the neighbourhood of £16m, though in the several years that followed there were two more large Hungarian loans.[67] Russia in the early seventies was clearly a lively customer for money, and as long as it was not in conflict with British policy, Rothschilds were happy to organize loans for the Czar's government. When official policy changed, so did theirs. This, rather than any strong Austrian predilections on the Rothschilds' part, explains their actions.

Goverments and their shifts of policy complicated the Rothschilds' lives. An uncertain international situation was not good for the disposal of foreign securities, which made up the largest part of their business. Wars and rumours of wars badly depressed the market, which meant that the 1870s were a tricky time for the bank. It was necessary to look further and work harder for profits. In the 1870s Rothschilds were involved in a vast funding operation for the United States government, in which they and several New Yorks banks disposed of some £267m of United States bonds.[68] Lionel wrote to Disraeli of the 1876 operation:

> You will see our name in the American telegrams as connected with the new funding contract. This time we have 4½% bonds which are not so popular as 5%, but as the public will now invest their money in very few securities, we have no doubt of placing them with time and a little trouble.[69]

Time and trouble were worthwhile to keep in line with government policy. There was nothing to gain, and a great deal to lose by not doing so. The mutual interdependence between government and the bankers dictated the closest cooperation. As always, this was particularly true of relations between Disraeli's government and the Rothschilds. In the years after the purchase of the Suez Canal shares, Rothschilds became heavily involved in the Egyptian affairs. It must be stressed, however, that the pressure for that involvement continued to come from the government, not from the Rothschilds.

The Khedive's financial position remained precarious. Though the sale of the Canal shares had temporarily alleviated his problems, it had not removed them. Indeed, by advertising the weakness of his financial position, it had in a sense weakened it further. The purchase of the Canal shares, by increasing Britain's stake in Egypt, had naturally also increased her desire to promote a stable regime there. It became a critical interest of the British government to remove the Khedive from his difficulties, and the Prime Minister wanted Rothschilds to assume the leading role. The Rothschilds were not so keen. In March 1876 Lionel wrote to Leo, who was attending the wedding of Laury's daughter Bettina in Paris:

> Dizzy has just left. He sees the difficulties of our putting ourselves at the head of a large financial operation and told them so today in the Cabinet . . .[70]

Probably the greatest difficulty was reaching agreement with the Paris Rothschilds, who were no less intent on keeping in line with the policy of their government than the English Rothschilds were with theirs.

Alphonse had already explained the official French view at some length on 15 January:

> The French government says the Suez Canal affair has already prejudiced us and is seen in Europe as having been directed against us. Should England now accentuate even more her politics of intervention in Egyptian affairs, coming to the rescue of the Khedive by means of another financial operation . . . the position of the French government might become very delicate, with French political credit strongly affected.[71]

What the French wanted was joint intervention by the two countries, but on terms which the British government felt – no doubt rightly – were calculated to promote French prestige and interests. Alphonse made clear that he was speaking from the

157

highest authority, though in the above instance he did not identify it. There is no doubt of the source of the replies from London. As Lionel wrote to Leo on 25 March:

> Diz was here and I have written to Alphonse what our goverment wants. They want the French to make a good plan and not one that will put money in their pockets, and without doing the *Khedive any good*.[72]

With the continued mediation of the London and Paris Rothschild houses an accommodation was finally reached, and international supervision of Egyptian finances established, in which France and Britain played the dominant roles. Britain did not in fact appoint a representative until 1877, and the control proved too weak to be effective. Hence in 1878 there was a further reorganization in which stronger measures were recommended and a British Treasury official actually appointed to be Minister of Finance. On 22 June 1878 Alphonse was able to congratulate his London relatives on the fact that Egyptian government securities 'have risen this day considerably on the appointment of Mr Rivers Wilson as the Minister of Finance and of N. M. de Rothschild as the financial agents of Egypt'.[73] It was this that lay behind the Egyptian state loan of 1878, in which the London and Paris houses presided over the issue of £8.5m in stock secured on the domain lands.

Egyptian problems were by no means over. Disraeli would continue to call on the Rothschilds for their assistance – and they on him to smooth their way. But this is another story, for the Egyptian State Domain loan would be the last great service Lionel rendered to his old friend. On 3 June 1879 Lionel died, probably of a heart condition arising from rheumatoid arthritis.

There had been no warning. Natty had been in Paris on business. On his return, he wrote to 'My dearest Lord Beaconsfield', as Disraeli had become in 1876:

> The loss we have all sustained is so great, I may say inexpressible, and the sudden blow had so stunned us all that we can do nothing but think of the best and kindest of fathers.
>
> I was with him late on Friday night and during the whole of Saturday taking his instructions previous to my departure and I admired and appreciated then as I always

have done, the greatness of his judgment and the lucidity of his mind. He always laid the greatest store in your love and friendship and hoped and trusted it would be extended to his sons.[74]

It would be.

Lionel was almost the last of his generation. Nat, blind and crippled, had died in Paris in 1870. Mayer died in 1874, Anthony in 1876. Charlotte, who had suffered a mental breakdown in 1877, seemed unable to comprehend that her husband was dead.

The new generation which was to take the place of the old, though it did not lose its powerful base in the financial world, was to be powerful in a more conventional sense and with more conventional symbols. Hannah would marry an Earl and a future Prime Minister. Natty would become a peer in his own right and a figure in the political as well as the financial world. The Rothschilds had come into the fullness of their inheritance.

CHAPTER SIX

Roseberys and Rothschilds

IT IS NOT EASY to get early family impressions of Hannah Roths-child, the future Lady Rosebery, or at any rate not ones on which much reliance can be placed. Her mother, Juliana, was not especially popular with the other Rothschild ladies. Lionel's baroness got on well enough with her, and their sons, though vastly amused by her exaggerated hypochondria, were extremely fond of Juliana. She was young, only nine years older than Natty, intelligent and full of fun, and Mentmore was a pleasant place to be. Mayer, Uncle Muffy, was universally beloved. Horses, hounds, and hunting were great attractions. Indoors, Juliana kept things lively with parlour games, even if she did sometimes overdo acrostics.

As for Lionel's daughters, they were not much younger than Juliana, and a good deal older than Hannah. Leo was only five years older, but he was a boy. All in all, there is not much recorded interest in the little girl born in 1851.

The Aston Clinton Rothschilds, of course, had their own difficulties with Mentmore. Anthony and Mayer did their best to ignore their wives' differences, but not always successfully. Louise never forgave Juliana for marrying Mayer instead of her own brother Joe. As always, Louise's better nature struggled against this animosity. She made every effort to hide it from her children, and Connie and Annie seem well into their teens to have been unconscious of any strains with Mentmore, though there would sometimes be a month at a time without any visits between the houses. When there were, there was not much interest in Hannah. Beyond patronizing notice of Hannah's performances in the amateur theatricals so popular at Mentmore, Connie's only remark about her in her 1858 diary was amaze-ment that a thirteen-year-old boy like Leo, only two years younger than herself, was silly enough to make the effort to play with a seven-year-old girl.[1] She would later find a great deal to say about Hannah, almost all of it bad, but that was after a series of family marriages to aristocratic young Christians, the last being Hannah's own to the fifth Earl of Rosebery. The first had been Annie's to the Hon. Eliot Yorke, a younger son of the Earl of Hardwicke, in 1873, and much bad feeling had arisen from it.

It was not, of course, a marriage without precedent. Hannah Mayer's marriage to Henry Fitzroy had set one in the previous generation. But, despite their philosophic acceptance of Hannah Mayer's choice, the family emphatically rejected this as a precedent to follow. The feeling of her elders clearly made an impression on the fifteen-year-old Connie, as her comment on the death of little Arthur Fitzroy in 1858 suggests:

> I cannot help thinking that all the misfortune and distress which have overwhelmed poor Aunt Hannah Mayer have been a punishment for having deserted the faith of her fathers and for having married without her mother's consent. All the grief that she caused to that mother she now feels doubly herself.[2]

The faith of their fathers had not lost its strong hold on any of the English Rothschilds. Though not excessive, their religious observances were regular. The sabbath was a day of rest, and when in Town it was usual on Saturdays to attend synagogue. In the country, there were prayers at home. The great religious holidays were strictly observed. No food passed their lips on the Day of Atonement. At Passover the whole family gathered for the Seder at 148 Piccadilly, as they had once gathered a few doors away at 107 while the first Hannah had lived.[3] Nor, as Macaulay had noticed, was any form of pork ever in evidence on a Rothschild table. Oddly perhaps, there were sometimes pigs on Rothschild farms. Such was Anthony's passion for breeding livestock, that he seems not to have been able to draw the line at pigs. There is some suggestion that the need of a Silesian pig had to do with sniffing out truffles in the Aston Clinton woods, but there would hardly seem to have been the same justification for the purchase of an Irish pig![4]

Anthony's brothers shared his enthusiasm for breeding livestock, but he surpassed them all in his devotion to shooting pheasants, and distinguished shooting parties assembled at Aston Clinton to pursue the sport. Among others, the Prince of Wales was his guest, as he was the Prince's at Sandringham. Anthony also became the Prince's confidential financial adviser; and when he died in 1876, the Queen wrote to her son: 'You will be very sorry for poor Sir Anthony Rothschild who was so very kind and loyal and so fond of you and a very good man.'[5]

But of his nephews' friends, it was not only the Prince who began to frequent Anthony's house. Other friends from their Cambridge days also came. None became closer to his daughters than the young Yorkes, whose house at Wimpole had been a gathering place for the Prince's set. Wimpole and its sons and daughters became particularly dear to Connie, and for reasons not entirely clear she decided to cement the relationship with Annie.

On 29 April 1872, her birthday, Connie noted in her diary:

> I was a little fool some years ago and behaved like one. If it had not been so, I might have been married and comfortably settled. I am now moving heaven and earth for Annie. She has no notion of what I am doing.[6]

From her earliest diary, Connie had demonstrated a pronounced tendency to believe that every man she met was in love with her, beginning with *both* her cousins Natty. A careful reading of each tiny volume might reveal more about the truth of her assumption that she had been crossed in love. That for 1872 certainly amply justifies the truth of her last assertion. On the 7th of June she hoped that Eliot was falling in love with Annie. On the 30th on a visit to Wimpole she thought that they were falling in love with each other, but 'I do not know how to bring matters about'. She went on:

> Oh dear Wimpole, happy blessed place. I wish I could be a Christian. I love the faith and the worship.[7]

She was certainly in love with Eliot, noting of a visit he paid her shortly after she had finally determined that Annie loved him:

> Eliot came, sat down, cried, took my hands, kissed them. I kissed his forehead. He raised his lips and touched mine. How I would go through fire and water for him. I love him so.[8]

Connie was evidently highly neurotic, yet the strong attractive powers of English 'Society' on an impressionable young girl would under any circumstances have been great. Her parents had clearly not anticipated the consequences of the life into which their daughters had been launched. When Connie began giving hints to her mother in July, long before it was entirely clear to the principals that marriage was their destiny, Louise had simply 'smiled in such an incredulous way'. In October when first Connie and then Annie openly declared how matters stood, their mother was 'inconsolable'. After three days in a 'terrible state', she finally agreed that Eliot should come to Aston Clinton, make his formal proposal, and attempt to secure Anthony's consent.

For the President of the United Synagogue and of the Jews' Free School – for Anthony was a member of the family more or less in charge of their relations with the community – this was likely to be a traumatic experience. It was. Connie recorded that Eliot spoke to her father after dinner: 'Then came the scene. I shall never forget it.' Next morning, Anthony went up to Town, 'to face New Court'. He returned in the evening, '*very* plain quite against it'.

Next morning, however, on Connie's advice, Annie went to her father 'and had it out with him. He gave his consent.'[9] It was a decision which caused him much pain and anguish.

His family's attitude was not the least of Anthony's worries. After a brief revival of his spirits, he returned from a visit to Mentmore, 'looking gloomy. He had been suffering from Natty.' The regular inhabitants of that house were even stronger in their opposition. On a subsequent visit, Juliana never even put in an appearance. Later, Mayer, encountered in London, 'would not speak to us or get into our carriage'. As for Hannah, Connie's conclusion was: 'Hannah is a brute.'[1]

Connie is not specific about the behaviour that lay behind this judgment, and it would seem to be a harsh one on a young woman of twenty-one deeply devoted to her own parents and doubtless a good deal influenced by their strong disapproval. Given Hannah's own later marriage, it is perhaps not surprising that Connie's reaction was bitter. Equally, however, it suggests that one should not place too much reliance on her assessments of her cousin.

As they had over Hannah Mayer's marriage, it did not take the family long to come round. By the New Year, Juliana was her usual cheerful self, while at 148 Piccadilly, Lionel received both his nieces kindly. But Anthony continued to suffer. Annie's first

wedding took place at the Mount Street Registry Office on 11
February. None of the family attended. Connie was prostrate,
and 'Papa looked so sad. We all felt it dreadfully, Annie included.' Connie was able to go down to Wimpole for the church
wedding the next day, but it was not a ceremony she remembered with pleasure:

> I was partly the cause of it. I hope, trust, it may all turn
> out well. May God protect us all.[11]

The marriage was a happy one, tragically cut off by Eliot's death
only five years later.

As far as the family was concerned, the storm over Annie's
marriage seems to have cleared the air. Their emotions spent, the
two subsequent marriages were taken calmly, if not enthusiastically. In November 1877 Connie married Cyril Flower, who had
been Leo's closest friend at Cambridge. Flower, who had had the
reputation of being the most 'beautiful' man of his day at the
university,[12] was probably not sexually attracted to women. He
was also already ill with diabetes, which would kill him in 1907.
This may have increased his testiness and petulance, which
matched Connie's own. A Liberal politician who held minor
office, Flower's greatest recommendation seems to have been his
unswerving loyalty to Gladstone. The tart remark in Cokayne's
Complete Peerage on the peerage bestowed on him in 1892 is not
unfair: 'An advanced Liberal, ennobled on Gladstone's recommendation, and certainly not one of his most successful efforts to
adorn the Upper House.' It was something perhaps to be Lady
Battersea, but it is unlikely Connie got much else out of the
marriage.

Hannah married Rosebery the year after the Flowers' wedding, in 1878. Connie's assessment of the recently married
couple in 1879 was that, '*He* is very pleasant'. In the same year,
she put her cousin down variously as 'most selfish' and a 'cold
uncongenial hostess'. She added of a visit by Gladstone to
Mentmore: 'Hannah was silenced. She takes no interest in big
subjects and he takes no more in gossip.'[13]

The novelist Henry James, another visitor to Mentmore, was
perhaps as acute an observer. He was vastly impressed by
Mentmore

> where everything is magnificent. The house is a huge
> modern palace, filled with wonderful objects accumu-

lated by the late Sir Meyer de Rothschild, Lady R's father. All of them are precious and many are exquisite, and their general Rothschildish splendour is only equalled by their profusion.

He was not as impressed by Hannah, but his reasons were different from Connie's, and his assessment disagrees with hers. He found Hannah 'large, fat, ugly, good-natured, sensible and kind'.[14] As a judge of female beauty, there is no need to defer to James, but most would allow that he was a shrewd judge of character. The evidence on the latter point is all in his direction, though he too would seem to have underestimated Hannah.

Given the attitude of the Rothschild women, early impressions are probably best left to the male Rothschilds, and, such as they are, they reveal a not unimpressive personality. Ferdy had remarked at the time of the Prince of Wales's visit to Mentmore on Hannah's calmness amidst the frenzy of everyone else's preparations; and it must have taken considerable self-possession for a girl of seventeen to have done the honours of the house, receiving the prince at the door and conducting him to her mother, vainly sheltering from the draughts in the drawing room.[15] The previous year her proud father had reported from Paris that 'the Empress was very gracious to Hannah, put several questions to her and said how grieved she had been on hearing of the sad loss which the family in London has met with',[16] referring to Evelina's tragic death.

Hannah, though shy by nature, had therefore been moving with poise and apparent ease through 'Society' long before she married Archibald Primrose, the fifth Earl of Rosebery in 1878. Largely since her father's death in 1874, entirely since her ailing mother's death the year before the marriage, Hannah had also been her own mistress, among other things adding to the large Bucks estate that had been left to her. After riding over a new acquisition in May 1877, she wrote to her Uncle Lionel: 'My new tenants seemed delighted at their land belonging to me which was pleasant to hear. Some of them had evidently been hoping a Rothschild would be a purchaser of it.'[17] She was clearly aware of the family's high reputation as landlords, and of the social responsibilities of being a Rothschild. Connie's version of a self-centred, self-indulgent girl, divorced from the real world, cannot be taken at face value.[18]

Nor is it possible to accept an even more prevalent impression, strongly tinged with anti-semitism, of a somewhat fat and ugly heiress, married by a handsome young peer for her money, and barely tolerated by him thereafter. Giving Henry James his due, it is true that by no one's standards, did Hannah have the stunning beauty of her cousins Laury and Evelina, but the picture by an unknown artist which hangs in Rosebery's bedroom in Barnbougle, of Hannah in the Great Hall at Mentmore, reveals an undoubtedly pretty and attractive girl. Photographs demonstrate that the later portraits by Leighton, and the particularly fine one by Watts, did the mature woman no more than justice. If unquestionably plump, Hannah had a serene and handsome beauty, much less forbidding than that of many Victorian matrons.

What is more, the impression is unfair to Rosebery. He was hardly poor to begin with, the possessor of a vast Scottish estate, another handsome house, The Durdans, at Epsom, and an income in excess of £30,000 a year. True, marriage to Hannah probably more than quadrupled his income and brought him an even grander house at Mentmore, not to mention one at Newmarket, and 107 Piccadilly – the latter soon abandoned for Lansdowne House, rented from the Marquess, and then a permanent new residence at 38, Berkeley Square.

It is impossible to say that financial considerations played no part in determining Rosebery's proposal to Hannah on 3 January 1878. Indeed, it is difficult to say what went on in his mind. His diary is entirely silent on the matter. There is no entry for the year 1877 after 12 July. On 1 January 1878, he takes up the diarist's task again, noting that he spent the day shooting at The Durdans, and then dined at the Turf Club, which he did not leave until 2 a.m. Then there is no entry until the laconic 'Engaged to be married at 4.20 p.m.' on the 3rd. After that, there is nothing until about a month after their marriage, on 20 March, when they left for a Continental trip.[19]

An intensely introspective and thin-skinned man, Rosebery, while often brutally frank in his diary, seems not to have confided in it until he was certain in his own mind of his opinions and motivations. It is clear that it was no spur of the moment decision that took him down to Mentmore with a sapphire locket, to propose formally and be accepted on the spot.[20] Much soul-searching had undoubtedly preceded the event. But there was more than one question on which he might have searched his soul.

Among surviving correspondence, there are several letters from his mother, widowed when her eldest son was only four and long since married a second time to the Duke of Cleveland. The Duchess had been born a Stanhope, and, like her son, had inherited the, in her case somewhat brittle, brilliance of her Stanhope and Pitt ancestors. She and her eldest son did not get on. Rosebery was not in the habit of asking her advice in advance, and he did not in this case, simply announcing his engagement to his mother. This did not, however, prevent the Duchess taking violent exception to the proposed marriage, founded on religious grounds. Rosebery's replies to her letters have not survived, but her final letter to him gives some idea of the nature of his to her:

> Do not for a moment suppose that I ignore the sacrifice your future wife makes in marrrying you. No two persons of different religions can marry without making a very great sacrifice, and – pardon me for adding, grieving and disappointing those who love them best. Even in the widely different instance of a marriage between a Roman Catholic and a Protestant this would, to a certain extent, be the case. You must also of course expect to be unkindly judged by the world. But I fully believe that you have, as you tell me, fully weighed and considered every aspect of the question, and I do not intend to recur to it again . . .
>
> P.S. After all, there is one thing that I want to say. I have taken it for granted that your children are to be Christians; but it would be a great comfort to me to hear this confirmed by yourself.[21]

Clearly, Rosebery did not let Hannah's cause go by default.

Her decision had probably not been reached without anguish. No comment from Hannah has survived, but tucked in the box of correspondence and mementoes of her engagement is a clipping from the *Jewish Chronicle* of 5 October 1877, the month before Connie's wedding. The paper expressed 'the most poignant grief', and it went on to put the rabbinical query: 'If the flame seized on the cedars, how will fare the hyssop on the wall: if the leviathan is brought up by the hook, how will the minnows escape?'[22]

There is no evidence that any living Rothschild put such a question to her, but her dead father must have been very much on Hannah's mind. She had doted on him, as indeed had the whole family. Ferdy had written on 8 February 1874 in response to a letter of sympathy from Rosebery, that 'this is a loss we shall feel as long as we live. The genial spirit, the youthful and kindly disposition of my uncle endeared him to us and made him the centre of all our amusement which can never be replaced.'[23] Mayer's kindness and good nature were proverbial in the family, and even Connie seems to have found it in her heart to forgive him his actions at the time of Annie's wedding. But that so sweet-tempered a man could have acted as he did was a measure of the strength of his feeling on the subject. Hannah bore his mother's name, and his mother's injunctions in his student days at Cambridge had clearly never been forgotten – Mayer would never have compromised his Jewish faith.

It must have been difficult for Hannah to get round this. Whether she consciously decided to act on her own judgment or deluded herself into thinking that her father would have approved is unclear. She made as few compromises as possible. There seems never to have been any question in anyone's mind of her giving up her own personal faith, but the marriage itself was a compromise.

It was made easier by the fact that her parents had known and liked Rosebery, and that he was an intimate friend of Ferdy's, who before the building of Waddesdon had a small house at Leighton close by Mentmore. They moved in the same racing circles. It has generally been supposed that Disraeli introduced the future husband and wife at Newmarket in 1869, but Connie seems to have been the source of this story and her memory is not always accurate. It is possible. The first correspondence between the two families is in the autumn of 1871. Ferdy was already calling Rosebery by his affectionate Oxford nickname, Ladas, after his first horse of that name – the one which had precipitated his early removal from the university; the second won the Derby in 1895. But 1871 was 'The Baron's Year'. In November, Juliana, besides inviting Rosebery to Mentmore, informed him of the imminent arrival of a 'little parcel which the winner of the Derby and Leger begs you to accept with his kind regards'.[24] A Mentmore horse also won the Oaks in the same year. Rosebery's marriage brought him not only a fortune, but a famous stud as well.

It also brought them great happiness. Robert Rhodes James has given, on the whole, a highly accurate as well as sympathetic account of the marriage, but one judgment on Hannah might be open to misunderstanding: 'One cannot avoid the impression of Hannah Rosebery following nervously in Rosebery's footsteps throughout their married life, utterly devoted but consumed with alarm lest she made some dreadful mistake.'[25] Especially as this is followed by some alleged heavy-handed humour of Rosebery's at Hannah's expense – about Hannah and the rest of the heavy baggage – it might give rise to a somewhat patronizing and inaccurate assessment.

Some years later, when Hannah's name was proposed as a member of the committee that was to manage Queen Victoria's Jubilee Institute for Nurses, Sir Henry Ponsonby commented for the Queen's benefit: 'The names are good, though there are some strong opinions among them. Lady Rosebery is very determined.'[26] That Hannah was utterly devoted to Rosebery is quite true, and that she was sometimes nervous lest she had put a foot wrong is also true: but often her anxiety arose from the strength of her personality, not its weakness. An example of this is found in her several heated exchanges with Mrs Gladstone. In attempting to ease the path of *her* husband, the older lady sometimes felt it necessary to comment rather too frankly on Hannah's, about his dilettantism or his excessive ambition, whichever suited her argument best. The strength of Hannah's response on the first occasion ought to have convinced Mrs Gladstone that it was unwise to criticize Lord Rosebery to his wife. Hannah, for her part, worried that she had lost her temper. But neither learned. Mrs Gladstone continued to tell Hannah her version of the truth, and Hannah continued to lose her temper.[27] Her worries were primarily that her temper might do Rosebery harm, or that she might misrepresent or inadequately represent, his position.

When Hannah had written to Lord Granville announcing her engagement, that seasoned politician had replied: 'He is a charming and most agreeable man, and one, who if *you keep him up to the mark*, is sure to have his page in history.'[28] There is no doubt that Hannah tried to do just that. She was intensely ambitious for her husband, and provided him with what their friend Disraeli (Hannah had asked him to stand in her dead father's stead at her marriage and give her away) called 'feminine inspiration'. Disraeli meant absolute devotion, and that is what Hannah gave

Rosebery. It had the effect Disraeli envisaged. Eddie Hamilton said of Hannah that she had 'in a notable degree the faculty of getting other people to work and of quickening their energies'.[29] Certainly Rosebery strove for her as he never had before, and never would again. It was while she lived that his greatest successes took place, or were prepared.

Yet, in spite of all the evidence of Rosebery's devotion to Hannah, the impression has persisted that he was somehow ashamed of her, and that he vented his feelings in some rather crude and heavy-handed humour at her expense. No one seems actually ever to have heard for themselves this humour with Hannah at its butt – the stories just appear, without any definite attribution of time or place. They are by no means impossible. Growing up without a father and alienated from his mother, Rosebery was always shy and introverted, never quite at home as a boy with those of his own age. As sometimes happens in such cases (with his great-uncle William Pitt, among others) his way of showing intimacy in later years was often rough and juvenile. Rosebery, for example, seems never to have known when to stop teasing. Ferdy Rothschild was extremely attached to him, but he complained bitterly on one occasion: 'For the last 12 years when you and Harry [probably Ponsonby] and I meet, I am the incessant butt [sic] of your chaff, which no doubt you think amusing, but is not always equally gratifying to myself.'[30] Yet this evident insensitivity was not incompatible with what at other times could be the most tender care and understanding. On another occasion, Ferdy wrote: 'I am a lonely, suffering and occasionally very miserable individual despite the gilded and marble rooms in which I live. There is but one thing in the world which I care for; and that is the sympathy and the confidence of the few persons that I love.' Foremost among them, Ferdy said, was Rosebery.[31] For the twenty years of their acquaintance, Rosebery ministered with great tact and kindness to the often querulous and morbidly sensitive aging widower of Waddesdon, as Ferdy's letters to him eloquently testify. Rosebery was a man of contrasts, but he was not one intentionally to injure those he loved.

Nor was Hannah injured. There was a dignity and integrity in her personality that would have protected her. She spent several years after their marriage making an intensive study of her father's house and collections. The resulting book she had privately printed, and the letter she wrote to 'My husband' on the occasion says much of both of them, and their relationship:

> I hope you will take this first copy of the description of some of your possessions to The Durdans. It is not a catalogue, for I have only endeavoured to give the means of identification of those works of art which appear to me of particular interest.
>
> In time to come, when like all collections this will be dispersed, and I hope this will be long after my death, this book may be of value. It has been of particular interest to me, for it was commenced in the wish to indicate the monument of taste, which my father made, which I consequently cherish, and whilst caring for the beautiful things besides, it enabled me to honour his memory. And thus in now handing it over to your care I feel yours are the only hands which are fitted to hold what he, whom I consider was as perfect as any mortal may be, cared for. I could not speak this. Excuse a letter.[32]

Whatever Hannah's reasons for insecurity, being Mayer Rothschild's daughter was not one of them.

Hannah would live to see her husband a political phenomenon, and Foreign Secretary in his early forties. She would not live to see him Prime Minister. In October 1890 Lady Rosebery became seriously ill with typhoid fever, complicated by Bright's Disease. Early on the morning of the 25th her doctor told Rosebery that there was no hope. He tried to keep it from her, but without success. Quite composed, she said simply: 'I will struggle hard for life for your sake.'

But what struck him even more was something else:

> When I told her in the day that Lady Jersey was believed to have typhoid, she said, 'Oh poor thing, poor thing, she will have to go through all I have gone through. Telegraph to her Archie and tell her how sorry I am for her' – which of course I did at once.[33]

Then she seemed to rally for a while, and Rosebery's hopes came ebbing back. But the recovery was illusory. In the second week in November she had a relapse. On the 18th Rosebery recorded: 'She had been delirious for fully a week, only waking up with a wonderful smile whenever I came into the room.

"Archie! This *is* nice", in her old sweet childish way.' About ten o'clock in the evening she spoke to him clearly: 'Archie, Archie I am going home.' Relentless honesty forced him to add: 'She probably still thought she was in Paris where she had fancied herself last week. But these were the last words I heard her say.'

She died at 5.50 the next morning. Rosebery wrote: 'I went down to the Castle and watched a beautiful dawn of melting grey, until it was time to see the children.' The next day he noted simply, 'I moved to the Castle'.[34] And Barnbougle Castle, half a mile down the hill from Dalmeny House, remained his favoured abode thereafter. His bedroom has been kept exactly as he left it. There are two decorations on the wall of the small, sparsely furnished room. Over the fireplace is the large picture of Hannah as a girl. At the foot of his bed hangs a large and elaborate wooden crucifix. The waves lap at the base of the tower below his window, and the window itself commands a magnificent view over the Firth of Forth, looking towards where the dawn broke on 19 November 1890.

Perhaps with some reluctance, Rosebery decided that Hannah must be buried beside her father at the Jewish cemetery at Willesden. Principal Donaldson, who had been her mentor in Scottish history and culture, told him there was no doubt that was her wish, which decided the matter.[35] The Queen, who had come to know and like Lady Rosebery, had anxiously noted the ups and downs of her illness in her Journal, and she sent Sir Henry Ponsonby to the funeral on the 25th. He sent a full report on what he obviously found an entirely new experience on his arrival back at Windsor. He was struck by the fact that there were no women at the funeral except as spectators, and that the men kept their hats on in the chapel and at the grave. He was also struck by the fact that 'Lord Rothschild gave the orders and asked Sir Henry Ponsonby to express to Your Majesty the thanks of the family.' They were all there, as were Gladstone, Lord Spencer, Sir William Harcourt, and about twenty members of the London County Council, of which Rosebery had been the first Chairman. Ponsonby was impressed by the simple dignity of the service and the short sentence in Hebrew at the grave: 'May she go to her appointed Home.' 'Lord Rosebery,' he reported, 'never spoke but remained close to the coffin till it was lowered into the grave. Lord Rothschild led him back to the chapel but he looked down the whole time.'[36]

What was Rosebery thinking as Natty led him away? The clue is perhaps given in a letter he wrote to the Queen from Mentmore three days later:

> There is . . . one incident of this tragedy only less painful than the actual loss: which is that at the moment of death the difference of creed makes itself felt, and another religion steps in to claim the corpse. It was inevitable, and I do not complain; and my wife's family have been more than kind. But none the less it is exquisitely painful . . .
>
> . . . Love such as my wife's cannot perish . . . it is with me as much as my skin, as the air I breathe; and . . . so it must be to the end. Great love I firmly believe never dies or runs down, but is part of the poor heritage of mankind . . .
>
> But perhaps the dearest thought to a bereaved soul is contained in the lines Your Majesty wrote in my wife's album, and the lighting upon which has given me the desire to write tonight
>
> > 'I hold it true whate'er befall
> > I feel it when I sorrow most
> > 'Tis better to have loved and lost
> > Than never to have loved at all.'

★   ★   ★

The relationship between Rosebery and the Rothschild family has always been a focus of intense interest to those who believe in the close and sinister connection of high finance and politics during the period. Rothschilds was a great banking house with large interests in the areas where British imperialism was at its most active during the last two decades of the nineteenth century, Egypt and South Africa. Not only was Rosebery one of the most important politicians of the time, he was also an avowed imperialist. Rosebery was married to a Rothschild. Many have found the logic of the situation inescapable.[38] But like many plausible cases, this one needs more careful examination.

That the relationship was in some ways a very close one is evident. It was not a direct financial one in the sense that the Roseberys maintained an interest in the bank. Only the son of a partner could become one, and only with the consent of all the other partners. Daughters of partners could leave their capital in the firm and receive interest on it, or they could withdraw it over a period of years. Hannah chose the latter option, and after their marriage Rosebery seems to have pressed on the legal proceedings to bring this about.[39] This did not, however, bring even temporary damage in personal relations, and Rosebery continued to seek and receive advice on investments from Rothschilds.[40]

Relationships are not, however, based only on share portfolios. That between Rosebery and the Rothschilds was close in other ways as well. Hannah's death did not end Rosebery's active membership in the large and growing cousinhood that populated the Vale of Aylesbury. Rothschild houses were becoming more numerous. On 1 May 1872 Connie noted in her diary that her Uncle Lionel and Natty had gone to look over Tring Park. A week later she noted with enthusiasm: 'Great news. *Tring P.* is bought and will belong to Emmy.'[41] The children of the two Louises were almost as close as their mothers, and Aston Clinton was delighted to have the Nattys only a couple of miles away at Tring.

Lionel had decided to provide country houses for all his sons. Shortly afterwards, Ascott was acquired for Leo. The extensive rebuilding began before Lionel died. Alfred's exotic chateau at Halton would not be begun until after his death. Meanwhile Ferdy had purchased Waddesdon and was in the process of building his own great and perhaps rather more pleasing chateau there.[42]

The denizens of the several houses met regularly to hunt, to shoot, or simply to gossip. Sundays had a routine all their own. On 10 February 1884 Leo described their activities to his mother. Natty had ridden over that morning from Tring. They then did their usual rounds, and 'as Dizzy said the variety of a Sunday proprietor is tremendous when he discourses on his horses and his cattle, so no doubt we were no exception to the rule'.[43] Mentmore was and remained a regular part of the Sunday circuit.

There were therefore many things that tied Rosebery to the Rothschilds. Hannah's death and his emotional response did nothing to loosen the ties, and in some ways strengthened them.

On the other side, there is no doubt that the Rothschilds took a keen and sympathetic interest in Rosebery's political career. It is also true that the imperialist opinions he articulated were theirs as well. What is more, they had held such opinions long before their young relative by marriage took them up. It would, however, be quite wrong to assume a simple cause and effect relationship. The question must be closely examined in the light of the Rothschilds' own history, and of how their opinions came to be formed.

Before beginning such an examination it may help to clarify one or two points. In the first place, it is important to define more precisely the meaning of imperialism. The term first began to be used widely in the 1880s, and Rosebery was clear from the beginning that distinctions had to be drawn. 'Imperialism, sane Imperialism, as distinguished from what I might call "wild cat" Imperialism, is nothing but this – a larger patriotism,' he declared in 1885. Imperialism was not mere mindless expansion for the sake of expansion, rather it was the protection of real and tangible British interests. 'If,' he continued, 'a Liberal Imperialist means that I am a Liberal who is passionately attached to the Empire,' then he was quite willing to accept the label.[44]

The Empire he had primarily in mind was the Indian Empire with its vital lifeline through the Suez Canal. The distinction he was making is one that has been taken up by some modern historians, who argue convincingly that what was once thought to be a new imperialist phase in the last quarter of the nineteenth century was merely the pursuit of traditional policy by a new means. Throughout the century, Britain had been intent on securing her route to India. This had been her purpose in the Crimean War. It had been Disraeli's purpose in purchasing the Suez Canal shares. What was new in the last quarter of the century was that, both because of the collapse of the indigenous regimes on which she had relied and of competition from other European states, Britain was forced to seize territory in order to protect that route.[45] The policy was Palmerstonian and Disraelian, only the methods were new.

As will be seen presently, such an explanation aptly fits the manner in which the Rothschilds, as well as Rosebery, first came to espouse 'imperialist' opinions in the 1880s. It does not perhaps fit quite as well as an explanation of British policy in South Africa in the 1890s. That is a question to which we shall come later. But, because of their close connection with Cecil Rhodes, among others, South Africa does suggest another issue as far as the

Rothschilds are concerned: to what extent did the Rothschilds attempt to influence government policy, and if they attempted it, to what extent did they succeed?

There had been suggestions of the sinister influence of the Rothschilds from the beginning. With the third generation of the family, however, the trickle of suggestion became a steady stream, and one that has never stopped. To give an example of contemporary comment, there is Wilfred Scawen Blunt's confident assertion that the Rothschilds, using Bismarck as their catspaw, were responsible for the deposition of the Khedive of Egypt and his replacement by his son in 1879. Parker T. Moon, a sober and distinguished Professor of History at Columbia University writing in the 1930s, went even further. According to him, the Rothschilds 'utilized their political influence to bring about the conquest of Egypt'. Such allegations were to be followed by equally persistent suggestions that the Rothschilds must bear the responsbility for the Boer War.[46]

If Rothschild influence on foreign and imperial affairs has not been underestimated, neither has the role they played in domestic politics. Speaking of the breakup of the Liberal Party in 1886, for example, A. B. Cooke and John Vincent have said that 'somewhere in the background, the Rothschild interest was closely involved'.[47] Similarly, Roy Foster, in his recent biography of Lord Randolph Churchill, has emphasized their intimate connection with that politician and his brief meteoric career.[48]

All the events mentioned above, beginning with the deposition of the Khedive in late June 1879, took place after a crucial change at N. M. Rothschild & Sons. On 3 June, after a telegram had announced the death of her Uncle Lionel, Connie noted in her diary:

> Natty is now head of the house, master of the firm, owner of a large property. How will he and Emmy bear their great responsibilities?[49]

It is on Natty, Sir N. M. as he had become after he succeeded Anthony to the baronetcy in 1876, Lord Rothschild as he would become in 1885, that attention must now be focused. In order to understand his actions after he assumed the direction of the bank, it is necessary to go back to the mid-1870s. For from Natty's close relationship with Disraeli in that period stemmed a great deal of what followed. It was responsible for his deep involvement in the affairs of Egypt. It strongly affected his views on foreign and imperial policy generally, and the Disraelian stance he adopted in turn significantly affected his attitude toward the Liberal Party and its breakup.

CHAPTER SEVEN

Disraeli,
Gladstone and Lord Rothschild

IN A HASTY AND UNDATED NOTE from the Turf Club, Natty wrote
to Monty Corry on one occasion during Disraeli's second government:

> One of those stupid things took place in the House this
> afternoon which vex me more than anything else.
>   I got into the House just as the division was taking
> place and as I did not receive a hint from anyone found
> that I had voted in the majority and it was a censure of the
> Government.
>   I write this to you although you know I would sooner
> have cut off both my hands than do such a thing.[1]

A Liberal by long association, Natty had become a Conservative
by conviction.

At any rate, he had become a supporter of the Conservative
Prime Minister, and though the Liberal associations continued,
he was in many ways one of the staunchest. In March 1879, for
example, following embarrassing British reverses in the Zulu
War, Natty wrote to warn Disraeli of the danger of Conservative
abstentions on a Liberal vote of censure to be moved by Sir
Charles Dilke, another friend of Natty's. 'I shall be in the
company of prominent Liberals tomorrow,' he went on, 'and
will call on you Monday evening.'[2] Clearly, on this as on other
occasions, the Rothschild information network was at Disraeli's
disposal.

It remained as wide as ever, domestically as well as interna-
tionally, for there was never any chilling of social relations with
the Liberal leadership. 'What do you say to the visitor who is now
with dear Ma, whilst I am writing this', Lionel had wryly written
to his children in Paris in the middle of the violent Liberal attacks
on the Rothschilds over the Suez Canal shares. 'I have just heard

that the famous Mr. Gladstone is with her drinking tea and eating bread and butter. I doubt whether he will come to see me.'[3] Warm social relations with Gladstone continued. In July 1880, Ferdy was highly amused when Disraeli, whose London home was then with Alfred in Seamore Place, had to be hustled off to dine with Natty so that Alfred could invite Gladstone to meet the Duke of Cambridge![4]

Little or no effort, however, was made to accommodate to Gladstone's political opinions. Everyone knew that Natty was a warm supporter of the foreign policy Gladstone so bitterly denounced. To use Granville's description to Gladstone in 1877, Natty was 'a red hot Turk'.[5] As for Natty, despite the continuance of their personal friendship, he could hardly find words strong enough to express his disapproval of the former Liberal Prime Minister. In December 1879 Natty had been pursuing one of his favourite avocations, reading history. He had found a speech of Walpole's which he recommended to Disraeli's attention. The words, he thought, were particularly applicable to 'that arch fiend Gladstone'.[6] There is therefore every reason to believe in the genuineness of the parting salutation of a letter Natty wrote to Disraeli on 30 December of the same year. He had just reported widespread Liberal disgust with Gladstone: 'That he will do you good and himself harm is the wish of ever yours . . .'[7]

Natty's attitude towards Disraeli was in fact as close as he ever came to hero worship. Never to anyone else did he express sentiments of regard and affection so ardent and unrestrained as to him 'whom I hope I may be permitted to call my dearest friend'[8], and the opening salutation 'My dearest Lord Beaconsfield' became a frequent one in his letters.

There was more than one reason for this deep attachment to Disraeli. One was enthusiasm for what he understood to be Disraeli's ideas, or some of them. In November 1880 he wrote to thank Disraeli for a copy of what would prove to be his last novel:

> You once told me never to thank an author for his work until it had been read thoroughly. Under these circumstances I ought not to write. Although I have read Endymion once, I know I shall not fully appreciate it until I become as fully acquainted with it as I am with the pages of your great trilogy. One of these days 'when the flag of St. George's waves over the plains of Rassclas' and

Cyprus is a flourishing colony, 'Those who have failed in literature and arts' will no longer talk of your works as the dreams of a poet or the imagination of a visionary but will acknowledge as I have always done that you are one of the greatest of British statesmen.[9]

Perhaps it was modesty that prevented Natty from recognizing what is generally held to have been the portrait of his parents, under the guise of the Neuchatels, and their home in the novel. Or perhaps he simply did not recognize it. He can be forgiven for as usual in Disraeli's novels, in so far as he is evoking anything real, it is a pastiche of Rothschilds and their houses.

As for the earlier novels, it is evident that, though he referred to the trilogy, it was not *Coningsby* and ancient institutions, or *Sybil* and the sufferings of the poor that struck Natty's imagination, but *Tancred*. For it is in the last novel that an Eastern Emir advises that the Queen transfer her court to Delhi, and promises to secure for her the Levantine coast, and Alexandria if she wishes it. It is possible to derive almost anything from Disraeli's novels, but Natty was not alone in seeing in such allusions an anticipation of the policy of assuring Britain's greatness by securing her position in the Middle East, a policy which Disraeli undoubtedly pursued in the 1870s.[10]

The Rothschilds had been closely involved in the implementation of the policy from its dramatic beginning in the purchase of the Suez Canal shares, and they continued to be. This is partly what lay behind the New Year's greetings Natty sent to the Prime Minister at the end of 1879:

> You know my dear Lord Beaconsfield the great affection my brothers and myself have always entertained for you. That feeling has been greatly strengthened by the very great kindness we have received from you during the past year, a year in which we have had the misfortune to lose a beloved father.[11]

Partly no doubt this was sentiment responding to the kind of sentiment that had sent Monty Corry posting up to London from Hughenden, where a telegram had brought the news of Lionel's death. Disraeli wrote to 'My Dearest Children':

> I am quite overwhelmed – and cannot trust myself to say more.

I send this by a faithful messenger who will bring back to me how you are, in this the most trying moment of your lives![12]

Disraeli had given affection, but his 'very great kindness' had also been of a quite practical sort. The new partners of N. M. Rothschild & Sons had felt in need of a Prime Minister's support. They had asked for it, and they had not asked in vain.

It would be misleading, however, to start with the assumption that it would be a matter of the Prime Minister using government influence to pull Rothschild chestnuts out of the fire. The question at issue was one in which the government had a most intimate interest – Egypt. It was furthermore a question in which government continued to be keen to secure Rothschild cooperation. And it was by no means always evident who was pulling whose chestnuts out of the fire.

Briefly put, the situation as far as the British government was concerned was that they desired the financial stability of Egypt, but with as little direct responsibility for themselves as possible. This was the aim of the 1878 arrangement of Egyptian finances. Under this arrangement, Rivers Wilson, an official of the British Treasury, had become Egyptian Minister of Finance. Technically, this was the doing of the Khedive, not of the British government. At the same time, however, the British Foreign Secretary, Lord Salisbury, used Rivers Wilson's presence in the Egyptian cabinet as an excuse for suspending the arrangements for European oversight of Egyptian finances established earlier. Rivers Wilson was not the formal representative of the British government, yet he was part of an informal pledge of the British government's interest in the matter. Had not such a pledge existed, the British and French Rothschilds would never have agreed to issue the £8.5m loan for which the British government had been extremely anxious.[13]

It was the sort of delicate arrangement on which diplomacy is wont to sustain itself, and often flourishes. It did not, however, find fruitful ground in the complexities of Egyptian politics. In the second week of April 1879 the Khedive overturned the arrangements which had been so carefully devised to keep his regime solvent and stable. Among other things, he dismissed Rivers Wilson and the other European members of his government, and in effect resumed direct control of the Daïra, or domain lands, which had been put under the supervision of a special commission of management as a security for the Rothschild loan.[14]

Rivers Wilson had his own plan for dealing with the situation, which he outlined in a telegram to the Rothschilds on 8 April:

> Pray consider whether, as your loan was made on the faith of the establishment of a new regime, a declaration from you withdrawing the loan would not be desirable. Such a step would have an important effect. It is evident that the only means of avoiding financial and political (? crisis) is the immediate removal of the Viceroy by a firman from the Porte, supported by the Powers, and at the same time the nomination of his eldest son. I hope you will urge this on Her Majesty's Government as the only possible solution.[15]

Rivers Wilson, then, was asking the Rothschilds to do two separate things. He was asking them to exert direct pressure on the government of Egypt by withdrawing their loan. He was also asking them to use their influence with the British government to secure the removal of the Egyptian ruler, the Khedive (still technically the viceroy of the Sultan). Either action would obviously fit the theories of those who believe that financial power directs political action. In one case, a great merchant bank was to browbeat a weak foreign government into submission. In the other, it was to get its own government to secure the reconstruction of that foreign regime.

The Rothschilds declined to do either. Rather they referred the matter to the highest authority. On 10 April Eric Barrington wrote from the Foreign Office to someone in the Prime Minister's entourage, probably Monty Corry:

> Natty Rothschild who brought me the enclosed telegrams for Lord Salisbury expressed a wish that Lord Beaconsfield should see them. The Rothschilds object strongly to Wilson's proposal to withdraw the loan, which they would consider a very dishonourable proceeding. They wish to work in close cooperation with Her Majesty's Government.[16]

In fact, the solution adopted was the second one Rivers Wilson proposed. The Khedive, under pressure from the British and French governments seconded by the Germans and Austrians, submitted to removal by the Sultan and was duly replaced by his eldest son. There is, however, no evidence that the actions of the British government were urged upon them by the Rothschilds. They had laid Rivers Wilson's plan before the government, it is true. But there is no ground for supposing that the government chose to act on the plan for any other reason than that they found it most expedient for the achievement of what had been their aim all along. Salisbury stated the government's aim very plainly: 'They are bound, both by duty and interest, to do all that lies in their power to arrest misgovernment, before it results in the material ruin and almost incurable disorder to which, it is evident by other Oriental examples, that such misgovernment will necessarily lead.'[17] Nor is there any more evidence that Rothschilds played a part in bringing about Bismarck's intervention. There are only two passing references to Egyptian affairs in Bleichröder's letters to New Court in June 1879, hardly the basis for assuming any deep conspiracy conducted through their usual channels to Berlin.[18]

Rothschild requests for assistance and acknowledgements of their successful applications begin later, during the long negotiations among the European powers to settle the precise shape of the new regime in Egypt. The first such is in a letter from Natty to the Prime Minister on 21 August.

> We are very pleased to hear of the satisfactory reply which has been received from Vienna and which is naturally owing to the strong representations which have been made by her Majesty's Government. We therefore are much indebted to Lord Salisbury and to you personally. My dearest Lord Beaconsfield we can never sufficiently convey the assurance of our deepest gratitude.[19]

On the 16th Edmond from Paris had already acknowledged to his English cousins the 'copy of Lord Salisbury's letter, evidence indeed how much your Government takes our interests to heart'.[20]

It is unclear precisely which letter of Lord Salisbury's is referred to. What is, however, clear from Rothschild correspondence in the period is that 'our interests' consisted primarily in promoting agreement between the British and French governments, without which the actual disbursement of the 1878 loan jointly undertaken by the London and Paris houses would have been most difficult and embarrassing. Equally clear from the correspondence of Salisbury during the period is, that for reasons of state quite unconnected with the Rothschilds, close cooperation with the French was the basis of his policy. Salisbury's aim was to perpetuate the so-called Dual Control of the two countries, and to exclude other countries, such as Austria, from a significant voice.[21]

What would have particularly concerned the Rothschilds was the establishment of an international commission of liquidation which would have the task of laying down the guidelines for the deployment of Egyptian financial resources. In so far as Austrian insistence on the rights of other powers stood in the way of the proposal to the Khedive of a decree establishing such a commission, and thus a settlement of the Egyptian debt, it would naturally have been of concern to the Rothschilds. They, however, were perhaps more inclined to be conciliatory and accommodating than their governments.

On 30 August Natty wrote to Disraeli that he had hoped to be 'able to pay you a visit this week and to announce to you that the Egyptian question was as far as we are concerned quite arranged'. But there had been an important hitch. Austria and Italy wished to incorporate in the decree a clause that all claims on Egyptian finances previous to the Rothschilds' should be paid in full. 'We have replied that we can have no possible objection,' but Natty was afraid that the responsible officials in Paris and 'here the Pedants of the Treasury' would be strongly opposed. Apart from anything else, what the Austrians and Italians were proposing would, as Natty pointed out, have virtually annihilated the Commission of Liquidation. He had called on the Assistant Under-Secretary at the Foreign Office, Sir Julian Pauncefote, who was of the opinion that some concessions would have to be made to Austria and Italy and promised to do all he could to expedite matters. But, Natty told the Prime Minister: 'A word from you would, I am sure, prove most efficacious. You have already done so much for us that you will not I trust mind doing this also.'[22]

Natty was not pretending to sacrifice Rothschilds interests. On the other hand, it would be impossible to read his request as a mere self-interested plea. What it was, was a suggestion which might help to expedite the settlement of a matter of as much concern to the government as to the Rothschilds. The same was true of his last request. In December Greek intransigence stood in the way of a Khedival decree setting up the Commission. The Greeks were, however, willing to adhere to the decree if France guaranteed that Greek subjects would be placed on the same footing as French citizens. Natty received word that the French Foreign Minister was prepared to act along these lines, but would propose a joint declaration with Britain, Germany, Austria and Italy: 'As the declaration will settle this most troublesome affair, we hope most sincerely, dear Lord Beaconsfield, that you will not mind using your great influence in getting the English Government to adhere at once to the proposal which is about to emanate from the French Government.'[23]

By mid-December all difficulties had finally been removed and Alphonse could congratulate his English relatives that everything was 'finally in order and the Egyptian business which has given us so much trouble will now become for us, I sincerely hope, a source of satisfaction'.[24] But it was not only the Rothschilds who were gratified that a settlement had finally been reached. It had also been a great object of their respective governments. Eric Barrington had said that it was the Rothschilds' wish to work in 'close cooperation with Her Majesty's government'. Their wish was realized. The events of 1879 illustrate once more, and even more forcefully, the extent to which the Rothschilds became part of the foreign policy apparatus during the Disraeli ministries. It would seem fair to say that they did not take undue advantage of the privileged position they occupied during these years. True, it will always be possible to argue about whether the profits they made were excessive, for this is in part a matter of opinion. What does seem clear, is that far from attempting to steer British foreign policy in directions profitable to themselves, they rather accommodated themselves to that policy. More than that, they attempted, and not unsuccessfully, to facilitate official policy and ease its course.

With the Gladstone government which followed in April 1880 the situation was a good deal more complicated. In November of that year, Natty wrote to Bleichröder that 'we are not on intimate terms with the present cabinet'.[25] As far as their relations with the Prime Minister on public matters were concerned, this was putting it mildly. This is made clear by the part Natty took in the Smyrna affair.

The Congress of Berlin in 1878, as part of its arrangement of Balkan affairs, had agreed on certain Montenegrin boundary adjustments. The Turks attempted to evade implementing them. What Natty saw as a crisis in the autumn of 1880, was brought about by the firm determination of the Liberal Prime Minister to force the Sultan to do so. Writing to Disraeli in October, Natty, who had just returned from the Continent, said that there was general agreement there that the crisis had been brought about not only by Gladstone's policy, but also by his 'arrogance'. Since his return to London, he had 'heard from good authority that Gladstone has proposed to other powers to seize Smyrna and collect the revenues of that town until the Porte gives way'.

Natty mentioned in passing that 'the revenues of Smyrna are I believe hypothecated to the guaranteed loan'. He referred to the 1855 loan which Rothschilds had issued; but precisely because it was guaranteed, this was primarily the problem of the guarantors, Britain and France, not of the Rothschilds. What mainly concerned Natty was that the combined authority of the great powers, the so-called Concert of Europe, could not be brought into action in this instance. With the exception of Russia and Italy, he thought it likely the other powers would refuse to back the British government. As with anything that disrupted international harmony, this was naturally of concern to those who dealt in foreign securities. 'In the stock exchange,' Natty reported, 'they say tickets for the European concert are very much offered.' But concerns of this sort are by no means confined to the Stock Exchange.[26]

Even more interesting than the letter Natty wrote to Disraeli were two he wrote soon after to Bleichröder. One was written the next day, 8 October:

> Our government waits for an answer concerning the occupation of Smyrna – only Russia and Italy so far have agreed, Russia with great pleasure as you may imagine. If the other powers disagree, nobody knows what will happen. As passionate and irritable a man as Gladstone may do anything. If he goes on alone with Russia and Italy, this would make the worst impression and be very unpopular. There is only one man who could manage this damned business – it is Prince Bismarck who has put into order the Egyptian business. It is desirable that he should take matters in hand.

The second letter was written on the 15th:

> Gladstone would like to go it alone but he cannot do it
> without asking the other ministers for their advice. Eng-
> land will not act without Germany, and never alone with
> Russia – I have good reason for my opinion. The best
> informed people tell me that Bismarck is stronger in
> foreign policy than ever before.[27]

The plain fact of the matter was that Natty was attempting to
persuade a foreign power to undermine the policy of a British
Prime Minister. It would seem equally plain that he was doing so
with the encouragement of some of Gladstone's close colleagues.

In order to attempt to understand what was going on, it is
necessary to recall the tangled web of intrigue that proceeded the
breakup of the Liberal party in 1886, on the occasion of the first
Irish Home Rule controversy. The issue was by no means
confined to Ireland. An influential school of historians today
would argue that there was never in fact more than one issue –
office and power – in the constant manoeuvre for which the
ostensible issues are no more than pawns.[28] This, however, is not
a question that need be of great concern here. Natty never aspired
to be quite such a 'High Politician', and the issues were of real
concern to him.

The divisions in the Liberal party went back at least to the
mid-1870s. It is safe to say that, though the Rothschilds had
undoubtedly surpassed all other Liberals in the closeness of their
attachment to Disraeli, they would have had close competitors in
their dislike of Gladstone as a public man. In 1875, following the
defeat of his government in the general election of the previous
year, Gladstone had claimed to step down as Liberal leader, and
Lord Hartington had theoretically taken his place. But in 1876,
whatever the theory, the Grand Old Man had swept back to the
leading position in the party on the crest of the wave of the
Bulgarian Atrocities agitation. His views were not shared by
most of his former colleagues in government. Granville, who
had been Foreign Secretary, while he remained personally loyal
to Gladstone, did not agree with his violently anti-Turkish, and
hence pro-Russian position. Neither did Hartington, who also
had personal reasons to feel aggrieved. From this time, a powerful, if not always stable and consistent, opposition to Gladstone
grew up within the party. It centred around Hartington, who

was generally agreed to be the obvious successor, and Natty was part of it. Gladstone's popularity with the broader party, both inside and outside Parliament, made it evident that it was impossible to block his return to the premiership in 1880. It did not, however, prevent persistent attempts thereafter to block his policies and, if possible, ease him out of that office. Natty in October 1880 was playing a part in these attempts.

The propriety of his actions is open to question. Rothschilds had come to hold a significant place in the conducting of British foreign policy. Admittedly, this had not been entirely by their own doing, and the wisdom of placing private merchant bankers in such a position is also questionable. But, whatever the answer to the broader question, it was evidently one thing to use that position with the knowledge and indeed at the desire of the Prime Minister, as had been the case with Disraeli, to advance his policies. It was quite another thing to use Rothschilds' position behind the Prime Minister's back, to attempt to subvert, or at least to modify his policy, as Natty was attempting to do in this instance with Gladstone.

Having said this, however, it is essential to be clear about what was *not* taking place. Though acting through his banking connections, Natty was acting not as a banker, but as a politician. Except in the most generalized sense, Rothschild financial interests were not involved. What Natty was questioning was the broad direction of British foreign policy. At the time of the change of government in April, he had assured Bleichröder that the continuity of foreign policy would be maintained.[29] By proposing to act with Russia against Turkey in this instance, Gladstone was obviously suggesting a reversion to his previous views. To those who disagreed with him these views remained objectionable for precisely the same reasons they always had been – they were held to threaten vital British interests in the Middle East.

It is also important to notice that, while Natty was in one sense passing on confidential government information, it was not information given in confidence. True, it was information which the ministers most responsible for foreign affairs did not wish him to have. Granville, who reported to Gladstone that he had surprised Alfred and the German Ambassador discussing Smyrna on 8 October, was exceedingly annoyed that the Rothschilds had got wind of it.[30] Clearly, however, Natty was making use of information deliberately leaked for the purpose by other members of the Cabinet who, like him, wished to undermine Gladstone's policy. Nor was this sort of thing exceptional. Cabinet solidarity is perhaps never more than a convenient fiction, but in this period of Liberal rule which Cooke and Vincent have aptly labelled 'Government by Dispute', the degree of intrigue was extraordinary. No one, certainly not the Prime Minister, was above it. If Natty did not rise above the ordinary level of political behaviour, neither did he fall below it.

As it turned out, Natty's initiative in the Smyrna affair did no harm, and may have done some good. At any rate, contrary to his fears, the Concert of Europe worked in this instance, and the united threat of all the powers, including Germany, to occupy Smyrna caused the Sultan to yield and made actual occupation unnecessary.[31] Thus, save for the Sultan's, all points of view on public policy would presumably have been satisfied.

If information transmitted by Natty through Bleichröder was conducive to this end, then it was beneficial. Not that Bismarck would have acted out of deference to Rothschild opinions, any more than he ever acted out of deference to Bleichröder's. There is no reason to suppose that Bismarck's actions were ever dictated by anything other than his conception of the political interests of the German state he had created, or that he ever looked on any banker as more than a pawn in the political game.[32] But the Rothschilds, who had clearly been impressed by his intervention in Egyptian affairs in 1879, believed that he could be brought into play to support British interests in the Middle East and used their contacts to promote this end. They were sometimes successful.

Whatever Rothschild differences there were with the Prime Minister and the Foreign Secretary, the Liberal government found themselves no more inclined, or perhaps able, to do without the Rothschilds than their Conservative predecessor. One area where their need for Rothschild cooperation remained as great was in Egypt.

Detailed studies of what led up to the military occupation of Egypt by Gladstone's government in 1882 agree that the decision was based primarily on political and strategic imperatives, and that financial interests as such were unimportant.[33] There is no need to modify this conclusion. The Rothschilds may well have been consulted. This would seem likely from the fact that in the early months of 1882 Natty was intimately involved in negotiations carried on by government officials who played a key role in the shaping of policy towards Egypt – Dilke, Parliamentary Under-Secretary at the Foreign Office, and Rivers Wilson, whose official position was now at the National Debt Office. The negotiations, it is true, had to do not directly with Egypt, but with the revision of the commercial treaty with France. Rothschilds played their usual role, with Natty conveying to Alphonse the views of Dilke and Rivers Wilson, and Alphonse returning the views of the French ministers.[34] Given the people involved, and the fact that an Egypt riven by internal strife was likely to have been much on the minds of those concerned with the relations of the two European powers so delicately balanced there, it is likely that the question was discussed among the English negotiators. But there is no evidence what, if any, political advice Natty gave, much less that it was taken.

There can be little doubt that he approved of the government's action, and he had clear and definite views as to the consequences – certainly a good deal clearer than those of the government itself. On 7 September Granville reported to Gladstone that Hartington's private secretary, Reggie Brett had

> written to Dilke to tell him that Tissot had asked Nat Rothschild what were the plans of the Government as to Egypt, and whether we should like to renew the Treaty of Commerce – and that Rothschild had answered that he could not say as to the second question, but as to the first, it was clear that England must secure the future predominance. To which Tissot answered 'naturally'.[35]

Roundabout though the means of communication were, there is every reason to believe that they accurately reflected Natty's views at the time. They would certainly soon be his views. He believed that the unilateral British occupation of Egypt, suppressing the revolt of Arabi Pasha and bolstering up the Khedive, an action in which the French had felt unable to participate, meant British supremacy in Egypt. Hartington would have accepted this conclusion. Gladstone never would. Despite the alleged acquiescence of the French Ambassador in London, it was a conclusion his government would bitterly resist for some time. In the end, Natty would be proved right, but the history of the question in the next few years would be governed by the uncertainties of the British and the anger and resentment of the French, with Bismarck stirring things up as suited his purposes.

Rothschilds delicately manoeuvred among these conflicting opinions. What the Liberal government, like its Conservative predecessor, primarily wanted from the Rothschilds was money to shore up an Egyptian regime which it, in its turn, had taken, under Britain's wing. It was not disappointed, though because of the animosities between the European powers, the negotiations were long and complicated before anything approaching a permanent solution could be arranged. An official loan could not be floated until 1885. In the meantime, with Egypt approaching bankruptcy, money had had to be found in the previous year. Rothschilds had provided monthly advances to a total of a million pounds on the security merely of a private note from the Foreign Secretary.[36]

Nor were credit facilities the only ones Rothschilds put at the government's disposal. They were willing that these should be deployed to maximum diplomatic advantage. This willingness is illustrated by an interview between Granville and Natty on 17 December. The latter called at the Foreign Office to say that he had received an application from the Egyptian government for a renewal of the temporary loan for another two months. Natty indicated that it was his desire not to embarrass the government's negotiations and suggested that knowledge of a renewal might not be helpful. 'Sir N. de Rothschild observed,' Granville recorded, 'that it might be our policy to press their house to do whatever was necessary to make Egypt bankrupt, and the idea of this would possibly have a good effect on the Powers.' Natty reckoned that no reply was required for a fortnight, and he promised to make none until he was advised by the government. After a week's deliberation it was decided to ask for Rothschilds' agreement to the request of the Egyptian government.[37]

The official loan the following year was jointly guaranteed by Britain, Germany, Austria-Hungary, France, Italy and Russia. The amount of the issue was £9,424,000, and it was undertaken by N. M. Rothschild & Sons. Not surprisingly, with such impressive international backing, it was a huge success.[38]

Given the government's close reliance on Rothschilds throughout, a charge by Gladstone in January 1885, when agreement with the other powers still seemed far away, that negotiations had been 'bitched' by leaks to the French through the Rothschilds seems rather odd.[39] What were supposed to have been leaked were proposals made by Lord Northbrook, a member of the government who had been sent on a special mission to Egypt the previous year. In fact, all the pertinent details of his proposals had been published in *The Times* on 20 November 1884, at least two days before he discussed the situation with the Rothschilds, a discussion urgently requested of them by the Foreign Secretary.[40]

True, they had known of his proposals earlier. But the only leak of which there is any evidence appears to have been officially inspired. On 5 November, Brett, Hartington's secretary, had sent Natty a detailed list of questions aimed at eliciting Bismarck's opinion of Northbrook's scheme.[41] Since the government was attempting at this point to enlist the German Chancellor's support, there is no reason to suspect a partisan motive. By this time Natty's German correspondent was probably Bismarck's son, Herbert, copies of whose correspondence Alfred was supplying to Hartington the following spring.[42] Certainly the Rothschilds were involved in promoting the contacts between Rosebery and Herbert Bismarck which were thought to have played an important part in achieving a settlement in the spring.[43]

As the Suez Canal shares episode has already illustrated, it would have been quite uncharacteristic of Rothschilds, situated as they were in a confidential business relationship with the government, to have leaked privileged information, even to their French cousins. Furthermore, in 1884–5 there is abundant evidence that, leaving aside the views of the English Rothschilds, the last thing the French Rothschilds wished to do was to stir up trouble. They deplored the animosity between their two countries over Egypt. They were even willing to contemplate, what would have been anathema to their government, a formal British protectorate. Alphonse wrote after the disaster at Khartoum in January 1885, where Chinese Gordon died at the hands of the followers of the triumphant Mahdi, that though he thought it an unlikely eventuality in the state of European politics:

> Whatever the decision of the English government, it can only benefit the holders of Egyptian funds and bills. Should England declare her protectorate over Egypt,

BARON ROTHSCHILD AT THE TABLE OF THE HOUSE OF COMMONS
The Jews' battle for recognition of their right to sit in their country's legislature
was largely a symbolic one

BARON ROTHSCHILD'S NEW MANSION
Giant reconstruction between 1859 and 1863 merged 147 and 148 Piccadilly into
one palatial residence

BARON LIONEL DE ROTHSCHILD
IN OLD AGE

MARRIAGE OF THE EARL OF ROSEBERY AND MISS HANNAH DE ROTHSCHILD
Disraeli gave the bride away

Egyptian credit would obviously benefit, as England would become jointly liable for Egypt's external obligations.[44]

Given the fact that no European government was anxious for Egypt to become bankrupt, there would either be some sort of British guarantee of a loan, or there would be an international guarantee. As bankers, the Rothschilds were perfectly willing to contemplate either. Nor had they much doubt that they would ultimately get the business. On 13 February Alphonse replied to a letter from the London house that he quite agreed it would be wrong to approach governments about the loan. Rothschilds should wait to be approached. He thought, and rightly, that their existing dominance in Egyptian finance gave them a position and prestige governments would not wish to ignore.[45] For a time after an international guarantee was agreed on, it seems to have been under consideration that the several European governments should separately approach the Rothschild houses in their respective countries. The Rothschilds, however, were clear among themselves that London was the most important market. In the end, the London house officially issued the loan.[46] Whatever the theory, however, the practice was usually much the same. Once governments had reached agreement, the several Rothschild houses got together and arranged the business details as suited themselves.

Ironically, one of the things that made the Rothschilds most feared, their international connections, frequently allowed each house to indulge its own particular patriotism, with relative impunity. They remained an international partnership until 1909. Its terms were a closely guarded secret, its existence an open one. The effect, however, may still be a cause for surprise. But the 1885 loan is a clear illustration, as the Suez business had been, that though governments might differ and each Rothschild house remain entirely loyal to its own, when the dust had settled no Rothschild was much hurt in his pocketbook.

There had been, it is true, a certain amount of competition among the houses in the past. Great success, such as the London house had enjoyed in the early and middle years of the century, had accorded it a slightly higher rate of interest on its capital. But by the latter part of the century such competition had become relatively unimportant in the partners' thinking. Business sought them out, there was plenty to go around, and the cooperation that had always been close became even easier.

Secure in its international connections, the London house was also secure in its relations with successive British governments. At least, this was the case as far as Egypt was concerned. Governments came to depend on the Rothschilds as much as the Rothschilds depended on government. It was an easy cooperation, in which neither side had much cause to fear the other. As bankers, Gladstone's governments found the Rothschilds as reliable partners as Disraeli's governments had.

As politicians, it was a different matter. From Gladstone's point of view, the Rothschilds in this respect left much to be desired. From the Rothschilds' point of view, he left almost everything to be desired.

On 29 November 1885, just after the end of Gladstone's Midlothian campaign and on the eve of the final breakup of the Liberal party on the Home Rule issue, Natty wrote to the man who would become leader of the dissidents, Hartington:

> Gladstone's name might well be changed to Ichabod. I enclose a note on the subject.

The note said:

> Eli's grandson was called Ichabod or 'The glory is departing from Israel' being born after the defeat of the Israelites by the Philistines.
> Samuel, Chap. IV, Verse 21.[47]

Natty was fond of allusions to Jewish history and folklore, and there were times when the point of long and involved stories from the Talmud were probably in need of rather more explanation than he gave. Hartington may or may not have been in need of instruction in the Old Testament. At any rate, the point is clear enough. Natty had lost all confidence in Gladstone. It should perhaps be noted that this was some two weeks before the famous 'Hawarden Kite' suggested that the Liberal leader had made a definitive shift towards Home Rule. But of course Natty had ceased to have confidence in Gladstone long before this. His disillusionment went back for at least a decade, and he would seize the opportunity which would soon afford itself to make a break that had been coming for a long time. It was a break clearly foreshadowed by his long Conservative associations, and particularly by his close relationship with Lord Randolph Churchill in Salisbury's minority government which was in power at the time.

Ironically, the final break would come only six months after Gladstone had proposed Natty for a peerage in his retirement honours the previous June. But the two sets of events are probably not unconnected, if only in a symbolic fashion.

Gladstone's motives in proposing the peerage may have had something to do with issues raised in a letter Reggie Brett wrote to Lord Richard Grosvenor, the Liberal Chief Whip and Patronage Secretary, on 29 October 1884:

> Although it is no business of mine, perhaps you will allow me to suggest that some special civility should be paid by you or Mr. Gladstone to Natty Rothschild. He is not a very robust Liberal, but I suppose there is not much object in letting him drift, and still less in driving him over to the Tories.

According to Brett, Natty had been particularly offended by proceedings in which leading Liberals closely connected to the government, including a somewhat radical relative of the Duke of Bedford, had apparently been attempting to substitute Ferdy for Natty as Liberal M.P. for Aylesbury:

> If it is thought that the Rothschilds can be played off one against the other, and that because Ferdinand may be a more acceptable or more pliant colleague, he can be put forward at Natty's expense, a very great mistake is made.
>
> The Rothschilds have held together for generations, and discipline in their family is differently understood from what it is in that of the Russells. If the Liberal party breaks with Natty, it breaks with the whole clan, and there is I imagine nothing to be gained by such a proceeding.[48]

The details of the intrigue, if intrigue there was, are unclear. Ferdy was certainly looking for a seat, and would succeed to Natty's, at the latter's own request. But if anyone thought he would be more pliant, they would be sadly mistaken. Brett would be proved right, the Rothschilds did maintain a united front. But this would not necessarily have been clear to everyone in the autumn of 1884.

A peerage for Natty may well have seemed the ideal way to advance several objects, to mollify Natty, please Hartington (whose secretary Brett was), and clear the way at Aylesbury for Ferdy. At any rate, Gladstone's secretary Eddie Hamilton recorded that, at a meeting on retirement honours on 10 June, which he attended along with Hartington and Grosvenor among others, it was agreed that Natty was to be offered a peerage. The reason Hamilton advanced at the time was to add commercial strength to the Lords.[49]

This time the Queen did not stand in the way. According to Hamilton, at Gladstone's meetings with her, 'she made little or no difficulty; she had overcome the strong scruples she entertained respecting the proposal when Mr. G. made it during his first administration'.[50]

That proposal had been of Lionel in 1869, when the notion of a 'Jew peer' had been unthinkable to Victoria. The Queen's only recorded impression of Natty had been in 1881. On 4 May of that year, she had noted in her Journal: 'Saw . . . Lord Beaconsfield's two executors, Sir Nathaniel de Rothschild a handsome man of about 38 or 40 with a fine type of Jewish countenance.'[51] Perhaps her dead friend had taught her to have a juster appreciation of Jewish countenances.

In any case, the Queen approved, and on 9 July the new peer took his seat. He was supported by his old Cambridge friend, Charlie, now Lord Carrington, and by Rosebery. With his hat on his head and his hand on a Hebrew Bible he had brought for the occasion, Natty took the Jews into the House of Lords as his father had taken them into the House of Commons two decades before. The process of Jewish Emancipation was complete in every important respect. There was now no order of society from which a Jew was excluded.

Contemporaries saw the peerage in this light. Eddie Hamilton, for example, recorded his impression:

> Some people are turning up their noses at the Rothschild peerage; but I am very pleased it has been conferred. The stake which the remarkable family hold in this country amply justifies Royal recognition; and it removes the last remnant of religious disqualifications.[52]

Natty himself, in a restrained note of thanks to Gladstone, put the honour exclusively in this latter light. 'That the greatest champion of civil and religious liberty has bestowed for the first time a peerage on a member of our faith will greatly increase the value of the dignity.' Apart from the ordinary civilities, this was his only comment.[53]

Natty took care that the significance of the event should be lost on no one. The title spoke volumes. The day after Natty's letter to Gladstone, Alphonse sent his congratulations 'to Lord Rothschild'. The Jewish community in Paris was delighted, he said, not least because of the great pain such a title was bound to cause Russian and other anti-semites. The next day, he stressed again that it is 'with great pleasure that we note that you can retain our family name'.[54] Their elderly aunt at Aston Clinton also exulted: 'On Wednesday the 24th a peerage was given to Nathaniel who thus becomes Lord Rothschild! What changes in the last forty years, when the former title barely would have appeared on the envelope of a begging letter.'[55]

There was to be no hiding under a territorial title. No more than some reluctant Labour peers later, could Natty have avoided a territorial title altogether; and the full title was Rothschild of Tring. But it was simply as 'Lord Rothschild' that the new baron was to be known. Natty intended to make a point, and make a point he did every time he scrawled his lordly 'Rothschild' across the bottom of a letter.

In predicting that the new Conservative Prime Minister would raise no difficulties, Alphonse had remarked that Salisbury would thus show that 'he has laid aside old prejudice and although conservative, his administration is liberal all the same.'[56] The sort of Liberalism Alphonse had in mind was clearly of the old 'civil and religious liberty' variety, the by now rather old-fashioned term Natty had used to Gladstone.

The same definition of Liberalism also appears to be implicit in a long and interesting letter Ferdy wrote to Dilke at the beginning of the year. Dilke wrote on it:

> F. Rothschild wants to get into Parliament and I told him that he *is* a Tory and ought to stand as a Tory. This is his reply. He will never get in as a Liberal *nowadays*. I'm sure.

Ferdy had a different opinion, and his attempt to justify it is enlightening:

> I am not as you think by nature a Conservative. Conservatism has been the ruin of several foreign coun-

tries and liberal policies have been the making of England. To liberalism we – you – owe everything. On no point and in no manner do I incline towards Toryism in any form.

On the other hand . . . I deplore for the sake of the country I have adopted and I love truly, the restricted policy of the present Government, who have sacrificed if not the interests yet the magic power of the English flag and name to the narrower issues of Parliamentary reform. I am perhaps 'plus Catholique que le Pape' but I would that the Union Jack floated in every island of Polynesia, on every crag of the Himalayas, on every minaret of the East (this is a metaphor).

One would hope that the last explanation was gratuitous! But, Ferdy pointed out, for all the anti-expansionist rhetoric, 'You (I mean the Government) have to come [to] it after all in the long run. *Vide* the present expedition to Khartoum and augmentations to your colonies.' He referred to the relief expedition which would arrive too late to save Gordon, and probably to such acquisitions as those in New Guinea and Bechuanaland.

Having suggested the sort of Liberal policy he approved of, Ferdy went on to suggest the sort of which he disapproved:

Now if I do not call myself a Radical it is that I consider it unworthy of great leaders of men like Chamberlain and yourself to court popularity with the masses by advocating such trivial measures as the abolition of the game laws for instance and stimulating an unhealthy desire for social and pecuniary equality . . . instead of governing the people on broad principles and leading them into wider issues.[57]

A modern reader might well have as much difficulty as Dilke in identifying views such as Ferdy's as Liberal. They were, however, far from unique in the Liberal Party at the time Ferdy was writing, at the beginning of 1885. Their most prominent and coherent spokesman at that time was the future Lord Goschen, who defined his Liberalism in terms of a strongly patriotic line abroad, and strict economy and firm opposition to any sort of state interventionism at home.[58] Though opinion was just beginning to become explicitly and self-consciously concerned with the latter collectivist issue, Goschen's position might accurately be described as Palmerstonianism without civil and religious liberty. The Rothschilds had always been Palmerstonians, and, as Natty's peerage eloquently demonstrated, the old issues of civil and religious liberty were largely dead and buried. Liberalism was about to begin a process of drastic redefinition. It was a process that would take the Whig wing, followers of Hartington and Goschen, into Conservatism by way of Liberal Unionism. There was little question of the way the Rothschilds would go. The cause that had made them Liberals had been won, and there was everything in Liberalism as it would develop to repel them.

Natty was not given to, nor called upon for, statements of political faith. But it is clear from his comments on specific issues that, if he had indulged in them, his would not have been greatly different from Ferdy's. In February 1885, after the disaster at Khartoum had convinced Rosebery that it was his duty to accept Gladstone's offer of a Cabinet post, Natty wrote:

> I am truly glad you have consented to join the Government. Your clear judgment and patriotic devotion will help the Government and save the country.
>
> I hope you will take care that large reinforcements are sent up the Nile. The campaign in the Sudan must be a blatant success and no mistake.[59]

He was equally disapproving of Chamberlainite collectivism (or any form for that matter of what he, like many contemporaries, broadly labelled 'Socialism'). He told Rosebery in September that a speech of Chamberlain's in which he advocated such things as giving local authorities compulsory powers of land purchase to provide allotments, a burning symbolic issue, and equalization of taxation, would do 'an incalculable amount of mischief'.[60]

As his worst critics have always known, Natty was an imperialist and a rigorous anti-collectivist. Yet it would not be many years before he would join Cardinal Newman in bringing the great London dock strike of 1889 to a peaceful and constructive solution. He had already helped to defuse what might have become an explosive imperial issue.

There was one occasion during the second Gladstone government when there was a serious threat of war with another European power over an imperial question. That was the Pendjeh crisis of 1884–5, when Russian and Afghan troops clashed over a border dispute and the Indian Army prepared itself on government orders to step in if necessary. By the beginning of April 1885 matters between the British and Russian governments appeared to have reached an impasse, and there were powerful voices in the British press calling for war.

It was at this point that Natty began to take a hand. On 7 April Reggie Brett, recently resigned as Hartington's secretary but remaining in close touch with the man he still referred to as 'my Chief', wrote to Natty: 'I see that The Times scoffs at your idea that . . . there need be no war between England and Russia. But you are right notwithstanding.'[61]

Natty took steps to effect his idea. On 12 April Eddie Hamilton noted in his diary that de Staal, the Russian Ambassador, had put out an unofficial feeler:

> What has transpired is this: M. de Staal is a good deal influenced by N. Rothschild. Yesterday or the day before he says to N. Rothschild: 'What would the British Government (or your country) be satisfied with?' The reply he gets is: 'Probably nothing short of the recall of General Komaroff and the immediate recall of the Russian forces from the debated country. Do this, and you will get a boundary line not unlike the one which you Russians have drawn for yourselves.'[62]

De Staal thereupon sent a proposal along these lines to Brett, who in turn forwarded it to Gladstone. It would not be the end of the crisis by a long way. But Hamilton noted in his diary that it was 'something to have got anything out of the Russian Embassy, however unofficially it may be put forward'. The Cabinet thought so too, and agreed to accept de Staal's memorandum as a basis for negotiations.[63]

It would not be the last time that the voice of moderation issued from New Court. Natty was not an undiscriminating imperialist, and he was not a man of violence.

CHAPTER EIGHT

Randolph,
Rhodes, and Chamberlain

BRITISH IMPERIALISM in the 1880s was not confined to Egypt, and in the 1890s the main focus of public attention would shift to South Africa. An examination of the Rothschilds' role in Egypt tends to confirm the view of that school of historians who see British imperialism in the period as dominated by political and strategic, as opposed to financial, considerations. Certainly in Egypt the financial interest represented by the Rothschilds appears to have played a distinctly subordinate role – or, in terms of the metaphor used by Hobson, they seem to have been only a cog in the political machine, and definitely not its governor.

But what of other areas? One thinks immediately of South Africa, which many have seen as the classic case of imperialism dominated by financial interests. Those who emphasize strategic interests would draw a distinction between 'British' and what they see as the indigenous South African imperialism, represented most notably by Cecil Rhodes; and they would argue that the former, mainly concerned for the safety of the alternate route to India around the Cape of Good Hope, was dragged along somewhat reluctantly by the latter, which, most would agree, had something to do with diamonds and gold. A mastery of the subtleties of the argument are not, however, essential to a study of the Rothschilds. There is no doubt that they were deeply involved with Rhodes and diamonds, and gold; and some, following Hobson, have been confident that they were behind Joseph Chamberlain and a British government which finished in the Boer War what Rhodes had started with the Jameson Raid.

Before turning to South Africa, however, there is an earlier case some might see as equally self-evident to be considered. There are certain similarities with the later case, for not only is it a question of influence over a prominent politician, precious stones are also involved – in this instance Burmese rubies.

The politician is Lord Randolph Churchill, who burst on the official scene as Secretary of State for India in Salisbury's first government in 1885, and then went on to an even greater role as Chancellor of the Exchequer in Salisbury's second government – until a disastrous decision to resign in December 1886 ended his official career forever. The case is stated succinctly by Roy Foster in discussing strange omissions in Winston Churchill's biography of his father. The younger Churchill never even mentioned Lord Randolph's

> growing intimacy with Rothschild, to whom he 'turned for everything' by 1888, to whom he entrusted Cabinet secrets, the interests of whose firm he pressed in Persia, India, and Burma, who was – to general discomfiture – his closest adviser as Chancellor of the Exchequer, and to whose bank he owed £66,000 when he died.[1]

If ever there was a case of a politician under the thumb of his banker, this might seem to be it.

In fact, as Foster's own compelling study helps to illustrate, there is good reason to doubt it. Foster comments on the paucity of evidence about the Churchill-Rothschild relationship. He is quite right. Not only are there remarkably few letters from Churchill to Natty still extant (Natty's correspondence not preserved in bank archives was almost totally destroyed), there are not many letters from Natty to Churchill in the latter's papers. What is more, such as there are throw little or no light on the questions alluded to in the above quotation, at any rate no direct light. One can only make inferences from other evidence.

The very lack of evidence might seem to point toward a sinister influence someone was attempting to hide by destroying the proof. But the scarcity of Rothschild letters, and especially Natty's letters, is by no means unique to the Churchill Papers. In almost every collection where one would expect to find a great deal, one in fact finds very little. This is true of the papers of Hartington, Rhodes, Rosebery, Lansdowne and Arthur Balfour, to name some with whom Natty was on intimate terms. One finds rather more in Disraeli's papers, and, oddly some might think, most of all in Salisbury's papers. For, if one expected to find that patrician politician above contact with mere bankers, one would be much disappointed. Salisbury's papers demonstrate conclusively that not only was Natty constantly seeking advice and information, but also imparting it.

It would be quite wrong, however, to assume that the greater the bulk of evidence, the closer the degree of intimacy. The reason for the relative richness of the Salisbury archives is almost certainly other, rather lying in the fact that Salisbury spent a great deal of time at Hatfield and had a trusted private secretary at the Foreign Office, Schomberg McDonnell, who kept him informed with a steady stream of letters and memoranda. Among other things, he reported on extensive conversations with Lord Rothschild.

Even more than most politicians, Natty's favoured means of communication was by word of mouth. The Rothschild brothers were well known even in their own family for their assiduous calling to chat and gossip. On one occasion, Ferdy reported to Rosebery that Natty had called early one morning to pump him, among other things, on Rosebery's views and likely political actions. Alfred followed later in the morning. 'What a pity the Inquisition has been abolished,' Ferdy remarked. 'What touts my relatives would have been!'[2]

The point of course was not mere idle social chit-chat, but the gathering, and in some cases the imparting of information.

For a variety of reasons Natty and his brothers would have found this more easily and conveniently done by conversation than by letter. For one thing, they were not only politicians but busy bankers with wide international connections. The latter involved them in extensive correspondence. Natty wrote long letters every day, sometimes more than one, to his relatives in Paris and Frankfurt. He wrote several letters a week to Vienna, and to Bleichröder in Berlin. And these were only the regular items in a voluminous business correspondence.

This would have limited his time and energy for political correspondence, especially as there were alternative means to hand. For another thing that made Natty different from other politicians was the fact that he spent relatively little time outside the metropolis. Most politicians were out of London and separated from their colleagues for a good deal of the year between August and February. Hence the correspondence that flowed during those months. Natty, on the other hand, aside from a couple of weeks at some watering place, English or Continental, spent almost all his time within easy reach of New Court, as his father had done before him. But, whereas Gunnersbury was within driving distance of the bank, Tring was not. Natty usually spent what we now call the weekends at Tring, but out of season, when his family had departed for the country, he spent his weekdays 'a solitary hermit in London', as he described himself to Rosebery in November 1886.[3] From Piccadilly he could make his morning calls in the West End on his way to the City. These would often include the Foreign Office or the War Office, and if the principal was not there a trusted lieutenant such as 'Pom' McDonnell or Reggie Brett usually was. They could both pass on to and relay information from their chiefs, and it is clearly not by chance that a good deal of information on Natty's thoughts and actions comes by way of them. For Rhodes, L. Maguire at the Exploration Company Limited, one of several through which Rhodes conducted his enterprises and only a few doors away from the bank in St. Swithin's Lane, served much the same purpose. Of course such means of communication were also more discreet and less binding than committing oneself to paper, but the saving of time and energy to the principals at both ends was at least equally important.

It seems therefore unwise to assume that a lack of evidence in itself constitutes a kind of evidence, and much safer to confine oneself to such evidence as does exist. A bank account is one source, but here, as Foster's work makes clear, Churchill's indebtedness to the Rothschilds waxed as his influence waned. His maximum use to them in a business way would have been when he was Secretary of State for India in Salisbury's first government in 1885 (though it appears that in every instance where he attempted to promote their interests he failed, and the Burma Ruby Mines Ltd. was not to be floated until four years later[4]). He would have been of relatively little use after his official career ended in December 1886 with his resignation as Chancellor of the Exchequer in Salisbury's second government. Yet his period of heavy indebtedness to the Rothschilds postdates his period in office by several years. His debts to the bank did not reach £11,000 until the end of 1891, and the great leap to almost £67,000 came after that. Heavy Rothschild investment in Churchill came only in what Foster has aptly termed the years of 'Wilderness Politics' after 1888. Up to that year his debt to the bank had accumulated to only £900.

Certainly at the end of his official career Churchill did not talk or act as if he had been bought and paid for. Just after the most crucial decision of his political life, to resign from Salisbury's government, he told Brett that, though he was actually going to Blenheim, he would give out that he was going to Brighton:

> I asked if I could tell Natty. He said no, because he is furious with Alfred Rothschild, who it appears is talking strongly against him.
> 'He complains that I did not consult the Rothschilds. After all I am glad to have them as friends, but I am not yet Rivers Wilson, and am not yet in their pay.'[6]

There is no reason to believe that Rivers Wilson was either.

The 'literary evidence' in the Churchill Papers has little or nothing to do with Rothschild business interests or with Randolph's debts. It is mainly concerned with broad questions of domestic and foreign politics. Natty's overriding concern as reflected in his letters was to build up and preserve what would become the anti-Gladstone, Unionist coalition of Conservatives and disgruntled Liberals. He long considered Churchill as crucial to the cause, probably largely because he saw him as the one politician on that side of the question likely to be able to compete with Gladstone on anything like equal terms as a great popular leader. 'I hope,' he wrote to Churchill at the time of the general election in June 1886 after the defeat of the first Home Rule Bill, 'that you will take my advice and have a go at the Grand Old Man on his own dung hill.' And the next day: 'I shall call at Connaught Place on Saturday . . . and try to impress on you the necessity of public speaking in Scotland.'[7]

Evidence continues of the primacy of the anti-Gladstonian cause in Natty's mind. On 3 October 1886, Brett wrote to Hartington that he had seen Natty and Randolph in the past couple of days:

> They seem to conduct the business of the Empire, in great measure, *together*, in consultation with Chamberlain. But they all have in view apparently a main object, which is the maintenance of the Unionist party. And on this account your wishes and opinions seem to be the prime factor in all their calculations.

He went on to report that 'the essential thing, as Randolph says is "to keep the Gladstone gang out of office" '.[8]

As far as the business of empire was concerned, the line Natty was advocating was one he had been suggesting to governments, Liberal and Conservative, from at least 1884. It was that a basic element of British policy must be good relations with Germany. He told Eddie Hamilton in August of 1884 that France was bent on reestablishing her position in Egypt, and that 'our only chance is to come to terms with Bismarck'.[9] He had done his best to promote good relations by encouraging contacts between Bismarck and the Liberal government in the negotiations over Egyptian finances in 1884–5. He provided similar good offices to Salisbury's government which came into office in the middle of the year.[10]

The central element in Bismarck's policy, as Natty was well aware, was the isolation of France, whose desire for revenge after 1870 Bismarck saw as the great threat to the European system he had established. 'France has been flirting with Russia,' Natty wrote to Rosebery in February 1887, 'the result anyone could have foreseen is that Bismarck will let Russia do what she likes in the Balkans.'[11] But, though Bismarck wished to keep on good terms with Russia and to keep her out of the arms of France, neither did he wish to alienate his closest ally, Austria. The result was a delicate game of balance in the Balkans. This mainly consisted of avoiding conflict between Russia and Austria by keeping the Balkan situation as stable as possible, while at the same time recognizing special Russian interests, as in Bulgaria.

Natty did his best to promote cooperation on both points. At the time of the second transition between a Salisbury and a Gladstone government, in the early months of 1886, the former had agreed to join in a naval demonstration to bring the current disturber of the peace in the Balkans, Greece, to heel. Just before Parliament met, while the Conservatives were still in power, Natty enlisted Brett's support in attempting to persuade the Liberals to do nothing to endanger Salisbury's Balkan policy, even to the point of delaying a discussion of Irish affairs.[12] And shortly after the Liberals came to power, Alfred reminded Rosebery, who became Foreign Secretary in this government, of the urgency with which Berlin viewed the matter.[13]

During Salisbury's second government, which came to power in June after Gladstone's first defeat on Home Rule, the key question was Bulgaria. The establishment of a strong Bulgarian state had been a great object of Russian policy in the 1870s, but once an independent Bulgaria had been established, it showed a distressing tendency, from the Russian point of view, to be independent of Russia as well as of Turkey. Those who wished to stand well with Russia therefore would be ill-advised to give any aid or comfort to an anti-Russian government at Sofia. Since Bismarck wished to stand well with Russia, the same applied to those who wished to stand well with him.

It was these considerations that lay behind the policy Natty urged on Churchill in 1886. Unfortunately, such a policy ran dead against the one preferred by the Foreign Secretary, Lord Iddesleigh, the former Sir Stafford Northcote. Natty did not even pretend to take Iddesleigh's policy seriously. He rejected with horror a request from the Foreign Office for a £400,000 loan to bolster up the provisional government at Sofia. 'Was there ever such *folly*!', he wrote to Churchill on 27 September. A week later he pressed similar views in person on the Foreign Secretary, who, as he told Churchill, he found 'cackling like an old hen'.[14]

Churchill, and Natty was evidently hand-in-glove with him, used both the Foreign Secretary and his policy roughly. There was, however, a point to the line they were pursuing. Support of Bismarck's policy in the Balkans was calculated to get his support for Britain in Egypt. More than that, it might well mean his exercising restraint on Russia. 'Bismarck has I think isolated France,' Natty wrote to Rosebery in December, 'and I should not be in the least astonished if he made England and Russia staunch friends.'[15] The alternative to the policy Natty advocated had already been tried, and it had not been pleasant. If Bismarck could not keep Britain and France apart by drawing the former into his orbit, he would keep them apart by stirring up trouble between them, in Egypt, for example. All in all, the most hopeful course lay in cooperation with Germany, or so it seemed to Natty.

Natty was not alone in this view, however. Not only was it taken up by Churchill, whether from conviction or expediency, it also had the support of a much weightier statesman, and one with considerable experience in foreign affairs. In the same letter to Hartington in which he observed that Randolph and Natty together, in consultation with Chamberlain, seemed to be conducting the business of the empire, Brett had also remarked that in advocating their common line, Churchill had 'had no difficulty with Lord Salisbury who is content to adhere to the

German alliance, but with Lord Iddesleigh and with some of the English agents abroad, there has been a good deal of trouble'.[16] Brett was quite right as to Salisbury's views. Iddesleigh would soon be dead, hounded to death some said by Churchill, and cooperation with Germany would be the cornerstone of Salisbury's policy for the rest of the decade.[17] The two intriguers were in good company, and Natty at any rate had a cause to advance beyond the intrigue itself.

Natty's objective was a strong foreign policy calculated to advance Britain's imperial interests. This was probably the main factor in his strenuous efforts for the Unionist cause. He had not liked Gladstone's recent Irish policy either – 'confiscation' was what he called the land bill of 1880 –[18] and he seems to have made the usual equations between Home Rule, which would weaken the empire at its heart, and wider imperial concerns. But it was Gladstone's foreign and imperial policy that had most profoundly alienated Natty, and at this time at any rate his concern continued to centre in these areas.

That his efforts in the Unionist cause were strenuous cannot be doubted. So were Alfred's. They were also largely behind the scenes. From the beginning of 1886, when the cause can first be called 'Unionist', the Rothschilds worked hard to promote good relations between the Conservatives and the several factions of Liberals who would ultimately become the Liberal Unionists. Their efforts took a variety of forms. Early in January 1886 Alfred was deputed to convey to Hartington Salisbury's willingness to serve as Foreign Secretary in a Hartington government – an unlikely eventuality, but a complimentary suggestion.[19] At the end of the month, the same source was assuring Churchill that Hartington had not surrendered on the Home Rule issue.[20] And not only did the Rothschilds serve as intermediaries between the several parties. In the June general election New Court became a centre of activity for those promoting Liberal Unionist candidates.[21] In these senses, Cooke and Vincent are quite right when, in discussing the breakup of the Liberal party, they observe: 'Somewhere in the background, the Rothschild interest was closely involved, whether at a spiritual level only none can say.'[22] Obviously, they were involved at every level.

As has already been suggested, it was also the Unionist cause, or at least the concerns that lay behind their support of the Unionist cause, that to a great extent explain early Rothschild interest in Randolph Churchill. Letters from Natty to Churchill in March 1887, following the latter's decision to resign, demonstrate both Natty's continuing concern for the Unionist cause and his realization that Churchill, though a brilliant, was a not entirely reliable ally in any cause. Churchill's obvious willingness to follow almost any political course that seemed expedient caused Natty deep concern. Churchill had, Natty wrote, completely misjudged the situation. There would be a coercion bill for Ireland, and 'as Joe supports it, you should do the same'. Several days later he wrote that Hartington as well as Chamberlain supported the Conservative government, 'most enthusiastically and energetically'. Natty could not believe, so he said, that Churchill could be coming back to support Gladstone:

> and so I congratulate myself that you are coming back to speak for and support the Government. You will have plenty of time between now and Easter, and you can take your old place as the most prominent speaker on the Tory side, where I feel sure you will be welcomed. But I am equally convinced that you would damage yourself irretrievably if you acted the part of a frondeur.[23]

Unfortunately, a *frondeur* was precisely what Churchill was, and always had been.

Natty did not object to a politician with no principles so long as he used his talents in the right cause. It took him a long time to give up Churchill. As late as September 1888, Natty was still writing about meeting 'to arrange your plan of campaign'.[24] By then, however, the wilderness years had set in. This naturally raises the question of why the Rothschilds began in these years to give Churchill increasingly heavy financial support. Part of the reason may have been that most of the money went into speculations in South African ventures in which they were all deeply involved; and that Randolph's name could still add lustre to the schemes of men such as Cecil Rhodes. Another part of the reason was personal friendship. Long after Natty had given up Churchill as a serious politician, he continued to value him as a friend. In January 1893 he wrote how much he was looking forward to seeing Churchill at Tring: 'There are no end of things to talk over – Panama land, Home Rule etc.' One of the last letters in the Churchill archives is a little note from Lady Rothschild bearing best wishes and accompanying some small gifts for the last fruitless voyage in search of health.[24]

All this is not to argue that there was not something a little dangerous in the relationship between Churchill and the Rothschilds, but it was probably more a matter of personality than of purse-strings. It would be true to say that of all the politicians in the Rothschild circle, Churchill was the one with whom they were on easiest and most intimate terms. It was not that they knew him better than, for example, they knew Disraeli or Rosebery. They certainly did not. The relationship, however, was entirely different. Disraeli's age and stature as a politician naturally gave him a somewhat special position. Rosebery's youth did not prevent him, particularly when in office, from maintaining his distance from the Rothschilds, a policy which they fully understood and were happy to maintain. On Rosebery's side, one of the things which long stood in the way of his taking office in 1884–5 was his link with the Rothschilds, and their close connection with Egypt.[25] Natty was quite aware of these scruples and of the reasons for them. In January 1886, in discussing with Brett whom the Liberals might put in the Foreign Office, he thought Rosebery 'out of the question owing to his connection with the House of Rothschild'.[26] As a consequence, when Rosebery did take office, their relationship assumed an almost chilly correctness on both sides.

An example from 1893 will make the point. In the previous year, when Gladstone had formed yet another government, the Rothschilds had been extremely anxious that Rosebery should take the Foreign Office. As usual, they were concerned with maintaining a continuity of foreign policy; particularly in Egypt, where it was feared that Gladstone if left to himself might finally fulfil his promises to withdraw. They were not alone in their fears, and, aside from urging him personally, they helped to mobilize pressure from, among others, the Prince of Wales and perhaps from the Queen herself.[27] The pressure was successful in the end, and Rosebery proved to be as firm as his supporters had hoped he would be, strongly asserting the British position in a difficult situation which followed the accession of a young Khedive.

Rothschild cooperation was close – but not intimate. Early in 1893, Brett wrote to Rosebery:

I saw Natty and Alfred, and told them that you were much obliged to them for having given you all the information at their disposal, and therefore wished them to know, before reading it in the papers, that the Egyptian garrison was to be reinforced. If they wished to let Sinadina [Ambrose Sinadonia, an associate of the Rothschilds in Egypt] know anything they might say that the 'Government were about to take measures to ensure the maintenance of order'; but they were not to give the news to anyone else, until they themselves heard it from another quarter.

Of course they were delighted and most grateful. Natty wished me to tell you that all the information, and any assistance, which he can give you is always at your disposal.[28]

The latter promise was kept, but always with the most punctilious correctness on both sides. Paradoxically, some might think, of all the ministers of the period, Rosebery was probably the one least accessible to the Rothschilds. Nor, though their opinions were close on most foreign policy questions, can it be argued that Rosebery owed his views to them.

The difficulty with Randolph Churchill was that, when not in a fit of pique, he was all too accessible to the Rothschilds, and that some of his opinions – or what passed for opinions – would clearly seem to have come from them. As Dr Foster has shown, in the constant political manoeuvre that constituted his political life, Churchill was apt to take up the ideas of others as suited his purpose. He was also a man of great enthusiasms and little judgment. The Rothschilds provided him, as they had provided Disraeli, with a vast information network and with alternative means of influencing policy. Undoubtedly they also discussed with him, as it was in their interests to do with ministers, their business ventures. There was nothing new in the substance of their relationship with Churchill. The difference was in personality. Harnessed to independent opinions and policies, as in the cases of Disraeli, Rosebery, and Salisbury, the Rothschilds were a most useful adjunct in the conduct of foreign policy. In Churchill's case, they were harnessed only to a vaulting ambition. It is not necessary to believe that Churchill supported an expansionist policy in Burma merely to promote Rothschild interests in rubies, much less that they asked him to, in order to believe that there was something at least potentially dangerous in the relationship. It is difficult to point to any particular damage that arose from their association. Indeed on the foreign policy issue, they, or rather Natty, for the views were his, almost certainly had the better case. The danger lay in the ease with which the ideas were taken up. Perhaps Natty should have seen this. But to be the mentor of a major politician is heady stuff, particularly if one believes in the causes one is advocating. The danger signs with Cecil Rhodes were much clearer, and Natty would be a great deal more cautious.

The broad outlines of Rhodes's life are well known. How the young vicar's son went out to South Africa to grow cotton, only to be caught up in the diamond fever. How, doing an Oxford degree the while, his organizing genius laid the basis for a monopoly of the diamond fields. The great struggle with Barney Barnato to achieve that monopoly, with its successful conclusion in the formation of De Beers. How Rhodes then secured large holdings in the new gold fields in the Transvaal. But how the pursuit of wealth was always subordinate to the pursuit of power. In 1889 came the formation of the British South Africa Company to settle what would become Rhodesia, but then to push as far north as possible, perhaps even to make a link with Cairo. In 1890 Rhodes became Prime Minister of the Cape Colony. From then on, all his resources, business and political, would be concentrated on the expansion of a British South Africa, British in its culture, South African in its energy and enthusiasm – and, beyond that, in the distant future, on the expansion of a wider British culture throughout the world. The first objective would receive a temporary check in the disastrous Jameson Raid of December 1895 on the Transvaal, which ended Rhodes's political career at the Cape; but left him with a country of his own, a reputation little dented, and a future that would almost see the British government at the end of a bitter and bloody war realize his dreams of a British South Africa. The second objective would give rise after his death to the Rhodes Scholarships.[29]

Rothschilds first became associated with Rhodes in 1887 during the great struggle with Barnato for control of the diamond industry. In August, after an interview with Natty at New Court, Rhodes was promised their backing, a million pounds backing.[30] It was neither a new departure, nor a snap decision. As their interest in Burmese rubies demonstrates, the Rothschilds had been watching the gem trade for some time. They also sought expert advice on the future of the trade, especially in the vast and expanding American market,[31] and they had their own advisers on the spot in South Africa. As usual, the Rothschild international network was brought into play, and with its backing, Rhodes and De Beers ultimately triumphed.

Rhodes was immensely impressed with Natty on their first acquaintance, and in long letters he poured out his plans and hopes and asked for Rothschild assistance on all kinds of questions. On 20 January 1888, he wanted Natty's advice on a syndicate he had in mind. He also wished him to take a share of what would become the British South Africa Company, and he wanted him to use his influence with the government to prevent Colonial Office interference with Rhodes's projects, and to keep Rhodes's ally, Sir Hercules Robinson, British High Commissioner at the Cape. Nothing was held back.[32]

In June came an even greater mark of Rhodes's favour and confidence. Natty was entrusted with the project that would ultimately become the Rhodes Scholarships, but which started as an idea for a fantastic secret society to spread British power and influence throughout the world. After providing for his family, Rhodes proposed to leave the vast bulk of his fortune to Natty for the promotion of this society. The flavour of the whole project is suggested in a cryptic postscript Rhodes added to the note to Natty which accompanied the copy of his will: 'In considering question suggested take constitution Jesuits if available and insert "English Empire" for "Roman Catholic Religion".'[33]

But Rhodes's early enthusiasm for Natty clearly wore off. In February 1891 Reggie Brett met Rhodes at the house of W. T. Stead, the editor of the *Pall Mall Gazette*, and Rhodes opened his mind to Brett. He told him that he intended to remain firm in the territorial claims of the British South Africa Company in Manicaland, in spite of the Portuguese, and even in spite of Lord Salisbury. He also confided to Brett that he was 'a Dutchman at the Cape just as a Jesuit is a Chinaman in China'. And he impressed on Brett that the Jesuits were his ideal. He went on to talk of a 'federation of English speaking races', which his proposed 'secret body of workers or helpers' was to effect. And he told Brett that he had left his fortune to Natty for this purpose.

But he had come to have serious doubts: 'He now thinks Lord R. honest but without sufficient brains.'[34]

What Rhodes had in mind is probably suggested by a letter Natty wrote to him on 15 January 1892. Rhodes's letter to which it was a response has not survived, but it is evident that it was one full of complaints about British statesmen and proposing that De Beers' funds should be used to finance northward expansion, either by the Cape or by the British South Africa Company. Rhodes had only one object, and it was typical of him that he was not especially concerned about which of his several enterprises, business and political, were brought into play to achieve it. He did not find a sympathetic audience in Natty.

In response to Rhodes's complaint that Salisbury had betrayed him in a recent colonial agreement with the Portuguese, Natty observed:

> I think you are a little hard on Lord Salisbury when you say he treated you badly over the Portuguese business. You must not forget that at that time public opinion all over Europe was in favour of Portugal, and it would hardly have been wise for Lord Salisbury to incur the reproach, on the part of friendly powers, that this country was going to crush weak little Portugal for the sake of a no doubt important but undeveloped region in Central Africa. After all, could you have expected more or as much from a Liberal Government?

Nor was he much more sympathetic to Rhodes's complaints about remarks that Churchill had made after a recent visit: 'It was no doubt injudicious on the part of Lord Randolph to cry down Mashonaland; but you may be certain of one thing, namely that you have no warmer admirer than him, and perhaps it was as well that he should not have painted Mashonaland in too glowing colours, because it might have produced a rush into the country and in consequence increased your transport and food difficulties.' This was a shrewd blow, for one of Rhodes's persistent complaints and justifications for further expansion was that only bad communications were holding up the development of the future Rhodesia.

As for Rhodes's proposal to expand, apparently into Nyasaland and Bechuanaland, Natty pointedly refused to give any advice on the political aspects of the question:

We begin by saying that you are the only judge as to whether the Cape Government ought to take over the Northern Territories; that is not our business, and we do not wish to offer any opinion on the subject. You must know how far your Charter would be violated or not by such a policy, and whether it would meet with the approval of Her Majesty's Government.

The policies of the Cape government or of the British South Africa Company, and the relations of both to the British government, were not appropriate subjects for a banker's advice:

But what we do say, is, that if that is your policy, and you require money for the purpose, you will have to obtain it from other sources than the cash reserve of the Debeers Company. We have always held that the Debeers Company is simply a diamond mining company . . .

Rhodes might possibly be able to find a loophole, but he would be most unwise to take advantage of it. People were no longer willing to tolerate liberties with company funds, and De Beers might suffer as a consequence. 'Apart, therefore, from the question whether it is right or wrong to use the funds of the De Beers Company in this way, it would be very injudicious.'[35]

Clearly such caution and scrupulousness were not the kind of thing Rhodes wished to hear. He needed a confidant with more 'brains'. He was disappointed in Natty, and so perhaps would some others be who might expect Natty's advice to have been of a different sort.

Neither was there any attempt to keep Rothschild loaning policy in line with Rhodes's, though every care was taken to keep it in line with the policy of the British government – which was not always the same. On 9 June 1892 Natty wrote to the Prime Minister who was also Foreign Secretary, Lord Salisbury, seeking advice. Rothschilds had been approached by the South African Republic, the Transvaal, about taking charge of a loan. The original request had been for three million, of which one million was to be for the eventual purchase of a Portuguese railway line to be constructed from Delagoa Bay to the Transvaal frontier. But 'upon our pointing out to them that such an operation would meet with very great opposition in this country, they at once abandoned that part of the scheme'. Natty did not need to enquire whether the British government would approve independent access to the sea for a Boer republic. Governments had always opposed it, though at this point Rhodes was actually encouraging the railway's construction.[36] Natty had no intention of doing so. The remaining two million was to be devoted to public works, and to completing a network of railways within the Transvaal itself which would connect with those already built in the Cape Colony. The latter project, Natty pointed out, would be in the interests of a large amount of British capital already invested in the Transvaal, the most prominent example of course being the investment in the gold fields. Salisbury's opinion, however, 'I need hardly say will entirely guide our conduct in connection with the proposed operation'.

Salisbury found 'nothing in the proposed loan as you are good enough to explain it, which would appear in any degree objectionable to Her Majesty's Government – and, therefore, I should be far from wishing in any way to dissuade you from assisting it'.[37] It was duly floated. The Rothschilds were not only bankers to Rhodes, but to the Transvaal.

When, therefore, Rhodes in 1895 began plotting the coup in which it was hoped that an invasion of the Transvaal by the South Africa Company's police under Dr Jameson would coincide with an inspired rising of English and other foreigners, there was perhaps more than one reason why he did not confide in the Rothschilds. At any rate, he did not, a fact of which there is happily clear proof in what remains a murky affair. It was long uncertain whether Rhodes confided in Joseph Chamberlain, who became Colonial Secretary when the leaders of the Liberal Unionists joined a new Salisbury government in the summer of 1895. It has become increasingly clear that he had done, and the evidence which exonerates the Rothschilds further implicates Chamberlain. On 9 August 1895, Maguire wrote to Rhodes from the Exploration Company's office next door to New Court:

> Lord R. has called advising you to come home to see Chamberlain. This is on general grounds at the instigation of Brett, who thinks, no doubt with justice, that you could do good by talking over the general position with Chamberlain – neither he nor Brett know anything of Jameson's possible movements, and the position of the Protectorate has not been discussed with them.[38]

If the syntax leaves any doubt as to whom the 'he' refers, it would seem to be removed by the allusion to the Bechuanaland Protectorate. Rhodes had requested Chamberlain to consider transferring that to the chartered company a month earlier.[39] Maguire was reassuring Rhodes that Brett and Natty had not been brought into the secret.

With the disastrous failure of the Raid, for the rising never took place and Jameson's police suffered ignominious capture, Rhodes ceased to play a central role in relations with the Transvaal. British officials, however, soon took over where he had left off, with Chamberlain at the Colonial Office in charge. The main bone of contention was the position of the large foreign population in the Transvaal, the Uitlanders to whom the ordinary rights of citizenship were denied. The majority were British, and Chamberlain took up their cause. Matters reached a crisis in the late spring of 1899, and though negotiations dragged on through the summer they came to nothing. President Kruger finally broke them off on 9 October, with an ultimatum that amounted to a declaration of war.

Could war have been avoided? Natty thought so, and through the summer and right up to the eve of war the influence and facilities of New Court were bent towards this end. On 20 July 1899, McDonnell reported to Salisbury:

> I had a long conversation with Lord Rothschild last night.
>
> He had just seen Lewis, whose partner Marks is hand in glove with Kruger at Pretoria and has been working hard to make him give way.
>
> Lewis, who has known Kruger intimately for thirty years, said there was no longer any doubt that Kruger would give way on all points: and he added 'in fifteen years the Transvaal will be British. Kruger is the last remnant of the old Boer Toryism, and he is also the last President of the kind that the Transvaal will ever have'.
>
> This is merely interesting because Lewis has proved hitherto to be singularly correct in his forecasts.[40]

On the 24th of July, Natty forwarded a cable from Marks in Pretoria. Marks had seen General Joubert, and the Government Council had unanimously agreed to a list of concessions. Natty commented: 'I merely send you this, as I think it shows they will ultimately settle *all* outstanding questions, but you are better able to judge than I am.'

The government clearly judged differently, failing, or refusing, to see any signs of compromise on the Boer side.[41] But there was one last attempt from New Court. On 27 September, McDonnell forwarded to Salisbury copies of several cables Natty had left with him. One was 'sent by Lewis and Marks at the request of the Rothschilds, acting on the suggestion of the *Duke of Devonshire*, who asked Leopold Rothschild to draft it and actually added the words "without conditions" himself'. The Duke of Devonshire was the Rothschilds' old friend Hartington. The cable itself said, in part:

> N. M. Rothschild & Sons inform us action Government of Great Britain sending last Friday despatch . . . should be proof Government of Great Britain are anxious Peace. If agree to five years franchise *without conditions* Government of Transvaal have no reason to fear friendly discussion subsequently arranging details.

The immediate response was not positive. But two days later, on the 29th, Natty forwarded another cable, which conveyed the information that the President of the other Boer republic, the Orange Free State, had approached the British government. Natty commented:

> As a matter of course you will go on with your preparations, but it strikes me that if Steyn has asked you what you want, it must be with the knowledge of Kruger and would show a desire for peace.

McDonnell's response can be taken as the ultimate reply to Hobson and his belief that finance capital, and the Rothschilds in particular, pushed the politicians to war. Lord Salisbury

> wishes me to express his thanks to you for having given him the opportunity of seeing these messages: at the same time however he feels that, in justice to Mr Chamberlain, upon whom the responsibility for the negotiations rests, he cannot but deprecate very earnestly any further communications of this kind with Pretoria.[42]

The politicians, not the bankers, were in charge.

★   ★   ★

Hobson's case long seemed a most plausible one, and he had all, or most of his facts straight. The Rothschilds had no dominating influence with the press. But they did have large and evident financial interests in those areas where British imperialism was at its most active. They had also played an important role in the growth of a new armaments industry. In 1888 they presided over the first issue of shares for the Naval Construction and Armaments Company, fulfilling the same function in the same year for Maxim-Nordenfelt Guns and Ammunition Company.[43] The pieces of the puzzle were much as Hobson saw them. The difficulty is that they don't fit together.

Rothschilds took pains not to press any line of action too hard on the British government, and they clearly did not support an aggressive line. As for other governments, aside from the special case of Russia and its treatment of the Jews, there is only one possible instance in this period of the Rothschilds attempting to use their financial power to influence political action. That was with the government of Brazil, to whom the Rothschilds had long been the major bankers. It is, however, the exception that proves the rule.

In the autumn of 1895 the Brazilian government was acting aggressively on the question of Trinidad, to which they also laid claim. In pursuit of their claim they had occupied territory in British Guiana. On 21 October 1895, Natty called on McDonnell to urge that the British government, in the interests of British subjects in Brazil, impress on the Brazilians the necessity of settling outstanding disputes by peaceful arbitration. McDonnell replied, so he informed Salisbury, 'that it was for the Rothschilds to prove . . . the policy of withdrawing and that, if they could effect this, the main difficulty in the way of arbitration would be removed'. McDonnell went on to observe: 'There is no doubt the Rothschilds can do this; but they naturally want to make us do it.' Oddly enough the Brazilian Legation in London appears to have agreed that the best way of influencing the situation was for Rothschilds to cable direct to the Minister of Finance. The Legation even obligingly provided the wording of a cable delicately hinting to the Minister that it would be as well for Brazilian bonds if the matter were taken to arbitration![44] Whether such a cable was actually sent is unclear.

McDonnell was quite right in seeing that it was not in Rothschild interests to attempt to dictate to their customers. Neither was it in the personality of the man who was in charge at N. M. Rothschild & Sons. Natty was a man of peace.

CHAPTER NINE

'We, my dear Natty, We'

THERE IS A FAMILY STORY of an important meeting between the three partners of New Court and officials of the Treasury and the Bank of England. Lord Rothschild sat at one end of the table flanked by his brothers. After discussions had proceeded for a while, he suddenly announced; 'I have made up my mind.' Alfred tugged gently at his sleeve: 'We, my dear Natty, we.'[1]

The story is an accurate reflection of the relationship between the three brothers. Natty was the dominant partner in every sense. Not that the other two did not have strengths and personalities of their own. Alfred, whose blond good looks had served the A.D.C. well in female roles, was a man of considerable taste and discernment. It is sometimes felt that the fanciful château at Halton hardly reflects that taste. Admittedly it looks somewhat incongruous high on the Chiltern hillside between Wendover and Aston Clinton. It is not the place for a sixteenth century French château. Alfred, however, seems to have been rather more concerned with the inside than with the outer appearance. According to a description which appeared in the *Daily Telegraph* in 1889, probably inspired by him and included in his scrapbook, the architects were instructed to build a house 'the ground floor of which should consist of four stately rooms, identical in dimensions, radiating from a lofty and spacious central hall, and linked together by suites of smaller apartments, in which certain art treasures might be displayed to the best possible advantage'.[2] The sumptuous splendour of these apartments impressed even Nikolaus Pevsner,[3] and he saw them long after Alfred's day, without the magnificent collection of Sèvres, the walls stripped of their Romneys, Gainsboroughs, and Reynoldses, their Hobbemas, Bouchers, Cuyps, Watteaus, and Greuzes.

Alfred did more than indulge his taste. He also put it, and considerable energy, at the nation's disposal. He worked hard to persuade a parsimonious Gladstone government to buy the Duke of Marlborough's pictures when they were offered in the 1880s. The only success was with Van Dyck's equestrian portrait of Charles I, but that in itself was a considerable achievement.[4] He was also one of those most assiduous in courting Sir Richard Wallace, doing his best with Salisbury and Hartington to secure Wallace a peerage in 1888.[5] It was only fitting that in the 1890s Alfred should have been made in turn a trustee of the National Gallery and of the Wallace Collection.

Alfred was also clearly possessed of not a little skill in diplomacy. In 1892, when he was serving as a British representative to the international conference on Bimetallism, Sir William Harcourt paid him 'a compliment paid to someone – I forget whom – that his manner of refusal was more agreeable than other people's acceptances'.[6] It was a compliment that could never have been paid to Natty.

It is illustrative of the relationship between the brothers that when the Chancellor of the Exchequer in Gladstone's last government needed a Rothschild, a name which 'will carry a weight which no other name could command in the monetary world', he had turned to Natty, and Natty had volunteered Alfred's services. Harcourt was a trifle concerned, not having 'the advantage of knowing Alfred's opinions on these subjects, but I take it for granted he is a good staunch monometallist (what Mr Gladstone calls a "sane man") who will uphold to the death the single gold standard'. Natty replied there was no need to worry: 'Alfred is perfectly [sound] in all subjects, particularly so on Bimetallism.' At the same time he obviously told Alfred to write accepting the mission, which he did in a long and flowery letter.[7]

Contemporaries were well aware of where the power lay at New Court. On one occasion, Schomberg McDonnell wrote to Salisbury that he had been to the bank seeking advice from Lord Rothschild. Natty had given it, and then 'called up Alfred Rothschild (who always acts as Mr Toskins) and he said the same only more strongly'.[8] Natty provided the brief, but Alfred seems to have argued it effectively, and there were times when his emollient skills were sorely needed.

Leo was also overshadowed by his eldest brother, but he too had qualities the others lacked. Everyone who knew him is agreed on Leo's genuine kindness and unaffected good humour. He was the family pacifier. He also spent time looking after the family's political interests in Bucks. At political gatherings, according to Ferdy, he made an 'infinitely better chairman than his lordly brother. He is plucky and genial.'[9]

The role of bluff country squire was by no means entirely an assumed one. Leo was devoted to the country and its pursuits, and he was a famous sportsman. There can be little doubt that he was the moving force in founding the Gunnersbury stud. Lionel had little or no interest in horse racing, and grave reservations about Leo's while an undergraduate. It is therefore a tribute to Leo's charm and powers of persuasion that it was at this time that the stud was being formed. After he came down from Cambridge, Leo took it over completely, and he was the 'Mr Acton' whose horse won the Derby in 1869. The stud moved with him to Ascott, where it would continue to flourish. Leo, this time under his own name, would again be the owner of a Derby winner in 1904.

Ascott itself was probably the greatest success, at least the one aesthetically most pleasing, of the country houses of the three brothers. There was already a timber-framed house there, dating from about the turn of the seventeenth century, when the estate was acquired. The house was greatly enlarged, very successfully in the same style, by the architect Devey. Though Lionel was still alive when the house was begun, Leo was probably responsible for the choice of the architect. He certainly had artistic tastes, and had taken regular lessons from an R.A., Aster Courbold, while at Cambridge.

Despite his other interests, indeed in part because of them, Leo was also active in promoting the business and the wider political and religious objects of the family, which occupied an increasing part of their time and attention. It was probably because of their shared interest in horse racing that Leo was in charge of the correspondence with the bank's main associate in New York, August Belmont. At any rate, the breeding and racing of horses was one of the regular topics discussed, along with business and politics, in the letters Leo wrote. And more than one object could be pursued on an English racecourse.

Yet wherever the family went, and whatever its pursuits, Natty was the dominating figure in the background. It was perhaps as well that his brothers were as they were and could look after public relations, for geniality and expansiveness were not Natty's strong suits. He was economical of words, which added to an outward frostiness that could be glacial. Sir William Harcourt gleefully recorded the following account Natty had given him on one of his morning calls. Henry Chaplin had

> invited him to dinner and told him he had pressed Lord Salisbury on the subject of Bimetallism and that Lord Salisbury had said that there was no use his (Chaplin) moving in the matter unless he could get Lord Rothschild with him; to which Lord Rothschild replied, 'Then I can tell you it is no use your moving at all.'[10]

Sometimes Natty simply said nothing. Mrs James de Rothschild vividly remembers her first meeting with him. Jimmy, as he was known in the family, had taken his bride to 148 Piccadilly to introduce her to its head. It was out of season, and as usual Lady Rothschild had gone to the country and virtually shut up the house. Natty was in one of the drawing rooms amidst the dust covers, his back to the fireplace and his hands folded behind him. Jimmy introduced her. Without unfolding his arms or in any other way acknowledging her presence, Natty turned and started talking to Jimmy.

As on this occasion, his wife was often not there to ease the situation. The passion had gone out of their marriage. It had started in passion, and far from being arranged had been the result of their own deliberate decision, almost in defiance of the rest of the family. Emma had, as Connie enviously recorded in her diary, given herself 'to the man of her own choice, to the man of her heart'.[11] What happened thereafter is not easy to say. Natty clearly found it difficult to show affection. So it seems did she. Connie was not always an acute judge of character. But she was fond of Emma, and there is reason to believe that the character sketch she did of her in 1858, at Emma's own request, is broadly accurate. She began by saying that Emma had conquered selfishness, and had come to see that being provoking was not kind. But Connie thought Emma formed 'her opinions too hastily and does not judge kindly enough of the faults of others'. Connie went on:

> People call her cold . . . She is only reserved but not cold, her feelings do not lie at the surface and they are only roused by strong means. Her disposition is not very generous, but she is appreciative and kindhearted. She is

ROTHSCHILD HOUSES AND HUNTING HAUNTS, BUCKS

Their country homes were within easy reach of London enabling the Rothschilds
to combine their passion for hunting with an active business life in the City

'NATTY', FIRST LORD ROTHSCHILD

The resurgence of anti-semitism on
the Continent began in earnest almost
simultaneously with Natty's becoming
the head of the bank and the family and
was one of his major concerns for
the rest of his life

'The whole of British capital
having been exported to
the South Pole as a result of/the
Budget Revolution, Lord Rothschild
flees from St Swithin's Lane,.
and succeeds in escaping to
the Antarctic regions disguised
as a penguin.'
(*Westminster Gazette*,
6 December 1909)

intelligent, ingenious and persevering. Her imagination is small and I do not think her mind can easily produce.[12]

In some ways perhaps Emma and Natty were too alike, shy, aloof and outwardly cold. Partly because of her upbringing in highly orthodox and straight-laced Frankfurt, Emma was also somewhat narrow and prudish in her views. At any rate, the marriage cooled. Their third and last child, Nathaniel Charles, was born in 1877, when she was only thirty-three.

In due course, among other doors outside which Lord Rothschild's carriage was often seen to stand, was Lady Gosford's. She was generally thought to be his mistress. Whether she was in the full sense of the word is unclear. Alfred and the former Mlle Marie Boyer, who enjoyed a marriage of convenience with a gentleman of the unlikely name of Wombwell, provided the irrefutable proof in the form of a daughter, Almina, who married the Earl of Carnarvon. In their case, little effort was made to take advantage of the cloak of respectability so obligingly provided by Mr Wombwell, and it was generally known that Almina was the bachelor Alfred's daughter. Indeed her name proclaimed the fact – Marie was generally known as Mina!

Natty was more discreet. His private correspondence was destroyed, and when Lady Gosford appears in his more public correspondence it is merely as the recipient of innocuous favours. As he did for numerous other friends, he arranged special treatment for her on Continental railways, for example. Perhaps more revealing is the letter he wrote to the future Lord Haldane seeking information on where he could get a copy of Haldane's translation of Schopenauer for Lady Gosford, who was anxious to have one.[13] Probably as much as anything, the 'solitary hermit' craved company and good conversation.

It was a typically well-bred Edwardian relationship. Natty was friendly as well with the Earl of Gosford, who was in succession a Lord in Waiting to the Prince of Wales and Vice Chamberlain in the Household of Queen Alexandra, to whom Lady Gosford would in turn serve as a Lady in Waiting after her husband's death in 1922. The Gosfords often stayed with Leo at Ascott. Not surprisingly, Lady Gosford would appear to have been in sharp contrast to Lady Rothschild in appearance and personality. Of the latter, the Major-Domo at Chatsworth, an ex-Colonel of Carbiniers, once loudly enquired: 'Who is that? A foreigner I presume – rather beaky.' Connie, though admitting that Emma's nose was 'rather too long', summed up the general impression she created: 'Tall and thin, she looks extremely distinguée.'[14] Her photographs suggest that this was an accurate description. Lady Rothschild was handsome and distinguished, not beautiful. Lady Gosford was the beautiful daughter of an even more beautiful mother, the Duchess of Manchester, Hartington's mistress who would ultimately become his wife. And Lady Gosford was clearly not prudish.

Natty's friendship with Lady Gosford seems to have done nothing to harm his relations with his wife. Indeed their marriage appears to have been a happy one in much the same way his own parents' marriage had been, based on affection and respect after the passion cooled. Both enjoyed entertaining, and they invited a wide and distinguished circle of friends, to Piccadilly and to Tring.

Pevsner describes Tring Park as 'brick with French pavilion roofs; nothing outside specially splendid or showy'.[15] Significantly, there is no mention of its origins in a Wren house; Natty managed to obscure the older structure in the course of a significant enlargement of the house in 1889. There is certainly nothing unpleasant in the present house, which in the winter months can be viewed plainly from the London end of Tring High Street, which the park walls parallel for a considerable distance. The impression it gives is one of solid and substantial comfort – in a magnificent setting. The town of Tring is built on the lower slopes of the Chilterns; the house commands superb views of their heights, up towards which the park runs for some way. Natty found his aesthetic outlet in nature, in flowers and trees, as the park still testifies.

It was a lovely and appropriate setting for the steady round of late Victorian and Edwardian house parties which took place there. The Milners, the Chamberlains, and Rhodes came. Randolph Churchill was a frequent guest. The Gladstones came for three days in 1893, much to the consternation of the radical press, which feared that the aged premier might be corrupted by imperialist notions: 'It is not nice at this juncture, when the foreign secretary is closely connected by marriage with the same intriguing financial house, to see Mr Gladstone hobnobbing with Lord Rothschild.'[16] Arthur Balfour was another frequent visitor. Edward VII, as Prince and King, came more than once. On one of these occasions, a little girl who had waited a long time outside the Natural History Museum, Walter's creation, to see the famous personage was somewhat disappointed: 'The king looked just like Lord R.'[17]

Natty was a very English phenomenon. There can be no doubt he thought of himself as one. When Rhodes died early in 1902, Natty wrote to a select circle giving them advance information on how his vast fortune would be spent. Rhodes's latest biographer has observed that it was probably Natty's influence which was mainly responsible for transforming 'the mad scheme for a secret society into that which was to set up the Rhodes Scholarships'.[18] The latter scheme was announced in Natty's letter: 'Oxford will be able to offer inducements to Colonials, even Americans, to study on the banks of the Isis and to learn, as Rhodes did there, to love his country and to make it big and prosperous.' The rest of the fortune, Natty went on, 'his Trustees will have to spend in the interest of, and for the development of the Anglo-Saxon race'.[19] Clearly Natty thought there was nothing incongruous in a Jew undertaking such a task. Natty was an Englishman, above temptation.

It is a cruel and bitter irony that the resurgence of anti-semitism on the Continent began in earnest almost simultaneously with Natty's becoming head of the bank and the family. For the rest of his life the struggle to roll back a tide which left Britain itself by no means untouched, would be one of his major concerns. Anti-semitism hung over his life like a great black shadow, a cloud regularly crossing his mind. And of course he was not alone. Others might find it easy to forget that Lord Rothschild was a Jew. He never forgot it.

Bleichröder himself, Natty told Disraeli in November 1880, was one of the reasons for the outbreak of persecution in Germany in that year.[20] It was a theme to which he would often recur, and it is a measure of his preoccupation that when he wished to criticize the behaviour of another Jew he would frequently evoke this spectre. In 1899, for example, in the course of some disagreements about Ferdy's will with the latter's brother Salbert, Natty wrote to Alphonse: 'If the policy which he pursues in Vienna is at all similar to his conduct towards his relatives of late the only thing I can say is, "I am astonished there is so little anti-semitic feeling in Vienna".'[21] Salbert, as Natty had not failed to remind Alphonse, was the latter's son-in-law.

227

Jews had constantly to remember who they were, and to conduct themselves accordingly. There is no evidence that Natty acted any differently than he always had, or that he ever dreamt any change of conduct would be appropriate. Rothschilds behaved responsibly, but it was no part of his formula that they should sacrifice their dignity or yield in their pride. Indeed it was their duty to maintain both for the sake of their people. Natty was Lionel's son, and as the peerage showed, he never forgot that his own achievements had a wider significance. None of the family did. In 1890, when he declined reelection as a Director of the Bank on the grounds of ill health, Alfred observed: 'It is now 22 years since I had the honour and privilege of being elected a Director of the Bank of England, a compliment of which any one of us may justly feel proud; and in my individual case it was a double honour and a double privilege, since I was the first member of the Jewish Faith who was permitted to take part in the direction and management of one of the greatest financial institutions in the world.'[22] A Rothschild achievement was an achievement for all Jews, everywhere. Lest anyone forget, they pointed it out on every possible occasion.

That they felt the need to do so is another measure of how preoccupied they were with the Jewish question. Had there been any danger of their forgetting the importance of their every action, others would have reminded them. To quote the *Labour Leader* of 19 December 1891 on the subject of the Rothschilds:

> This blood-sucking crew has been the cause of untold mischief and misery in Europe during the present century, and has piled up its prodigious wealth chiefly through fomenting wars between States which ought never to have quarrelled. Wherever there is trouble in Europe, wherever rumours of war circulate and men's minds are distraught with fear of change and calamity you may be sure that a hook-nosed Rothschild is at his games somewhere near the region of the disturbance.[23]

The famous passage in which Hobson talks of the 'peculiar race' which, according to him, dominated European finance, and holds it inconceivable that any European war could take place without Rothschild approval, is the same kind of thing stated in slightly more acceptable language.[24] Good Liberal that he was, Hobson would undoubtedly have been shocked to be charged

228

with having fomented anti-semitism; this only made the sentiments he expressed the more dangerous. Nor were such opinions in any sense confined to the left, they were also to be found on the right of politics.[25] The fact that they were unfounded did not prevent them from being widely held.

The Rothschilds acted to stem the tide of prejudice not only as individuals, but as bankers. The Jewish question is the great exception to the rule that they never attempted to use their financial power to dictate political policy to potential customers. The Rothschilds had given up a lucrative Russian business in the 1870s in deference to the policies of their own government. They failed, indeed refused, to compete vigorously for it again because of the policies of the Russian government, which not only did not discourage, but actively encouraged, the pogroms that started again in the 1880s after a liberal interlude. Care was taken to leave the Czar's government in no doubt as to why its approaches were treated coolly. Walter, on behalf of New Court, wrote to Bleichröder, who was associated in the negotiations of 1890:

It is evident the Russian Government has entirely misunderstood the accusations brought against them. It is not the question of new laws being promulgated against the Jews but the putting in force of the existing ones which have been held suspended for some time and which are so harsh and oppressive that they may be the cause of many Jews becoming violent Nihilists. We hope you can use your powerful influence at St. Petersburg to prevent the Government from putting into force the old cruel and senseless laws.[26]

Negotiations continued sporadically, and the Rothschilds continued to make their scruples and their objectives plain. At the end of June 1906, Natty put the matter succinctly, as only he could, to the representative Count Witte, the Russian Finance Minister, had sent to bring New Court around. Natty reported to his Paris cousins the following conversation with the representative, DeBrandt:

As far as I understood him, the remedy is a very simple one. Make a big loan for Russia, and something may be done for the Jews! I told him that he was putting the cart before the horse, namely, that when the Russian Jew has liberty and equal rights, Russian finance would improve and the Treasury difficulties would be considerably less.[27]

It could not have been put more plainly. DeBrandt, Natty reported was taken aback, claiming that Bleichröder, Mendels-shon, and the French bankers had never mentioned the Jewish question in connection with finding money. He was given to understand that their attitude was of no concern to N. M. Rothschild & Sons. In October 1907, Natty observed to his French cousins: 'I do not flatter myself if I say that the name of Rothschild would undoubtedly add prestige to a Russian loan.'[28] Unless and until Russia's policy toward the Jews changed for the better, it was prestige a Russian loan would not get. It was as simple as that – or almost.

In fact, it had taken the English Rothschilds a while to adopt such a clear-cut position. They had been reluctant to cut the Russians off completely, and they had continued a considerable business with them. Natty made this plain in justifying to Brett his proceedings over the threatened Baring bankruptcy in 1890. Rothschilds took a leading role in the successful effort to save Barings, but not as large a role as the latter's senior partner, Lord Revelstoke would have liked, or as B. Currie, of the Bank of England, originally suggested. Currie's proposal was that Rothschilds 'and three or four others should lend the Barings four millions to tide over their difficulties'. After giving the situation careful thought, Natty told Brett, he had refused on these grounds:

> The Russian Government had months before begun to deposit with Rothschilds. They now have a large sum belonging to the Russian Government. No doubt they are alarmed at the Barings' speculations in Argentine, as the Barings formerly held all the securities of the Russian Government. The moment there was a suspicion of the Barings' house, Staal received a telegram ordering him to withdraw the Russian deposits. Had Natty supported B. Currie's original proposal, that order would have extended to the Rothschilds – it might have commenced a run upon them – a debâcle.[29]

Nor, up to 1894, had the Rothschilds by any means cut the Russians off from loans. In 1889 two issues of a total of almost

£78m converted Russian debts from securities bearing five percent to new ones bearing four percent interest. An issue of close to £12 m the next year had a similar effect, and in 1894 there was a new issue of some £11 m for a three and a half percent loan. In between, however, the Rothschild houses had abruptly withdrawn from a large conversion worth some $300 m because of a Russian decision to expel two-thirds of the Jewish community, about 20,000 people, from Moscow. Their action caused fury in St. Petersburg, and the officially inspired press attributed the so-called 'Rothschild incident' to 'strong pressure by the Israelite and Judeophile party in England, which, as it appears, has been irritated by certain administrative measures taken in Russia towards a portion of the Israelite population'. The Czar's government, it was promised, would not knuckle under to such pressure.[30] None the less, in private Russian officials were willing to suggest, as they had earlier, that loans would improve the situation of Russian Jews. Such assurances did not work after 1894. Russian officials who proposed them were treated to Lord Rothschild's salty aphorisms about horses and carts.

Yet, however firm a line Natty took with the Russian government, he was much less dogmatic in the advice he gave to his own. Early in January 1899 Schomberg McDonnell called at Rothschilds to enquire about the likelihood of a large Russian loan being raised in the English market. He reported the results of his enquiries to Lord Salisbury:

> Mr. Alfred Rothschild, who is extremely Russophobe says *No*, on no account.
>
> Lord Rothschild is less decided: he thinks his House could make or mar such a loan; if they brought it out it would not be particularly lucrative; and his inclination is adverse to the operation.
>
> But if the London market remains closed he is afraid that Russia may learn her own financial strength.

What concerned Natty was that the Russians would find the money they needed out of their own immense gold reserves.[31] There was another consideration as well. In discussing the Anglo-Russian agreement of 1907, Natty observed that he fancied 'some of our coreligionists will not be over pleased with this rapprochment, but I always tell them the cause of the Jews in

Russia will not be improved if it is supposed that they stir up enmity between England and Russia'.[32]

Natty took the broad view of one deeply versed in the ways of diplomacy towards the situation of the Russian Jews. For their sake, as well as for his country's, he wished to keep the Russians within reach of British pressure, which as far as money was concerned, meant Rothschild pressure. Neither did he wish to drive the Russians to extremes of any sort. A Rothschild loan could only be an effective carrot as long as it remained a possibility, and this meant that no doors should be closed completely.

Not only were the pressures the Rothschilds mobilized relatively subtle, they were also various. On 3 June 1908 Natty wrote to Paris about recent efforts for the Russian Jews:

> Our excellent brother Leopold saw His Majesty the King at Epsom yesterday and spoke to him on the subject. His Majesty promised to take the matter into his serious consideration and will consult with Sir Charles Hardinge . . . and with the English Ambassador in St. Petersburg what is the best course to pursue to bring about an amelioration in our co-religionists' fate. In accordance with His Majesty's desire we have written him a long letter explaining the facts as far as we know them.

The King was about to leave for Russia, and the Rothschilds wanted to have the question raised in the political discussions which would take place during the visit. They were not disappointed. It was decided that it would be impolitic for the King to raise the matter personally, but on 13 June Hardinge sent the Rothschilds a report of an interview between the British Ambassador and the chief Russian Minister, at which the former 'by His Majesty's orders . . . raised the question of the treatment of the Jews in Russia'. The latter, Stolypin, had been encouraging, though not specific enough for Natty's taste. On 16 June he reported further to Paris:

> I had a telegram from the racecourse at Ascot saying that the Meilach [Yiddish for King] was very pleased with his visit and had a very high opinion of the Premier. He thought that in a short time something will be done for the Jews . . .[33]

Obviously there were uses in having a brother who frequented the Royal Enclosure, and if the condition of the Russian Jews was little improved, it was not for lack of effort by highly placed friends. In December 1881, Natty had declined an invitation from Rosebery to go with him to look at 'some good yearlings, but what with City business and the condition of the Jews in Russia, I have my hands full'.[34] So it started, and so it would continue. Natty and his brothers worked hard for their fellow Jews.

There is a school of historians who believe that all of human activity, more especially the activity of the rich, is self-interested. Few would deny that there is some truth in this. As a sole explanation of all human endeavour it is, however, rather inadequate.

One application of this view would be in regard to the plight of the Russian Jews, and would see efforts to ameliorate their condition as arising from a desire to keep them in Russia, and therefore out of Britain where they might create an unpleasant situation for British Jews. This seems to ignore the fact that the Russian Jews themselves would have preferred to remain in Russia, and that the Rothschilds acted at the urgent entreaties of their representatives. It is true that there was a deep fear among British Jews, and the Rothschilds certainly shared this fear, that an influx of wretched and destitute foreigners would increase anti-semitism in Britain.

Yet it is unwise to read more than the obvious into an account Natty sent to Paris in the same letter in which he reported the impressions of 'the Meilach':

> Today the Senate of the University of Cambridge published the results of the examination in Mathematical honours, and a little Jew who was first educated at the Jews' Free School was Senior Wrangler. His father fled from Odessa some years ago. I believe he used to preach in a small synagogue. He is now foreman in a small tailoring business where he receives high wages and teaches in one of the small Cheders. Such a boy might have done benefit to Russia. I hope he will do well here.[35]

Some, however, would read more than the obvious into this account, not as regards the desirability of Russian Jews staying in Russia, but over what happened to them when they got to

Britain. *Embourgeoisement* was evidently Natty's ideal. There are some who see sinister implications in such an ideal. When, it is argued, the rich and powerful encourage those below them to adopt their ideals and follow their example, it can only be with the object of safeguarding their own position. What they have in mind is the preservation of the social system of which they form the top layer.

There was doubtless an element of this in Natty's thinking. As he had remarked to Disraeli in 1880, in discussing other reasons for German anti-semitism besides Bleichröder himself, one was 'the constant influx of Polish and Rumanian Jews who arrive in a state of starvation and are socialists until they become rich'.[36] Natty himself did not care for socialists, and therefore he would undoubtedly have been anxious to promote the process of their becoming rich.

But there was more than one reason to dislike socialists. Aside from holding what he admitted was an enviable position in the existing social and economic system, Natty was convinced that it was the only one that would work. Under such circumstances, not only was it more comfortable for those at the top if those who could rise did, it was in their own best interests as well. Besides personal example, another way to promote the rise of the able poor was to provide exemplary conditions, decent housing and the opportunity for a good education. The Jews' Free School had been a favourite Rothschild charity from the beginning. In the 1880s, with the influx of refugees from the pogroms, the family took the leading role in providing new housing that would be clean, healthy, and cheap. The Rothschild Buildings would be all these things. The story is that Charlotte on her deathbed in 1884 had enjoined Natty to do something about housing in the East End of London. It is quite possible. At any rate, the meeting which founded the Four Per Cent Industrial Dwellings Company took place under Natty's auspices at the bank in March 1885. He subscribed £10,000 of the £40,000 initial capital, and personally bought, for £7,000, the land on which the building would take place. Later the bank would take charge of new issues of stock for the company. The Rothschild Buildings, and many of the families who got a start there, have had their historian. His conclusion is that they were 'the ugly offspring of a reluctant paternalism'.[37] Perhaps.

In attempting to consider the various interpretations put on

Rothschild actions, in this as in other matters, there is the danger of going in circles. They are taxed with not wanting foreign Jews in England. They are taxed with trying to make them English when they got them there. And they are taxed with, having made them English, not being enthusiastic enough in encouraging them to depart for the new land of Israel. They were undoubtedly cautious and conservative. They were deeply patriotic Englishmen. And because they were deeply patriotic Englishmen, Natty and his brothers were not Zionists.

They were, in short, not untypical products of their class and time. This involved attitudes that were sometimes unattractive. They often took a patronizing attitude toward lower class Jews. They were also made uncomfortable by what they felt to be caricature Jews, which sometimes gave rise to what in non-Jews would be considered anti-semitic remarks about appearances and characteristics. But such attitudes must not be removed from their wider context, and they must be seen in the light of all the evidence. That evidence is overwhelmingly in favour of the conclusion that the Jews had no more loyal, devoted and hardworking advocates than the three brothers, particularly Natty and Leo. On occasion, they did their work in strange places, but a racecourse is as good a place as any other for good works. Sometimes better.

What might be called their class prejudices were not limited to the Jewish community, and most of Natty's ideas about that community obviously had a wider significance. It was, for example, not only Jewish socialists whom he disliked and distrusted. Many of his remarks on social matters are almost a caricature of what he called 'the well known Manchester doctrine of free trade and laisser faire', a caricature which is heightened by the characteristic brevity and bluntness of his expression. There can be no doubt about where he stood as between that doctrine, and what he clearly identified as the opposing one that 'it is the paramount duty of the state to care for and foster the well being of all its citizens'. A policy based on the latter doctrine might be 'to a certain extent . . . very laudable'[38] but to a very limited extent indeed!

Natty's opinion, expressed to his French cousins, of Asquith's Budget of 1907, provides an eloquent example of the line he took. According to Natty:

All this increased taxation and spoilation is simply to provide the means and ways for a new form of outdoor relief in the shape of old age pensions to the not too industrious working man. I do not intend to argue upon the right or wrong of this policy from a political economical view, either now or in public, but diminished incomes mean a diminution of capital and less Income Tax. Increased Income Tax means less money to save and less capital liable to death duty.[39]

Despite Natty's disclaimer, it was a succinct statement of classical political economy, as well as suggesting the notions that underlay it. Workers required the strongest, indeed starkest, incentives to work, and capital must be left as free as possible to find its own level, without any artificial channelling.

This was the core of Natty's position. He sometimes stated his views in even more provocative terms. Fulminating the next year about the spread of semi-socialist policies everywhere, he went on:

Here, not content with introducing measures which are a violation of common sense and of political morality and which have no chance of passing, the Prime Minister promised a deputation of political ladies yesterday that at some future period he would introduce a bill granting female suffrage and a variety of other privileges for which no one cares or wants.[40]

There would be few modern political sacred cows which Natty did not at one time or another kick.

As usual with Natty, his bark was a good deal worse than his bite. However unyielding the views he might express within his own family, it was no less true of his attitude towards domestic than towards foreign politics, that he shunned conflict. Whatever he might say, he was strongly drawn towards compromise and conciliation. It was basic to his nature, a matter of the heart rather than the brain, but no less strong for that; and it was naturally strongest in cases which came most directly under his own attention. One such was the London Dock Strike of 1889, one of the first great labour demonstrations of the modern period. It was a potentially nasty situation, which would certainly have been nastier still but for the evenhandedness of the Metropolitan

Police and the successful efforts headed by Cardinal Manning to bring the employers to a substantial recognition of the strikers' claims. Natty was part of these latter efforts. On 7 September 1889 Gustave wrote of their pleasure that the Cardinal had 'taken our Cousin Natty as an intermediary. It is most honourable and excellent that the workers should know the sentiments of our family in their favour.' And on the 9th Alphonse congratulated Natty on the success of the mediators' efforts.[41] It was perhaps as well the dockers did not know Natty's sentiments. His actions, however, were all they could desire in this instance.

On their Bucks estates, the family had always thrown theory to the winds. On 10 July 1853, Louise had noted in her diary Bernal Osborne's *obiter dictum* that there was 'no greater evil in the country than a *Lady Bountiful*; there may be some truth in that remark – let me not be carried away therefore by the indolent luxury of giving, but try and do real good at our little Aston Clinton.'[42] Her resolve did not last long, and she was soon back at her old ways, lavishly distributing food and warm clothing. Two schools and a village hall remain a tangible reminder of her residence there. Aston Clinton is, as Pevsner observes, 'a Rothschild village'.[43] It is, of course, only one of a number. From one end of the Vale of Aylesbury to another, tons of bricks and mortar provide solid memorials of Rothschild benefactions. Natty was not behind the rest of the family. He built several hundred model cottages, as well as Victoria Hall for Tring. The town also got a large public park. He even provided a private health and social security system. It was more than his strict laissez-faire principles ought to have allowed, to say the least.

His principles did, however, lead Natty to take a prominent role in opposition to the policies of the Liberal governments between 1905 and 1914. Interestingly, he did not oppose the government on what had become the key issue for most religious groups, state support of religious schools. Protestant nonconformists had been violently opposed to such support since the 1870s, and the Liberal party represented their views. The Jews, in contrast, benefited from state support and favoured it, another bond for some with the Conservatives. Natty, however, was not willing to make an issue of the matter. In December 1908 Leo wrote to his Paris cousins that it looked as if the government's education measure would pass and it would be a great blessing indeed if by its means education was placed outside the pale of recriminations. My dear brother Nathaniel who understands this question admirably thinks it is the duty of the Jews to accept the measure, to leave the secular education of Jewish children to the care of the State. But the community must take upon itself the entire responsibility of providing the necessary funds for the religious education of the children.[44]

Natty was willing to pay the price if by this means education ceased to be a political football.

It was on another issue, on which the Liberal stand was also calculated to appeal to their traditional constituency, that Natty earlier in the same year had first felt it necessary to clash strongly and publicly with the Liberal government. This was over its Licensing Bill. The bill's object was to advance the cause of Temperance, so dear to the heart of many Protestant Nonconformists. The method by which the Liberals proposed to tackle this old and vexed problem was, after a few years grace period, to terminate all licenses for the sale of alcoholic drinks. The idea was that the government itself would then take charge of licensing, which would be done rather more sparingly. The problem was that most of the licensed premises were the property of the large breweries. The premises would clearly be much less valuable without the licenses. Therefore it was felt by many, as Leo explained to his French cousins, that the bill would amount to

> virtually nothing but confiscation. The leading brewery companies hold most of the public houses and have issued debentures at a comparatively low rate of interest to the public. These have always been considered an excellent security.[45]

Natty chaired large public meetings of debenture holders to protest and otherwise put himself at the head of public opposition to the bill. It strongly coloured his attitude to Liberal measures thereafter, and to him, and probably to most of his contemporaries, was of greater moment than what have become the more famous social reforms undertaken later. For its Liberal supporters, Temperance had long been a vital issue. On the other side of the question, Natty, commenting on a Unionist victory in the Peckham by-election, explained the wider significance of the proposed measure:

> The Licensing Bill is deservedly most unpopular with all classes. Not only would it destroy the Brewing Trade and restrict the comfort and amusements of the public, but it was a measure which threatened all kinds of property and might have inflicted severe harm in banking and financial circles, and if the principle embodied in this measure had once been conceded, everything and everybody might be expropriated for the so-called benefit of the state and without any compensation.[46]

Such opinions lay behind Natty's deep suspicion of Liberal measures, as well as behind what might seem the singular judgment that the dying Liberal Prime Minister, Campbell-Bannerman, was 'an advanced radical'.[47]

Natty's public opposition to the government over the Licensing Bill seems to have given him a taste for this kind of thing, and a prominent role was also urged upon him by the Conservative leadership. Late in March 1909 he appeared with Arthur Balfour at a large meeting at the Guildhall to press the government to meet the German naval challenge with more Dreadnoughts. When the Chancellor of the Exchequer in the new Asquith government, Lloyd George, proposed his famous Budget to pay for the Dreadnoughts and for what Natty called the government's 'profligate' old-age pension scheme, it was Natty who took the chair at a meeting of City magnates to oppose it. This evoked the well-known response from Lloyd George. In a speech in his best Limehouse style, the Chancellor enquired whether there was anything at all, any social measure the Liberal government could undertake without first securing the consent of Lord Rothschild?[48]

Certainly there was not much the government did that won Natty's approval. Lloyd George's 'people's Budget' was anathema to him. Besides increasing death duties and introducing a super-tax on incomes, the Budget also proposed to tax unearned increment in land and mineral values. It was the latter proposal which was most contentious. Natty saw it as raising a crucial issue. It was a juncture, he wrote in a letter to Paris in December 1909, probably as critical as 1688, a political event as important as when Simon de Montfort first vindicated the rights of Parliament:

You can be quite sure, my dear Edouard, if the theory is to prevail that the unearned increment of land is to belong to the state, there is nothing to prevent the unearned increment of all kinds of other property belonging to the state. When men fight with their back to the wall, they fight with vigour and courage, and like the 52nd at Albufuera, cost what it may they do not intend to be beaten. It is hard work but we all intend to do our duty.[49]

It was uncompromising language.

Natty referred specifically to the Lords' resistance to the Budget, and he made up one of the large majority which threw it out and thus precipitated the first general election of the following year. Though it assured a victory for the Budget, little else was settled and new problems were raised by the results of that election. The Liberal party itself lost seats, so many that it lost its independent majority; that now depended in the final analysis on eighty-two Irish Nationalists. Both this latter fact and the circumstances which had precipitated the election in the first place, focused attention on the House of Lords, who had long stood in the way of Irish aspirations as well as of Liberal social reforms. Not surprisingly the government concluded that the Lords' power to block legislation must be removed.

The result was a prolonged constitutional crisis, exacerbated by the death of Edward VII and the succession of the shy and inexperienced George V. In the end the government produced a Parliament Bill which removed the Lords' powers over money bills altogether and gave them only a two years suspensory veto in other matters. The Lords would have none of this, and another general election took place.

It left the party balance virtually the same, which the Lords did not consider a sufficient mandate to warrant a constitutional revolution. The deadlock continued until the summer of 1911, when it finally became clear that, if necessary, a reluctant monarch would have to break it by creating enough new peers to pass the measure. Significant Unionist opinion in both Houses, well aware of the implications for the Union, favoured resistance to the bitter end, but Balfour and the Marquess of Lansdowne were not among those who took this line, and Natty followed his leaders, as he had throughout. Lansdowne, Natty reported to Paris on 24 July, had advised the Unionist peers to acquiesce in the bill and about two-thirds were prepared to do so. But, he went on, a minority

> talk of dying in the last ditch and . . . as numerically they might be stronger than the Government peers in the House of Lords it would then become necessary for Lord Lansdowne and others like your humble servant to support the Government, which to say the least of it would not be a pleasant task.[50]

Pleasant or not he was prepared to do it. However strongly he might on occasion speak, Natty was no 'Ditcher'.

He was horrified by the violent language and behaviour of some of his Unionist colleagues. In what Natty described as a 'disgraceful scene', the Prime Minister was howled down in the House of Commons. The Unionist leaders themselves were sometimes treated with scant respect. In describing the intrigues against Balfour and Lansdowne, Natty told his French cousin that

> the large majority of the recalcitrants are hot-headed young bloods and old bloods too, who do not weigh the consequences of their actions. However there is still time for them to repent and one must have patience and not lose one's head or one's temper.[51]

Keeping his head and his temper were things Natty had always been good at. This makes all the stranger, allegations that in the last great political crisis in which he played a part, Natty took a line which could leave little doubt that he had lost both. Yet in the last decade, at least three books have repeated the charge that in the Home Rule crisis of 1914, Natty promoted armed resistance in Ulster; that he encouraged civil war.[52]

Briefly stated, the background is this. The Ulster crisis of 1914 was in a sense an outcome of the events of 1910 and 1911. The political leverage which the elections of the former year had given to the Irish Nationalists was one of the reasons for the Parliament Act of 1911. That gave the Lords the power only to block the Home Rule measure first introduced in 1912 for two years. In 1914 time had run out. Meanwhile, in Ulster the response had been violent; and the introduction of the Home Rule measure had seen, in the formation of the Ulster Volunteers, the founding of a movement prepared for armed resistance if necessary. In the first six months of 1914, strong efforts were made in Britain itself to give full support to the Ulster position. These efforts centred around Viscount Milner, and it was in his papers that the evidence supposedly incriminating Natty was found.

It must be said at the outset that that evidence appears to be slight and unconvincing. It is difficult to be stronger than that, because the crucial documents seem to have disappeared. The only book to cite them is Professor Gollin's; the two others have followed him. They are not among Milner's papers at the Bodleian, at any rate not among his papers on the Ulster crisis or in any other obvious place, and were not there when the papers were catalogued.

One must therefore rely on Professor Gollin and his description of the evidence. Beyond promoting a public pledge that its signatories would take whatever means were necessary to support Ulster's resistance to the Home Rule scheme and incorporation in it, Gollin claims that Milner and his lieutenants collected a large fund of money to back their objective. One of the alleged subscribers was Lord Rothschild.

The evidence Gollin cites is two documents, undated and bearing no other identification than the endorsement 'Very Secret'. One contains a list of names with an identifying letter; the other a list of letters with a sum of money written beside each. Lord Rothschild was 'D', and the sum written beside 'D' on the other list was £10,000.[53]

On the face of it, undated and unidentified lists of this sort seem slight evidence for the case built upon them; but it is always difficult to judge evidence one cannot see for oneself. In Milner's correspondence promoting the pledge, Natty's name appears on several lists. Only one is identified, though not in a very illuminating way: 'Names on various lists and suggested in correspondence.' On all the lists, his name appears in association with some who refused to sign the pledge as well as with some who did, and it never appears associated with any sums of money.[54] So much for the evidence in the Milner papers.

The evidence which exists elsewhere, in the Royal Archives and in Natty's own correspondence, is strongly and clearly against his involvement in any such scheme as Gollin describes. In mid-February 1914 Natty was playing his usual mediating role, approaching such militant Unionists as Bonar Law, the Conservative leader, and Geoffrey Robinson, the editor of *The*

Times, on the King's behalf.[55] His own letters to his French cousins, while leaving no doubt of his horror and revulsion at the idea of coercing Ulster, give no hint that he would have supported violence. Quite the contrary, as for example on 19 March:

> It will be a bold man who would venture to prophesy what will happen at the last moment – will the Unionists maintain their present stubborn resistance, will the Government be less peremptory in its refusals, who can tell, but in the meanwhile it is very unpleasant, disagreeable, I may even say painful literature to read of warlike preparations being made on both sides and sailors and artillery men spoken of as if England was going to embark on a real and serious military campaign. Hitherto at the crucial moment common sense and good will on both sides have proved to be such very strong factors that the danger has been averted and the problem has been solved. Will history repeat itself on this occasion. I earnestly hope so . . .

And on 2 July 1914, he wrote:

> Some very prominent Anti-Home Rulers take no pains to conceal their disappointment and their anger at the course of events, or namely the Parliament Act which has made the passage of a Home Rule Bill a certainty – but the verdict of a great majority of Unionists can be summed up in a few words – 'It is our imperative duty to do everything which will in all probability prevent Civil War.'[56]

Somehow it is difficult to believe that Natty had ever done less than his duty.

The fears of July were tragically stilled by the guns of August, and the country once more pulled together against the common enemy. Natty eagerly did what he could, as financial adviser to governments, as head of the British Red Cross, and as Lord Lieutenant of Bucks. He died on March 31st 1915. Emma wrote to the King that the last time he was able to sign his name, 'it was to forward a recommendation for a young Buckinghamshire man for a commission!'[57] Natty quietly did his duty to the end.

Leo lived till 1917, Alfred till 1918. But the greatness had gone out of New Court.

EPILOGUE

The English Rothschilds reached the apogee of their influence under the first Lord Rothschild. It was not only Randolph Churchill who turned to him constantly. So, in varying degrees, did practically every major British statesman of his period. Even Lloyd George did in the end.

Natty himself cannot take all the credit, though he deserves a great deal. If it was not he who had made N. M. Rothschild a great power in the land – Nathan and Lionel had done that – he ably maintained its power and prestige. His influence as a politician and statesman in part rested on the position of the bank, but it also rested on his own personality and special political talents. True, talent cannot develop without opportunity. Natty was the first Rothschild whose education, and the friendships that had grown out of it, fitted him to be an habitué of the inner sanctums of power. Yet whatever his predecessors might have done given the same opportunities, Natty made the most of his. He made himself indispensable to governments of every hue.

Natty himself, then, was part of the reason that N. M. Rothschild & Sons' greatness and that of the family was diminished after his death, but it was also partly a matter of chance. If there were no individuals of the same stature to take advantage of opportunities, neither were there the same opportunities.

The two World Wars of this century have been paradoxical in their effect in that the victors often seem to have emerged more seriously weakened than the vanquished. Great Britain's position in the world was certainly lessened by the First World War, not least financially. British assets had to be poured into the war effort, at the expense of her foreign investments, and she had to seek loans abroad. The United States, particularly, benefited and by the 1920s it was clear that the financial capital of the world had shifted from London to New York. The position of N. M. Rothschild & Sons was bound to be diminished.

Nor were those who succeeded Natty at the bank of the sort

who would struggle hard to maintain its position. His elder son had given up almost before he had started, and though Walter kept up a nominal association with the firm until 1908, it had been evident for a long time that banking was not his metier. Zoology was, and the collection he assembled at Tring, now part of the British Museum of Natural History, remains a tangible monument to his stature in his chosen field. Only in the affairs of his co-religionists did Walter follow in his father's footsteps. It was to him that Natty's old friend Arthur Balfour addressed his famous Declaration about a future Jewish homeland, not so much out of friendship as out of recognition of inevitable pre-eminence. To what other British Jew than the reigning Lord Rothschild could Balfour have addressed himself?

Walter's younger brother, Nathaniel Charles, though it was by the latter name that he was usually known, would also have preferred a career in science. As it was, he had to become the world's foremost authority on fleas in his spare time. Bitterly disappointed in Walter, Natty had leaned all the more heavily on his younger son, concentrating his hopes on him. Charles was the dependable one, and Charles did his duty, and even did it with distinction, but at heavy personal cost. Naturally a depressive, the unwanted responsibilities of the bank and being *de facto* head of the family must have seemed almost unbearable, and when to this burden was added physical illness, the load became too much to bear. In 1923 at Ashton Wold, to which he had first been attracted by the rare butterflies found there, Charles took his own life. His daughter, Miriam, deals with this generation of Rothschilds in her forthcoming book on her uncle and his family circle, *'Dear Lord Rothschild': Birds, Butterflies and History*.

With Charles's death, the management of the bank passed to Leo's two sons, Lionel and Anthony. The times were difficult, and theirs was essentially a holding operation. It is with the present generation, since the last war, that N. M. Rothschild & Sons has once again become lively and competitive. This has occurred under the chairmanship of Lionel's son Edmund, and Anthony's son Evelyn. The financial daring and brilliance of the present Lord Rothschild's son Jacob has also played a large role. There have recently been differences of opinion within the firm, and Jacob has left to devote himself full time to his brainchild R.I.T., formerly Rothschild Investment Trust; but, while some question his judgment, no one doubts his outstanding abilities.

The present Lord Rothschild, Charles's son, though now chairman of the holding company that controls the bank, has not spent most of his career there. He has in fact had several careers, as a Cambridge zoologist, an executive of Shell, and a civil servant. He has always been lively and controversial, most recently as the author of *An Enquiry into the Social Science Research Council* (1982), undertaken at the request of Sir Keith Joseph, Secretary of State for Education and Science. As of this writing, the academic dovecotes are still fluttering – in relief.

Other members of the family are noted as scientists, authors, gardeners, art collectors and racehorse owners. The variety of interests and talents remains impressive. The Rothschilds are alive and well.

NOTES

INTRODUCTION

1. J. A. Hobson, *Imperialism: A Study* (1902), esp. p. 64. 'Does any one seriously suppose that a great war could be undertaken by any European State, or any great State loan subscribed, if the house of Rothschild and its connections set their face against it?'
2. See Fritz Stern, *Gold and Iron: Bismarck, Bleichröder and the Building of the German Empire* (1977).
3. Quoted in John Pope-Hennessy, ed., *Baron Ferdinand de Rothschild's Livre d'Or* (privately printed for presentation to the Roxburghe Club by Lord Rothschild, Cambridge, 1957), p. 189.
4. See Chaim Bermant, *The Cousinhood* (1971).
5. Todd M. Endelman, *The Jews of Georgian England, 1714–1830* (Philadelphia, 1979), p. 112.
6. Abraham Gilam, *The Emancipation of the Jews in England, 1830–1869* (New York, 1982).
7. RAL T27, (1805).
8. Ibid., T5, Mayer Amschel to Nathan, 29 Oct. 1809.
9. See, for example, the letter cited in fn. 7.

Chapter I

NATHAN

1. Joseph Aston, *The Manchester Guide* (1804), p. 27.
2. RAL, N. M. Rothschild to Mr Fox, 27 Oct. 1807. Signed by Hannah Rothschild in N. M.'s absence.
3. Charles Buxton, ed., *Memoirs of Sir Thomas Fowell Buxton* (1849), p. 289.
4. Various dates have been given, but this is the one suggested by Nathan's own remarks near the time. In June 1802 he said he had been in Manchester three years (RAL 218/1, Manchester Letter Book, 30 June 1802). In February 1803 he said 'nearly four years' (*ibid.*, 9 Feb. 1803). For the Manchester business address, see RAM, Manchester Letter Book, 1800–02, fos. 25, 40, and 60. For his house, see Lucien Wolf, *Essays in Jewish History* (1934), p. 270.
5. RAL 218/1, N. M. to Lyon de Symons, London, 20 Aug. 1803.
6. Buxton, *Memoirs*, p. 289.
7. Bertrand Gille, *Histoire de la Maison Rothschild: des Origines a 1848* (Geneva, 1965), p. 458.
8. RAL T 27/23, Mayer Amschel Rothschild to N. M. (1805).
9. RAM, Manchester Letter Book, 1800–02; RAL 218/1, Manchester Letter Book, 1802–4, *passim*.
10. *Ibid.*, N. M. to Messrs. Tiebens and Liebrecht, Antwerp, 11 Aug. 1802.

11. *Ibid.*, N. M. to G. I. Elias, Frankfurt, 31 Oct. 1802.
12. *Ibid.*, N. M. to J. A. Matti, Frankfurt, 29 Dec. 1802.
13. *Ibid.*, N. M. to S. Geisenheim, à Metz, 9 Jan. 1803; to Joseph Anson Steiner, Munich, 23 Feb. 1803.
14. *Ibid.*, f. 103. For more information on Nathan's activities in the textile trade, see Stanley Chapman, *The Foundation of the English Rothschilds: N. M. Rothschild as a Textile Merchant, 1799–1811* (1977).
15. See the Manchester letter books, especially RAL 218/1, N. M. to Harman & Co., 1803; to E. Coulson, Hull, 18 Aug. 1803.
16. *Ibid.*, *passim*. The first reference to Cohen is a letter to him on 20 Oct. 1801 (RAM, Manchester Letter Book, 1800–02, f. 64).
17. RAL RFam FP/11, marriage settlement between N. M. and Hannah, 21 Oct. 1806.
18. For the Cohens, see Wolf, pp. 233–9.
19. See, for example, *ibid.*, p. 31.
20. See fn. 8.
21. RAL T2/16, Moses Alexander to N. M., 21 Feb. 1806 (Judendeutsch).
22. *Ibid.* T27/265, Carl Mayer to Salomon Mayer and James Mayer Rothschild, 18 May 1817 [hereafter C. M., S. M., and J. M.].
23. *Ibid.* T62/54/3, 5 June 1817.
24. *Ibid.* 109/27, Louisa to N. M. (Sept. 1831).
25. *Ibid.* RFam FP/16/0000/111.
26. See, for example, RAL 109/33–1, *passim*.
27. Quoted in Wolf, p. 276.
28. *Ibid.*
29. RAL T2/39 and T2/53.
30. RAL T27/13, Selig [Solomon] Cohen to N. M., 16 March 1808 (Judendeutsch).
31. *Ibid.* T29/14, S. M. to N. M., 17 Aug. 1814 (German).
32. *Ibid.* T27/105, C. M. to A. M., 9 Sept. 1814 (Judendeutsch).
33. *Ibid.* 218/1, Manchester Letter Book, N M. to Harman & Co., London, 30 June 1803.
34. On this whole matter, see Count Corti, *The Rise of the House of Rothschild*, translated from the German by Brian and Beatrix Lunn (1928), p. 85ff. Corti had access to Continental archives since destroyed.
35. Buxton, pp. 288–90.
36. Ronald Fieve, *Moodswing: The Third Revolution in Psychiatry* (New York, 1976).
37. Chapman, p. 19.
38. RAL T27/61, J. M. to N. M., 17 Aug. 1811.
39. On the whole matter of Nathan's involvement in financing Wellington's armies, see Lord Rothschild, *The Shadow of a Great Man* (1982).
40. B[ritish] L[ibrary] Add. MSS. 57367, ff. 12–26, J. C. Herries, a memorandum drawn up for Lord Liverpool and Nicholas Vansittart, 12 June 1816.
41. RAL T37/74, J. C. Herries to Deputy Commissary General Luscombe, 18 June 1814.
42. *Ibid.* T37/8 and 36, N. Vansittart to J. C. Herries, 11 Jan. 1814; J. C. Herries to N. M., 17 March 1814.
43. *Ibid.* T37/56, 15 May 1814.
44. *Ibid.* T37/42.
45. Gille, p. 458.
46. RAL T37/80, J. C. Herries to N. M., 4 Aug. 1814.
47. *Ibid.* T37/89, memorandum made at Cadogan Place by Mr Herries and Mr Rothschild, 14 April 1815.
48. RAL 109/6/126/2, C. M. to J. M., 25 April 1817.
49. *Ibid.* 109/8/69/2.

50. BL Add. MSS. 57367, ff.12–26.

51. See Corti, *Rise*, ch. III.

52. RAL T37/136, J. C. Herries to George Harrison, 5 Oct. 1816.

53. *Ibid.* 109/7/116/5, A. M. to C. M., 27 July 1817; 109/8/45/ln.

54. Gille, p. 458.

55. RAL 109/9/211/3, 20 April 1818.

56. *Ibid.* 109/8/5/1, S. M. and J. M. to N. M., 6 Nov. 1817; 109/8/138/2, same to same, 22 Oct. 1817.

57. *Ibid.* A. M. to N. M., 15 July 1814; C. M. to N. M., Frankfurt, 1814?

58. *Ibid.*

59. RAL 109/8/138/2.

60. BL Add. MSS. 57370 f.27, acknowledgement by Arbuthnot of a private loan from N. M., 4 Aug. 1820.

61. *Ibid.* 57367, fos. 12–26.

62. *Ibid.* 57398, f.64.

63. Printed in Lord Rothschild, *Shadow*.

64. *Ibid.*

65. T3/328.

66. See Lord Rothschild, *The Rothschild Family Tree* (1981).

67. RAL RFam FP/11.

68. I am indebted to the geographical expertise of Mrs J. Wagerman of the Jews' Free School.

69. RAL 109/4/1/5, N. M. to his brothers, 2 January 1816 (Judendeutsch).

70. *Ibid.* 109/513/299/2, A. M. to S. M. and N. M., 3 Nov. 1816.

71. *Ibid.* 109/4/3/195, 2 May 1816.

72. Wolf, p. 31.

73. RAL, a P. S. on S. M. to Hannah, 24 Aug. 1815.

74. Wolf, p. 31.

75. RAL T6/113, M. B. Kitzenger to N. M., 15 Oct. 1832 (German).

76. *Ibid.* 109/4/1/5, N. M. to his brothers, 2 Jan. 1816 (Judendeutsch).

77. *Ibid.* 109/0/2/41, S. M. to N. M., 24 June 1814.

78. *Ibid.* 109/0/3/61.

79. Quoted in Count Corti, *The Reign of the House of Rothschild*, translated from the German by Brian and Beatrix Lunn (1928), pp. 147–8.

80. RAL T42/4, 10 Feb. 1818.

81. *Ibid.* 109/4/2/63, C. M. to N. M., 11 Feb. 1816.

82. R[oyal] A[rchives] Y57/10, Edward (Duke of Kent) to Thomas Coutts, 13 May 1818; RAL T6/4, Captain Couray to N. M., 7 June 1821. I am grateful to Her Majesty Queen Elizabeth II for permission to use material in the Royal Archives.

83. RAL 109/7/36/2, S. M. to N. M., 12 May 1817.

84. A. Aspinall, ed., *The Letters of King George IV, 1812–1830*, 3 vols. (Cambridge, 1938), II, 47–8.

85. *Ibid.*

86. *Ibid.*, III, 175.

87. Jules Ayer, *A Century of Finance, 1804–1904: The London House of Rothschild* (1905), pp. 16–37.

88. RAL 109/5A/100/2, A. M. to J. M., 3 Aug. 1816.

89. Aspinall, II, 524.

90. Hansard's *Parliamentary Debates*, 2nd series, XVIII, 542–3.

91. Alfred Rubens, 'The Rothschilds in Caricature', *Transactions of the Jewish Historical Society of England*, XX (1968–69), 76–87.

92. BL Add. MSS. 38576, f.84.

93. RAL 150/0/R (Letter Book), 20 Dec. 1825.

94. Quoted in Lord Rothschild, *Shadow*.

95. RAL 150/0/R, N. M. to de Rothschild Bros., 28 Feb. 1826.

96. T37/158, 27 Sept. 1826.

97. RAL 109/48, Hannah to

Nathaniel and Anthony, 26 Dec. 1841.

98. *Ibid.*, T6/1, L. Boquet to N. M., 6 July 1821; 103/0, Hannah to Lionel and Nathaniel, 23 July 1839. On Nathan and the Jewish community, see also Wolf, pp. 275–6.

99. Board of Deputies of British Jews, Minute Book 2, 16 April 1829.

100. *Ibid.*, 3 May and 6 May 1829.

101. See Richard W. Davis, 'Toryism to Tamworth: The Triumph of Reform, 1827–1835', *Albion* (Summer 1980).

102. RAL RFam C/4/106.

103. *Ibid.*, /110 and 109.

104. *Ibid.*, /111 and 112.

105. *Ibid.*, /114.

106. *Ibid.*, /130.

107. *Ibid.*, RFam C1/62 and 67.

108. *Ibid.*, RFam C4/148.

109. Rubens, plate X.

Chapter II

HANNAH AND HER CHILDREN

1. Rosebery Papers, Hannah to Mayer, 15 Nov. 1836.

2. *Ibid.*, same to same (October 1837).

3. *Ibid.*, same to same, 11 Oct. 1836.

4. *Ibid.*, same to same, 26 May 1837.

5. *Ibid.*, same to same, 9 Nov. and 15 Nov. 1836, 26 May 1837.

6. Corti, *Rise*, 400.

7. RAL 109/13, Hannah to Charlotte, 3 July 1827; Anthony to his mother, 3 Dec. 1827; 109/14/4, same to same, 5 Feb. 1828.

8. *Ibid.*, T6/94, 8 Jan. 1829 (German).

9. *Ibid.*, 109/30/40.

10. *Ibid.*, 109/23, Nat to his father, 4 Feb. (1831).

11. *Ibid.*, 109/38, Lionel to his parents, 2 July 1834.

12. Rosebery Papers.

13. *Ibid.*

14. *Ibid.*, n.d.

15. *Ibid.*, 2 Nov. 1837.

16. *Ibid.*

17. Rosebery Papers, n.d.

18. G. M. Trevelyan, *Trinity College: An Historical Sketch* (Cambridge, 1972), pp. 91–5.

19. RAL RFam FP/5/10, Trustees of Baron and Baroness Mayer de Rothschild.

20. *Ibid.*

21. *Ibid.*, 101/2, James to nephews, 6 Nov. 1839.

22. *Ibid.*, 109/39/43, Anthony to Nat, 24 Oct. (1835); 109/52/56, Nat to his brothers, n.d. (1842).

23. *Ibid.*, 109/39/13, 21 March 1835.

24. *Ibid.*, 109/39/43, 24 Oct. (1835).

25. E.g. *Ibid.*, 104/0/62, Nat to his brothers, n.d. (1840).

26. *Ibid.*, 103/0/45, Anselm to his cousin, 23 July 1839, Paris; 104/0, Nat to his brothers, 2 June 1840.

27. *Ibid.*, 109/31/38 (Anthony) to Lionel, 28 Oct. 1837.

28. *Ibid.*, 101/2, James to Nat, 29 June 1839 and 16 July 1839.

29. *Ibid.*, 103/0/40, Anthony to his brothers, 17 July 1839.

30. *Ibid.*, RFam C/1/64, Hannah to Anthony, n.d.

31. *Ibid.*, 103/0/25, Hannah to Nat and Lionel, 27 May (1839).

32. *Ibid.*, 103/0/38, Anthony to his brothers, 11 July (1839).

33. *Ibid.*, RFam C/4/32, Lionel to his wife, 17 Aug. 1842.

34. *Ibid.*, 109/39/13, Lionel to Anthony, 21 March 1835.

35. *Ibid.*, RFam C/4 *passim.*

36. *Ibid.*, RFam C324/1, Anthony to (Nat), 16 June 1836.

37. Quoted in Cecil Roth, *The*

Magnificent Rothschilds (1939), p. 33.

38. Rosebery Papers, Hannah to Mayer, 15 Nov. 1836; and Louise and Hannah to Mayer, 11 Oct. 1836.

39. RAL T8/74, Charlotte to Lionel, n.d.

40. *Ibid.*, RFam P/D/1, Charlotte on 'Nathaniel', p. 1.

41. *Ibid.*, same on 'Leonora', pp. 7–8, 65–6 and 70.

42. *Ibid.*, 106–109.

43. *Ibid.*, p. 111.

44. *Ibid.*, p. 108.

45. *Ibid.*, 103/0/38, Anthony to his brothers, 11 July (1839); RFam FP/11, Marriage Settlement of Baron Mayer de Rothschild and Miss Juliana Cohen, 25 June 1850.

46. Buxton, p. 290.

47. RAF 109/24/42, Lionel to his mother, 27 April 1831; T7/4, 3 Oct. 1834.

48. *Ibid.*, 109/55, Nat to his brothers, 16 March 1843; T8/198, Nat to brothers, n.d. (1849).

49. Rosebery Papers, Hannah to Mayer, 10 May 1838.

50. H. M. Colvin, *A Biographical Dictionary of English Architects, 1660–1840* (1954), p. 545; *D.N.B.*

51. RAL 109/57/43, 6 May 1844.

52. *Ibid.*, RFam C/1/44, Hannah to Charlotte (Lionel), n.d. (1845).

53. *Ibid.*, C/1/36, Hannah to her sons, 14 June 1844.

54. Corti, *Reign*, pp. 64–5.

55. *Ibid.*, pp. 120 ff.

56. RAL 109/24, Lionel to his parents, 23 April 1831; to his mother, 27 April 1831.

57. *Ibid.*, 109/20, Lionel to his parents, 20 Nov. 1830; 109/24/22, 27 April 1831; 109/30/21, Lionel to his parents, 12 May 1832.

58. *Ibid.*, 109/31/74, Anthony to his mother, 4 Dec. 1832.

59. Ayer, pp. 37 ff.

60. BL Add. MSS. 57401, f. 46, Herries to Henry Goulburn, 12 Sept. 1841.

61. RAL Lo4/1/37, Anselm to cousins, 21 March (1841): 104/1/118, Nat to his brothers, n.d. (1841).

62. *Ibid.*, RFam FP/5/10.

63. *Ibid.*, 109/69A, 13 June (1847).

64. *The Times*, 9 July 1847.

65. *Ibid.*

66. RAL 109/70/1, Nat to brothers, n.d. (July 1847).

67. *The Times*, 14 July 1847.

68. RAL 109/69/1, n.d.

69. *The Times*, 12 July 1847.

70. *Ibid.*, 17 July 1847.

71. *Ibid.*, 29 July 1847.

72. RAL 109/63/1, Salomon to Lionel, 4 Aug. 1847 (German); Betty to Lionel, 4 Aug. 1847 (French).

73. *Ibid.*, 109/71/1, Nat to his brothers, 23 Dec. (1847).

74. *Ibid.*

75. *Ibid.*, 109/72/1, Nat to his brothers, 14 Feb. (1848); 109/73/1, same to same, 10 May 1848.

76. *Ibid.*, 19 June 1848.

77. *Ibid.*, 109/70.

78. *Ibid.*, RFam P/D/1, p. 60.

Chapter III

LIONEL AND HIS BROTHERS

1. *Vanity Fair*, 22 Sept. 1877.

2. RA Queen Victoria's Journal, 14 Nov. 1846.

3. RAL 109/58/1, Hannah to Lionel, n.d. Monday 1846; Anselm to Lionel, 24 Nov.

1846; Anthony to Lionel, n.d.

4. *Ibid.*, 104/1/91, Anthony to his brothers, 22 July 1841.

5. Charles H. L. Emanuel, *A Century and a Half of Jewish History* (1910), *passim*.

6. *Ibid.*, p. 52; BL Add. MSS. 40584, f. 396, Lionel to Peel, 10 Feb. 1846.

7. RAL 109/69A/3, 17 June 1847.

8. *Ibid.*, RFam C/4/49, Lionel to his wife, n.d. (July 1848).

9. Corti, *Rise*, pp. 244–5 and 311–12.

10. University of Southampton Library, typed excerpts from the Journals of Lady de Rothschild, vol. I, p. 8 (n.d. November 1847) and 110 (26 June 1850).

11. See my *Disraeli* (1976), pp. 80–8.

12. Journals of Lady de Rothschild, I, 77 (7 July 1849).

13. An excellent summary of the public aspects of the controversy will be found in Roth, pp. 45–54.

14. Journals of Lady de Rothschild, I, 110.

15. *Ibid.*, II, p. 3.

16. *Ibid.*, pp. 15–16.

17. RA A26/52.

18. Bodleian, Disraeli Papers, R 233d, 3 June 1879.

19. RAL RFam C/1/35, Hannah to Charlotte (L.), 3 June 1844.

20. *Ibid.*, RFam C/143, n.d. (1845).

21. *Ibid.*, RFam C/2/53, 25 Feb. 1847.

22. Journals of Lady de Rothschild, I, 102 (11 Feb. 1850).

23. *Ibid.*, pp. 7–8 (November 1847).

24. *Ibid.*, II, 20 (11 Jan. 1853).

25. *Ibid.*, I, 55 (20 Feb. 1849).

26. RAL RFam C/2/42, n.d.

27. Journals of Lady de Rothschild, I, 8.

28. RAL RFam C/6/1.

29. *Ibid.*, C/16/8, Juliana to Charlotte (L.), n.d.

30. Journals of Lady de Rothschild, I, 102 (11 Feb. 1850).

31. RAL RFam C/2/9, Disraeli to Charlotte (L.), 23 Nov. 1867.

32. *Ibid.*, 110.

33. Journals of Lady de Rothschild, I, 47–8.

34. *Ibid.*, 11.4

35. *Ibid.*, II, 28.

36. *Ibid.*, I, 104–5.

37. *Ibid.*, II, 12 (18 May 1852).

38. RAL RFam C/4/53, Lionel to his wife, 4 Feb. 1858.

39. *Ibid.*, 104/0/139, 21 Nov. 1840.

40. *Ibid.*, 109/43, correspondence with Edmund Carrington and J. Gleinster.

41. *Ibid.*, 109/44/13, 14 Mar. 1840.

42. *Ibid.*, 109/52, Richard Dawes to Mayer, 15 Oct. 1842; Hannah Rosebery, *Mentmore* (privately printed 1883).

43. *Ibid.*, 109/56/28, J. S. Brown to Mayer, 26 Jan. 1844.

44. *Ibid.*, 109/58/171, Lionel to his brothers, 7 Sept. (1844).

45. See my *Political Change and Continuity, 1760–1885: A Buckinghamshire Study* (1972), pp. 162–3.

46. G. E. C., *Complete Peerage*, under Rothschild and Rosebery respectively.

47. Robert Gibbs, *Buckinghamshire: A Record of Local Occurrences*, IV (1882), 3–85, *passim*.

48. Lord Crewe, quoted in G. F. Chadwick, *The Works of Sir Joseph Paxton* (1961), pp. 188–9.

49. Journals of Lady de Rothschild, II, 2 (22 May 1851).

50. RAL T7/33, Hannah to Charlotte (L.), 5 Nov. (1846?).

51. J. R. Vincent, ed., *Disraeli, Derby and the Conservative Party: The Political Journals of Lord Stanley, 1849–69* (1978), p. 27.

52. Chadwick, p. 188.

53. *Ibid.*

54. The whole of the above description draws heavily on *ibid.*, perhaps the last description of

Mentmore while it was still a house.

55. Rosebery Papers, Hannah's proof copy of *Mentmore*, in which original documents have been pasted in.
56. *Ibid.*
57. Chadwick, p. 195.
58. Journals of Lady de Rothschild, II, 13 and 31 (1 June 1852 and 23 Aug. 1853).
59. *Ibid.*, I, 7 (29 Oct. 1847).
60. Thomas Pinney, ed., *The Letters of Thomas Babington Macaulay*,

VI (Cambridge, 1981), 227–8.
61. Davis, *Political Change*, chs. 8 and 9, *passim*.
62. RAL T6/33, 6 March 1853.
63. RAL RFam C/10/4, Anthony to Lionel, 27 Aug. (1868?).
64. C. R. Dod, *Electoral Facts, from 1832–1853* (1972), pp. 151–2.
65. Roth, pp. 52–3.
66. RA G45/6, 22 Feb. 1856.
67. Quoted by Pope-Hennessy, p. 189.
68. RA Queen Victoria's Journal, 10 April 1856.

Chapter IV

CAMBRIDGE AND 'SOCIETY'

1. Davis, *Disraeli*, pp. 94–5 and *Political Change*, ch. 8.
2. *Ibid.*, p. 200; RAL RFam C/4/ 243 and 244.
3. *Ibid.*, C/4/345.
4. *Ibid.*, 109/73/1, J. A. Smith to Mayer, 15 Oct. 1849; James Cartmell to J. A. Smith, 14 Oct. 1849.
5. RA F 35 A/47, Mayer to Prince Albert, 22 Oct. 1849.
6. RAL 109/73/1, Arthur Cohen to Mayer, 21 Nov. 1849.
7. *Ibid.*, RFam C/3/110, Natty to his parents, n.d. (1859).
8. On the Cambridge curriculum during this period, see D. A. Winstanley, *Early Victorian Cambridge* (Cambridge, 1955), esp. pp. 168, 208, 213, 217–18, and 281–2. There is also a good summary in the same author's *Later Victorian Cambridge* (Cambridge, 1947), ch. v.
9. RAL RFam C/3/90 (23 Feb. 1860).
10. Winstanley, *Later Victorian Cambridge*, p. 188.
11. *Ibid.*, p. 144, and *Early Victorian Cambridge*, p. 282.

12. RAL RFam P/d/1, Charlotte on 'Alfred', p. 36.
13. *Ibid.*, quoted in Charlotte on 'Nathaniel', pp. 7–8.
14. Lord Rothschild, *Shadow*.
15. Corti, *Reign*, 450.
16. RAL RFam P/D/1, Charlotte on 'Nathaniel', pp. 26–7.
17. *Ibid.*, pp. 34–5.
18. *Ibid.*, RFam C/3/78, Natty to his parents, 26 Feb. (1860).
19. *Ibid.*, RFam C/3/111.
20. *Ibid.*, RFam C/3/12.
21. *Ibid.*, RFam C/3/20, Natty to his parents, 24 Mar. 1862.
22. *Ibid.*, RFam C/3/55 and 134.
23. *Ibid.*, RFam P/D/1, Charlotte on 'Nathaniel', p. 3.
24. *Ibid.*, p. 6.
25. *Ibid.*, RFam C/3/7.
26. *Ibid.*, RFam C/3/78, Natty to his parents, 26 Feb. 1860.
27. *Ibid.*, RFam C/3/111, 3 and 5.
28. *Ibid.*, RFam C/3/75.
29. *Ibid.*, RFam C/3/12.
30. *Ibid.*, RFam C/3/133 and 93.
31. *Ibid.*, RFam C/3/84, 102, and 79.
32. *Ibid.*, RFam C/3/67 and 9.

33. RA M64/60 and 61.
34. RAL RFam C/4/237, 2 Nov. 1863.
35. *Ibid.*, RFam C/19/45. A remarkably complete run of Lionel's letters to Leo will be found in RFam C/4.
36. *Ibid.*, RFam C/3/72.
37. *Ibid.*, RFam C/4/325, 25 May 1867.
38. Winstanley, *Early Victorian Cambridge*, p. 83 n.2, wrongly assumes that these negotiations were on Alfred's behalf. See also RAL RFam C/3/62.
39. *Ibid.*, RFam C/3/13, 12 Feb. 1861; *The Times*, 18 Mar. 1857.
40. *Ibid.*, RFam C/5/44 and 45.
41. *Ibid.*, RFam C/3/106.
42. Davis, *Political Change*, p. 197.
43. RAL RFam C/3/34, Natty to his parents, 25 Jan. 1863.
44. *Ibid.*, RFam C/4/93.
45. See the correspondence in Agatha Ramm, ed., *The Political Correspondence of Mr. Gladstone and Lord Granville, 1868–1876* (1952), p. 47ff.
46. RAL RFam C/4/92.
47. RAL RFam C/3/50, Natty to his mother, 6 Mar. 1868; C/8/29, Ferdy to the same, same date; C/16/14, Juliana to the same, same date.
48. BL Add. MSS. 48651, The Diary of Sir Edward Hamilton, 11 Aug. 1889.
49. RA GV GG1/1, Albert Edward to Alfred, 17 July 1865.
50. RAL RFam C/6/7.
51. *Ibid.*, RFam P/D/1, Charlotte on 'Evelina', pp. 44–6.
52. *Ibid.*, Charlotte on 'Leonora', p. 111.
53. *Ibid.*, RFam C/3/139.
54. Rosebery Papers, 9 Nov. 1878.
55. RAL RFam C/6/16, Evy to her parents, 12 Sept. 1861.
56. *Ibid.*, RFam C/6/41, Evy to her parents, 12 Jan. 1864.
57. *Ibid.*, RFam C/6/5, Evy to her parents, n.d.
58. *Ibid.*, RFam C/6/60, 63, and 57.
59. *Ibid.*, RFam C/6/92, n.d.
60. *Ibid.*, RFam C/4/324.
61. *Ibid.*, RFam C/8/68, 19 Dec. 1866.
62. *Ibid.*, RFam C/20/62, Louise (M.C.) to Charlotte (L.), 7 July 1866.
63. BL Add. MSS. 47916, f. 137; 47917, 17 April 1867; RFam C/16/24. I owe my information on Emma's account to her granddaughter, the Hon. Mrs Miriam Lane.
64. *Ibid.*, RFam C/3/40.
65. *Ibid.*, RFam C/5/94 and C/19/17.

Chapter V

HIGH FINANCE
AND HIGH POLITICS

1. RAL T49/12, copy John Forsyth to Barings, 6 Aug. 1834.
2. *Ibid.*, August Belmont to NMR, 9/10 Aug. 1839.
3. Ayer, pp. 40–1.
4. RAL T6/167, U.S. Department of State to NMR & Sons, 14 March 1843.
5. *Ibid.*, T10, p. 58, Mayer Carl to his cousins, 19 March 1870.
6. Anka Muhlstein, *James de Rothschild* (Paris, 1981), pp. 223–5; David Black, *The King of Fifth Avenue: The Fortunes of August Belmont* (New York, 1981), *passim.*; RAL T8/176, Lionel to Anthony, 15 Aug. 1849.
7. *Ibid.*, T9/23, C. J. Bidwell to

NMR & Sons, 7 Nov. 1863.

8. *Ibid.*, 109/58/148, Lionel to his brothers, 31 Aug. 1844.
9. *Ibid.*, RFam C/4/65, 17 Oct. 1861.
10. RA Y90/22.
11. *Ibid.*, Z59/3, 26 July 1841.
12. *Ibid.*, Y153/66.
13. RAL T7/78.
14. Ayer, pp. 40–1.
15. RAL T7/58, Anthony to his brothers, 21 July (1846).
16. *Ibid.*, T7/67.
17. Ayer, pp. 42–3.
18. RAL 109/72/1, n.d.
19. Journals of Lady de Rothschild, I, 3 (February 1848).
20. *Ibid.*, p. 4 (25 April 1848).
21. RAL 109/72/2.
22. *Ibid.*, 10 June 1848.
23. *Ibid.*, T8/40, 29 March 1848.
24. *Ibid.*, 109/72/2, 19 June 1848.
25. *Ibid.*, T8/31, 20 April 1848.
26. *Ibid.*, T8/46, 17 April 1848.
27. *Ibid.*, B17–1848. The originals are in Judendeutsch and I owe the translations to the kindness of Dr Gershom Knight.
28. *Ibid.*, T8/83, 26 June 1848.
29. *Ibid.*, T8/249.
30. Ayer, pp. 42–3.
31. RAL T8/337, Anselm to James, 1 Nov. 1852.
32. The former in London, the latter in Paris.
33. See Ayer, pp. 44–9.
34. RAL T8/179.
35. *Ibid.*, T6/284 and 285.
36. T10/47, 20 July 1870.
37. Bodleian, Disraeli Papers R263, 22 Nov. (1880). On Bleichröder see Stern; Dr Gershom Knight of the Rothschild Archives has done work on the Bleichröder-Rothschild connection which will emerge in forthcoming publications.
38. RAL 109/70/1, Nat to his brothers, n.d. (1847); 109/71/1, Disraeli to Lionel, 8 Dec. 1847.
39. *Ibid.*, RFam C/2/44, same to same, 28 Jan. 1847; W. F. Monypenny and G. E. Buckle, *The Life of Benjamin Disraeli*, 2 vols. (1929), II, 418.
40. *Ibid.*, RFam C/3/48, 28 Feb. 1868.
41. *Ibid.*, RFam C/4/48.
42. Vincent, p. 301.
43. Harvard University, Graduate School of Business Administration, the Kress Library in Baker Library, Box XIV.
44. RA J82/157.
45. Bodleian, Disraeli Papers R215, 3 Sept. 1867.
46. RAL T10, pp. 49 and 52.
47. RA 166/70, 16 Oct. 1870.
48. RAL RFam C/15/4 and 8.
49. *Ibid.*, T10, p. 60, 6 Aug. 1870.
50. *Ibid.*, p. 62.
51. *Ibid.*, p. 53.
52. E.g. RAL RFam C/15/6.
53. *Ibid.*, 130 A/2, 16 and 26 Jan. 1908.
54. Ayer, p. 55. See also RAL, T10, p. 82.
55. *Ibid.*, 102 & 104.
56. The Marquis of Zetland, *The Letters of Disraeli to Lady Bradford and Lady Chesterfield*, 2 vols. (1929), I, 192.
57. RAL RFam C/2/18, 31 July 1873.
58. *Ibid.*, RFam C/2/28.
59. *Ibid.*, 101/10–11/2/164.
60. Lord Rothschild, '*You Have It, Madam*' (1980).
61. *Ibid.* For a fuller discussion of the broader political and diplomatic implications, see Robert Blake, *Disraeli* (1966), 581–7.
62. Quoted in Rothschild, *You Have It*, pp. 23–5.
63. For the information and quotations in the paragraph, see *ibid.*
64. RAL RFam C/3/80.
65. Bodleian, Disraeli Papers R244 and 226, 31 Mar. 1877 and 15 June 1878.
66. RA B52/25.

67. Ayer, pp. 52–8.
68. *Ibid.*
69. Bodleian, Disraeli Papers R218.
70. RAL T12/34.
71. *Ibid.*, 11.

72. *Ibid.*, 109/136/1.
73. *Ibid.*, T13/4.
74. Bodleian, Disraeli Papers R269, 7 June (1879).

Chapter VI

ROSEBERYS AND ROTHSCHILDS

1. BL Add. MSS. 47913.
2. *Ibid.*, fos. 112–13.
3. *Ibid.*, 47924, f. 59.
4. RAL C/6/54 and 67 and C/12/9.
5. RA Add. A2/13, 7 June 1876.
6. BL Add. MSS. 47924, f. 62.
7. *Ibid.*, fos. 82 and 94–5.
8. *Ibid.*, f. 49, 2 Oct. 1872.
9. *Ibid.*, 47925, fos. 10 and 52–60.
10. *Ibid.*, fos. 63, 77, and 70.
11. *Ibid.*, 47926, pp. 42–3.
12. RAL C/5/273.
13. BL Add. MSS. 47933, fos. 26, 22, 28 and 29.
14. Leon Edel, ed., *Henry James Letters* (1975), II, 318.
15. RAL RFam C/16/14 and C/8/29.
16. RAL T10, p. 9, Mayer to his brothers, Monday n.d. (1867).
17. *Ibid.*, T12/121, Hannah to Lionel, 10 May 1877.
18. Robert Rhodes James, *Rosebery* (1963), p. 82.
19. Rosebery Papers.
20. Rhodes James, p. 225.
21. Rosebery Papers, n.d. (early January 1878).
22. Rosebery Papers.
23. *Ibid.*
24. *Ibid.*, Ferdy to Rosebery, 22 Aug. 1871; Juliana to Rosebery, 24 Nov. 1871.
25. Rhodes James, p. 88.
26. RA Add. J/239, 18 May 1888.
27. Rhodes James, pp. 115 and 145.
28. Rosebery Papers, 11 Jan. 1878.
29. Quoted in Rhodes James, p. 124.

30. Rosebery Papers, 13 Nov. 1888.
31. *Ibid.*, n.d. and 17 Feb. 1881.
32. *Ibid.*, 31 May 1884.
33. *Ibid.*, Rosebery's Diary.
34. *Ibid.*, 18, 19 and 20 Nov. 1890.
35. *Ibid.*
36. RA F39/60.
37. *Ibid.*, F39/62, 28 Nov. 1890.
38. For examples of this kind of reasoning, see Colin Holmes, *Anti-Semitism in British Society, 1876–1939* (New York, 1979), pp. 83–5.
39. Rosebery Papers, Ferdy to Rosebery, 8 Sept. 1878.
40. *Ibid.*, Natty to Rosebery, n.d. (Feb. 1880).
41. BL Add. MSS. 47924, fos. 63 and 66.
42. Mrs James de Rothschild, *The Rothschilds at Waddesdon Manor* (1979).
43. RAL RFam C/5/211.
44. Quoted in Rhodes James, p. 158.
45. This thesis was first fully stated in R. Robinson and J. Gallagher, *Africa and the Victorians* (1961).
46. D. C. M. Platt, *Finance, Trade, and Politics in British Foreign Policy, 1815–1914* (Oxford, 1968), pp. 167, 155, and 5.
47. A. B. Cooke and John Vincent, *The Governing Passion* (Hassocks, 1974), p. 56.
48. R. F. Foster, *Lord Randolph Churchill* (Oxford, 1981).
49. BL Add. MSS. 47933, f. 36.

Chapter VII

DISRAELI, GLADSTONE
AND LORD ROTHSCHILD

1. Bodleian, Disraeli Papers R268.
2. *Ibid.*, R250, 22 March 1879.
3. RAL 109/136/1, Lionel to Leo and Laury, 25 March 1876.
4. Rosebery Papers, Ferdy to Rosebery, 29 July 1880.
5. Agatha Ramm, ed., *The Political Correspondence of Mr. Gladstone and Lord Granville, 1876–1886* (Oxford, 1961), I, 64.
6. Bodleian, Disraeli Papers, R258, 9 Dec. (1879).
7. *Ibid.*, 260.
8. *Ibid.*, 263, 22 Nov. (1880).
9. *Ibid.*, 264, 29 Nov. (1880).
10. Monypenny and Buckle, I, 860.
11. Bodleian, Disraeli Papers, R260, 30 Dec. 1879.
12. Alfred's Scrapbook, p. 80.
13. Platt, p. 166; A. W. Ward and G. P. Gooch, *The Cambridge History of British Foreign Policy* (Cambridge, 1923), III, 161.
14. Platt, pp. 166–7.
15. Bodleian, Disraeli Papers, R282b, copy telegram from Wilson to Baron Rothschild, 8 April 1879.
16. *Ibid.*, 282.
17. Quoted in Platt, p. 168.
18. Dr Gershom Knight kindly brought these two letters to my attention.
19. Bodleian, Disraeli Papers, R251.
20. RAL 101/6–7/2/75 (French).
21. Agatha Ramm, 'Great Britain and France in Egypt, 1876–1882', in Prosser Gifford and W. R. Louis, eds., *France and Britain in Africa* (1971), pp. 82–3.
22. Bodleian, Disraeli Papers, R252.
23. *Ibid.*, pp. 255 and 257, 1 and 8 Dec. 1879.
24. RAL 101/6–7/2/186, Alphonse

to his brother-in-law, 22 Dec. 1879 (French).
25. Harvard, Bleichröder Papers, Box XIV.
26. Bodleian, Disraeli Papers, R262, 7 Oct. 1880.
27. Harvard, Bleichröder Papers, Box XIV.
28. This is the view of Maurice Cowling, reflected in this period by Cooke and Vincent's *Governing Passion.*
29. Harvard, Bleichröder Papers, Box XIV.
30. Ramm, *Gladstone-Granville*, I, 194–5.
31. Ward and Gooch, p. 153.
32. See Stern, *passim.*
33. Platt, pp. 154–80; Ramm, 'Great Britain and France in Egypt'.
34. BL Add. MSS. 43912 (Dilke Papers), fos. 4, 5, 11, 12, 13, 19, 20 and 22.
35. Ramm, *Gladstone–Granville*, II, 241.
36. Ayer, p. 65.
37. BL Add. MSS. 44177 (Gladstone Papers), fos. 240–1, memorandum by Lord Granville, 17 Dec. 1884; Ramm, *Gladstone-Granville*, II, 299.
38. Ayer, p. 65.
39. D. W. R. Bahlman, ed., *The Diary of Sir Edward Walter Hamilton* (Oxford, 1972), II, 759.
40. *Ibid.*, p. 737; Alfred's Scrapbook, pp. 17 and 15, Granville to Alfred, 22 Nov. 1884 and Northbrook to Alfred, 22 Nov. 1884.
41. Churchill College, ESHR 2/6.
42. Devonshire Manuscripts, Chatsworth, 340. 1752, Alfred to Hartington, 25 April 1885.
43. *Ibid.*, Alfred's Scrapbook, p. 19,

Rosebery to Alfred, 4 Mar. 1885; Bahlman, II, 806–7, 815–16, 825.

44. RAL 101/12–13/2/29, 6 Feb. 1885 (French).
45. *Ibid.*, 101/12–13/2/36.
46. For the relevant correspondence, see *Ibid.*, 101/12–13/2/162–74.
47. Devonshire Manuscripts, 340.1838, A and B.
48. Churchill College, ESHR 2/6.
49. Bahlman, II, 880.
50. *Ibid.*, p. 896.
51. RA Queen Victoria's Journal, 4 May 1881.
52. Bahlman, II, 899.
53. BL Add. MSS. 44491 fos. 189–90; 25 June 1885 (French).
54. RAL 101/12–13/2/148 and 149a (French).
55. University of Southampton Library, Lady de Rothschild's Journal, II, p. 72.
56. RAL 101/12–13/2/147, 25 June 1885 (French).
57. BL Add. MSS. 43913, fos. 89–90, 14 Jan. 1885.
58. See Cooke and Vincent, pp. 85–6.
59. Rosebery Papers, 11 Feb. 1885.
60. *Ibid.* (25 Sept. 1885); Ramm, *Gladstone-Granville*, II, 399 n 3.
61. Churchill College, ESHR 2/7.
62. Bahlman, II, 834.
63. *Ibid.*, p. 835; Cooke and Vincent, p. 217.

Chapter VIII

RANDOLPH, RHODES, AND CHAMBERLAIN

1. Foster, p. 395.
2. Rosebery Papers, 6 Sept. 1878.
3. Rosebery Papers, 12 Nov. 1886.
4. Foster, pp. 194–5, 197, and 211; Ayer, pp. 70–1.
5. Foster, p. 349; RAL VI/10/78, p. 407.
6. Churchill College, ESHR 2/8, Brett's Journal, 26 Dec. 1886.
7. *Ibid.*, RCHL 1/13/1534 and 1537, 17 and 18 June.
8. *Ibid.*, ESHR 2/7, 3 Oct. 1886.
9. Bahlman, II, 666.
10. Salisbury Papers, Hatfield, Natty to Lord Salisbury, 18 Sept. 1885.
11. Rosebery Papers, 8 Feb. (1887).
12. Churchill College, ESHR 2/7, Brett, memorandum, 22 Jan. 1886.
13. Rosebery Papers, 4 Feb. 1886.
14. Churchill College, RCHC 1/16/1844 and 1833, 27 Sept. and 5 Oct.
15. Rosebery Papers, 16 Dec. 1886.
16. Churchill ESHR 2/7, 3 Oct. 1886.
17. Ward and Gooch, pp. 245–6.
18. Bodleian, Disraeli Papers, R264, Natty to Disraeli, 29 Nov. (1880).
19. Cooke and Vincent, p. 308; Churchill College, ESHR 2/7, Brett, memorandum, 29 Jan. 1886.
20. *Ibid.*, RCHL 11/1350, 30 Jan. 1886.
21. *Ibid.*, RCHL 1/13/1534.
22. Cooke and Vincent, p. 56.
23. Churchill College, RCHL 1/19/2416 and 2423, 19 and 25 Mar. 1887.
24. *Ibid.*, RCHL 1/29/4055 and 31/4525.
25. Bahlman, II, 730.
26. Churchill College, ESHR 2/7, Brett, memorandum, 29 Jan. 1886.
27. *Ibid.*, ESHR 2/9, 22 Aug. 1892.
28. *Ibid.*, ESHR 2/9, 23 Jan. 1893.
29. See John Flint, *Cecil Rhodes* (1976).
30. *Ibid.*, p. 86.
31. Bodleian, Harcourt Papers dep.

120, fos. 48–9, Ochs Bros., 83 Hatton Gardens, to Natty, 9 Jan. 1893.

32. RAL 20 Jan. 1888 T43, 17.
33. Rhodes House Library, MSS. Afr. tl, fos. 23–5, 2 June 1888.
34. Churchill College, ESHR 2/9, 3 Feb. 1891.
35. Rhodes House Library, MSS. Afr. 228, C3B 201a.
36. Flint, p. 162.
37. Salisbury Papers, Natty to Salisbury, 9 June 1892 and copy Salisbury to Natty, 10 June 1892.

38. Rhodes House Library, MSS. Afr. s. 228, C7A, 135.
39. Flint, p. 185.
40. Salisbury Papers.
41. *Ibid.*; Chamberlain's dismissive responses are in letters from him to Natty, 18 and 24 July and 13 Aug. 1899 in the Rothschild-Lane Papers.
42. Salisbury Papers.
43. Ayer, pp. 68–71.
44. Salisbury Papers; RAL 101/33/157.

Chapter IX

'WE, MY DEAR NATTY, WE'

1. I owe this story to Mrs James de Rothschild.
2. 9 July 1889.
3. *Buckinghamshire* (1960), pp. 152–3.
4. Alfred's Scrapbook and Bahlman, II, 601.
5. Devonshire Papers, 340.2178, Alfred to Hartington, n.d.
6. Bodleian, Harcourt Papers, dep. 166, f. 231, Harcourt to Leo, 24 Nov. 1892.
7. *Ibid.*, fos. 61–2, 66, and 68.
8. Salisbury Papers, 4 Dec. 1897.
9. Rosebery Papers, Ferdy to Rosebery, 24 Nov. 1885.
10. Bodleian, Harcourt Papers, dep. 167, fos. 26–7, memorandum, 14 Dec. 1892.
11. BL Add. MSS. 47197, 17 April 1867.
12. *Ibid.*, 47193, f. 76–7.
13. National Library of Scotland, 5197, f. 203, n.d.
14. Churchill College, ESHR 2/9, Brett's diary, 27 Nov. 1892; BL Add. MSS. 47193, f. 77.
15. *Hertfordshire* (1950), p. 253.
16. *Justice*, 2 Sept. 1893, quoted in Holmes, p. 83.
17. Sheila Richards, *A History of Tring* (1974).

18. Flint, p. 93.
19. RAL 0000/150.
20. Bodleian, Disraeli Papers, R263, 22 Nov. (1880).
21. RAL, 0000/89.
22. Alfred's Scrapbook, pp. 37–9.
23. Quoted in Holmes, pp. 83–4.
24. *Imperialism: A Study* (1937), pp. 56–7. The book was first published in 1902.
25. See Holmes, p. 84.
26. Harvard, Bleichröder Archive, box XIV, 11 Aug. 1890.
27. RAL 130/A/0, 23 June 1906.
28. *Ibid.*, 130/A/2, 7 Oct. 1907.
29. Churchill College, ESHR 2/8, Brett's diary, 25 Nov. 1890.
30. Ayer, pp. 70–77; C. C. Aronsfeld, 'Jewish Bankers and the Tsar', *Jewish Social Studies*, vol. 35 (1973), esp. pp. 95–6.
31. Salisbury Papers, 3 Jan. 1899.
32. RAL 130 A/1, Natty to his French cousins, 26 Sept. 1907.
33. RAL 130 A/2, 3 June and 16 June 1906; RA W 53/105, Hardinge to Natty, 13 June 1908.
34. Rosebery Papers, 11 Dec. (1881).
35. RAL 130 A/2, 16 June 1908.
36. Bodleian, Disraeli Papers, R263, 22 Nov. (1880).

37. Jerry White, *Rothschild Buildings: Life in an East End tenement block, 1887–1920* (1980), p. 24.
38. RAL 130 A/3, Natty to his French cousins, 5 March 1909.
39. *Ibid.*, 130 A/1, 15 Apr. 1907.
40. *Ibid.*, 130 A/2, 21 May 1908.
41. *Ibid.*, 101/20.
42. University of Southampton Library, the Journal of Lady de Rothschild, II, 30.
43. *Buckinghamshire*, p. 53.
44. RAL 130 A/2.
45. *Ibid.*, 29 Jan. 1908.
46. *Ibid.*, 25 Mar. 1908.
47. *Ibid.*, 6 Mar. 1908.
48. Quoted in Roth, p. 130. For Conservative pressure on Natty to take a leading role in opposing the government's measures, see Rothschild-Lane Papers, the Marquess of Lansdowne to Natty, 17 July, 10 Nov. and 25 Nov. 1909.
50. *Ibid.*, 130 A/5.
51. *Ibid.*, n.d. and 26 July 1911.
52. John Marlow, *Milner: Apostle of Empire* (1976), pp. 226 and 235 n. 19; A. T. Q. Stewart, *The Ulster Crisis* (1967), p. 188; A. M. Gollin, *Proconsul in Politics* (1964), pp. 187–8.
53. *Ibid.*
54. Bodleian, Add. MSS. Milner, c. 689, fos. 36, 148, 149, and 150.
55. RA GV K2553 (3)/84, 'From Lord Rothschild', 9 Feb. 1914.
56. RAL 130 A/8, 19 Mar. and July 1914.
57. RA AA 48/55, 3 Apr. 1915.

BIBLIOGRAPHY

List of Unpublished Sources Consulted

BL – British Library Add. MSS. 38756 (Liverpool); 40584 (Peel); 43912, 43913 (Dilke); 44177, 44491 (Gladstone); 47913, 47916, 47917, 47924, 47933 (Battersea); 48651 (E. Hamilton's Diary); 47367, 57370, 57401 (Herries)

Board of Deputies of British Jews, Minute Books

Bodleian Library, Oxford: Disraeli Papers; Harcourt Papers; Milner Papers

Carnarvon Papers, Alfred de Rothschild's scrapbook

Churchill College, Cambridge: Randolph Churchill Papers; Esher Papers

Devonshire Manuscripts, Chatsworth

Harvard University, Graduate School of Business Administration, the Kress Library in the Baker Library, Bleichröder Papers, Box XIV

Lansdowne Papers, Bowood

National Library of Scotland – Haldane Papers; Rosebery Papers

Rhodes House Library, Oxford, Rhodes Papers

Rosebery Papers, Dalmeny House

RA – Royal Archives, Windsor

RAL – Rothschild Archives, London, N. M. Rothschild & Sons

RAM – Rothschild Archives, Manchester, N. M. Rothschild & Sons

Rothschild-Lane Papers

Salisbury Papers, Hatfield

Southampton, University of, typed excerpts from the Journals of Lady de Rothschild, 2 vols. For the originals, see BL Add. MSS. 47949–47962 (Battersea)

List of Printed Sources Cited

(published in London unless otherwise indicated)

Aronsfeld, C. C., 'Jewish Bankers and the Tsar', *Jewish Social Studies*, vol. 35 (1973), esp. pp. 95–6.

Aspinall, A., ed., *The Letters of King George IV, 1812–1830*, 3 vols. (Cambridge, 1938)

Aston, Joseph, *The Manchester Guide* (1904)

Ayer, Jules, *A Century of Finance, 1804–1904: The London House of Rothschild* (1905)

Bahlman, D. W. R., ed., *The Diary of Sir Edward Walter Hamilton*, 2 vols. (Oxford, 1972)

Bermant, Chaim, *The Cousinhood* (1971)

Blake, Robert, *Disraeli* (1966)

Buxton, Charles, ed., *Memoirs of Sir Thomas Fowell Buxton* (1849)

Chadwick, G. F., *The Works of Sir Joseph Paxton* (1961)

Chapman, Stanley, *The Foundation of the English Rothschilds: N. M. Rothschild as a Textile Merchant, 1799–1811* (1977)

Colvin, H. M., *A Biographical Dictionary of English Architects, 1660–1840* (1954)

Cooke, A. B. and John Vincent, *The Governing Passion* (Hassocks, 1974)

Corti, Count, *The Rise of the House of Rothschild*, translated from the German by Brian and Beatrix Lunn (1928)

———, *The Reign of the House of Rothschild*, translated from the German by Brian and Beatrix Lunn (1928)

Davis, Richard W., 'Toryism to Tamworth: The Triumph of Reform, 1826–1835', *Albion* (Summer 1980)

———, *Disraeli* (1976)

———, *Political Change and Continuity: A Buckinghamshire Study* (Newton Abbot, 1972)

DNB – *Dictionary of National Biography*

Dod, C. R., *Electoral Facts, from 1852–1853* (1972)

Edel, Leon, ed., *Henry James Letters*, II (1975)

Emanuel, Charles H. L., *A Century and a Half of Jewish History* (1910)

Endelman, Todd M., *The Jews of Georgian England, 1714–1830* (Philadelphia, 1979)

Fieve, Ronald, *Moodswing: The Third Revolution in Psychiatry* (New York, 1976)

Flint, John, *Cecil Rhodes* (1976)

Foster, R. F., *Lord Randolph Churchill* (Oxford, 1981)

G. E. C[okayne], *Complete Peerage*

Gibbs, Robert, *Buckinghamshire: A Record of Local Occurrences* (1882), IV

Gilam, Abraham, *The Emancipation of the Jews in England, 1830–1860*

(New York, 1982)

Gille, Bertrand, *Histoire de la Maison Rothschild des Origines à 1848* (Geneva, 1965)

Gollin, A. M., *Proconsul in Politics* (1964)

Hansard's *Parliamentary Debates*

Hobson, J. A., *Imperialism: A Study* (1902 and 1937)

Holmes, Colin, *Anit-Semitism in British Society, 1876–1939* (New York, 1979)

Marlow, John, *Milner: Apostle of Empire* (1976)

Monypenny, W. F. and G. E. Buckle, *The Life of Benjamin Disraeli*, 2 vols. (1929)

Muhlstein, Anka, *James de Rothschild* (Paris, 1981)

Pevsner, Nikolaus, *Buckinghamshire* (1960)

——, *Hertfordshire* (1950)

Pinney, Thomas, ed., *The Letters of Thomas Babington Macaulay*, VI (Cambridge, 1981)

Platt, D. C. M., *Finance, Trade and Politics in British Foreign Policy, 1815–1914* (Oxford, 1968)

Pope-Hennessy, John, ed., *Baron Ferdinand de Rothschild's Livre d'Or* (privately printed for presentation to the Roxburghe Club by Lord Rothschild, Cambridge, 1957)

Ramm, Agatha, 'Great Britain and France in Egypt, 1876–1882', in Prosser Gifford and W. R. Louis, ed., *France and Britain in Africa* (1971)

——, ed., *The Political Correspondence of Mr. Gladstone and Lord Granville, 1868–1876* (1952)

——, ed., *The Political Correspondence of Mr. Gladstone and Lord Granville, 1876–1886*, 2 vols. (Oxford, 1981)

Rhodes James, Robert, *Rosebery* (1963)

Richards, Sheila, *A History of Tring* (1974)

Robinson, R. and J. Gallagher, *Africa and the Victorians* (1961)

Roth, Cecil, *The Magnificent Rothschilds* (1939)

Rothschild, Mrs James de, *The Rothschilds at Waddesdon* (1979)

Rothschild, Lord, *The Rothschild Family Tree* (1971)

——, *'You Have it, Madam'* (London, 1980)

——, *The Shadow of a Great Man* (1982)

Rubens, Alfred, 'The Rothschilds in Caricature', *Transactions of the Jewish Historical Society of England*, XX (1968–69), 76–87

Stern, Fritz, *Gold and Iron: Bismarck, Bleichröder, and the Building of the German Empire* (1977)

Stewart, A. T. Q., *The Ulster Crisis* (1967)

The Times, 1847, 1857

Trevelyan, G. M., *Trinity College: An Historical Sketch* (Cambridge, 1972)

Vanity Fair, 1877

Vincent, J. R., ed., *Disraeli, Derby and the Conservative Party: The Political Journals of Lord Stanley, 1849–1869* (1978)

Ward, A. W. and G. P. Gooch, *The Cambridge History of British Foreign Policy*, III (Cambridge, 1923)

White, Jerry, *Rothschild Buildings: Life in an East End tenement block, 1887–1920* (1980)

Winstanley, D. A., *Early Victorian Cambridge* (Cambridge, 1955)

——, *Later Victorian Cambridge* (Cambridge, 1947)

Wolf, Lucien, *Essays in Jewish History* (1934)

Zetland, Marquis of, *The Letters of Disraeli to Lady Bradford and Lady Chesterfield*, 2 vols. (1929)

INDEX

Note: The name "Rothschild" has been abbreviated to "R", except in headings.

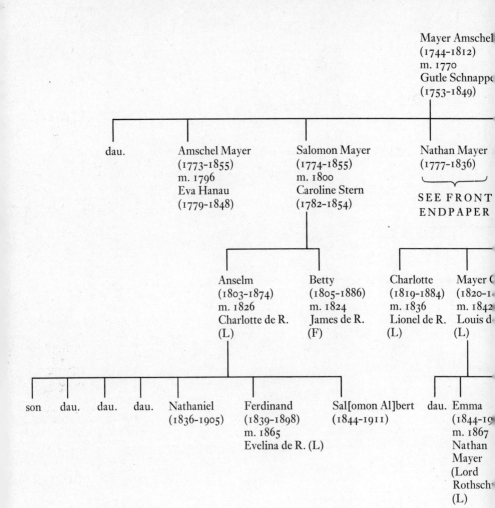

Mayer Amschel
(1744-1812)
m. 1770
Gutle Schnappe
(1753-1849)

dau.

Amschel Mayer
(1773-1855)
m. 1796
Eva Hanau
(1779-1848)

Salomon Mayer
(1774-1855)
m. 1800
Caroline Stern
(1782-1854)

Nathan Mayer
(1777-1836)

SEE FRONT
ENDPAPER

Anselm
(1803-1874)
m. 1826
Charlotte de R.
(L)

Betty
(1805-1886)
m. 1824
James de R.
(F)

Charlotte
(1819-1884)
m. 1836
Lionel de R.
(L)

Mayer C
(1820-1
m. 1842
Louis d
(L)

son   dau.   dau.   dau.

Nathaniel
(1836-1905)

Ferdinand
(1839-1898)
m. 1865
Evelina de R. (L)

Sal[omon Al]bert
(1844-1911)

dau.

Emma
(1844-19
m. 1867
Nathan
Mayer
(Lord
Rothsch
(L)